PSALMS *f*

PART II
Psalms 73–150

Also available in the Old Testament
for Everyone series by John Goldingay

Genesis for Everyone, Part I

Genesis for Everyone, Part II

Exodus and Leviticus for Everyone

Numbers and Deuteronomy for Everyone

Joshua, Judges and Ruth for Everyone

1 and 2 Samuel for Everyone

1 and 2 Kings for Everyone

1 and 2 Chronicles for Everyone

Ezra, Nehemiah and Esther for Everyone

Job for Everyone

Psalms for Everyone, Part I

PSALMS *for* EVERYONE

PART II
Psalms 73–150

JOHN GOLDINGAY

Published in the United States of America in 2014
by Westminster John Knox Press, Louisville, Kentucky

Published in Great Britain in 2014

Society for Promoting Christian Knowledge
36 Causton Street
London SW1P 4ST
www.spckpublishing.co.uk

Unless otherwise indicated, Scripture quotations are the author's
own translation.

British Library Cataloguing-in-Publication Data
A catalogue record for this book is available from the British Library

ISBN 978–0–281–06134–1
eBook ISBN 978–0–281–06784–8

First printed in Great Britain
Subsequently digitally printed in Great Britain

eBook by Graphicraft Limited, Hong Kong

Produced on paper from sustainable forests

CONTENTS

ACKNOWLEDGMENTS

The translation at the beginning of each chapter (and in other biblical quotations) is my own. I have already translated the Psalms in an earlier commentary (*Psalms*, three volumes, published by Baker Academic in 2006–2008); although I started from scratch for this book, sometimes I have adapted phrases from that commentary. I have stuck closer to the Hebrew than modern translations often do when they are designed for reading in church so that you can see more precisely what the text says. Thus although I prefer to use gender-inclusive language, I have let the translation stay gendered if inclusivizing it would obscure whether the text was using singular or plural—in other words, the translation often uses "he" where in my own writing I would say "they" or "he or she." Sometimes I have added words to make the meaning clear, and I have put these words in square brackets. At the end of the book is a glossary of some terms that recur in the text, such as geographical, historical, and theological expressions. In each chapter (though not in the introduction or in the Scripture selections) these terms are highlighted in **bold** the first time they occur.

The stories that follow the translation often concern my friends or my family. While none are made up, they are sometimes heavily disguised in order to be fair to people. Sometimes I disguised them so well that when I read the stories again, I was not sure initially whom I was describing. My first wife, Ann, appears in a number of them. Two or three years before I started writing this book, she died after negotiating with multiple sclerosis for forty-three years. Our shared dealings with her illness and disability over these years contribute significantly to what I write in ways that you will be able to see in connection with studying the Psalms but also in ways that are less obvious.

Not long before I started writing this book, I fell in love with and married Kathleen Scott, and I am grateful for my new life with her and for her insightful comments on the manuscript, which have been so careful and illuminating that she practically deserves to be credited as coauthor. I am also grateful to Matt Sousa for reading through the manuscript and pointing out things I needed to correct or clarify, and to Tom Bennett for checking the proofs.

INTRODUCTION

As far as Jesus and the New Testament writers were concerned, the Jewish Scriptures that Christians call the "Old Testament" *were* the Scriptures. In saying that, I cut corners a bit, as the New Testament never gives us a list of these Scriptures, but the body of writings that the Jewish people accept is as near as we can get to identifying the collection with which Jesus and the New Testament writers would have worked. The church also came to accept some extra books, such as Maccabees and Ecclesiasticus, that were traditionally called the "Apocrypha," the books that were "hidden away"—a name that came to imply "spurious." They are now often known as the "Deuterocanonical Writings," which is more cumbersome but less pejorative; it simply indicates that these books have less authority than the Torah, the Prophets, and the Writings, the Old Testament in a narrower sense. The precise list of the Deuterocanonical Writings varies among different churches. For the purposes of this series that seeks to expound the "Old Testament for Everyone," by the "Old Testament" we mean the Scriptures accepted by the Jewish community, though in the Jewish Bible they come in a different order, as the Torah, the Prophets, and the Writings.

They were not "old" in the sense of antiquated or out-of-date; I sometimes like to refer to them as the First Testament rather than the Old Testament to make that point. For Jesus and the New Testament writers, they were a living resource for understanding God, God's ways in the world, and God's ways with us. They were "useful for teaching, for reproof, for correction, and for training in righteousness, so that the person who belongs to God can be proficient, equipped for every good work" (2 Timothy 3:16–17). They were for everyone, in fact. So it's strange that Christians don't read them very much. My aim in these volumes is to help you do so.

My hesitation is that you may read me instead of the Scriptures. Don't fall into that trap. I like the fact that this series includes much of the biblical text. Don't skip over it. In the end, that's the bit that matters.

An Outline of the Old Testament

The Christian Old Testament puts the books in the Jewish Bible in a distinctive order:

Genesis to Kings: A story that runs from the creation of the world to the exile of Judahites to Babylon

Chronicles to Esther: A second version of this story, continuing it into the years after the exile

Job, Psalms, Proverbs, Ecclesiastes, Song of Songs: Some poetic books

Isaiah to Malachi: The teaching of some prophets

Here is an outline of the history that lies at the background of the books (I give no dates for events in Genesis, which involves too much guesswork).

1200s	Moses, the exodus, Joshua
1100s	The "judges"
1000s	King Saul, King David
900s	King Solomon; the nation splits into two, Ephraim and Judah
800s	Elijah, Elisha
700s	Amos, Hosea, Isaiah, Micah; Assyria the superpower; the fall of Ephraim
600s	Jeremiah, King Josiah; Babylon the superpower
500s	Ezekiel; the fall of Judah; Persia the superpower; Judahites free to return home
400s	Ezra, Nehemiah
300s	Greece the superpower
200s	Syria and Egypt the regional powers pulling Judah one way or the other

100s Judah's rebellion against Syrian power and gain of independence

000s Rome the superpower

Psalms 73–150

You might wonder why this second Psalms volume of The Old Testament for Everyone series begins with Psalm 73—why not put seventy-five of the psalms in each volume? The answer is that the Hebrew Bible divides the Psalter, the book of Psalms, into five smaller "books," beginning at Psalms 1, 42, 73, 90, and 107. You can see the marks of this division within the psalms in the special act of praise and the double amen that come at the end of Psalms 41, 72, 89, and 106. If the people who compiled the Psalter were going to structure it in this way, you might have thought that that they would put specific types of psalm in the different books—say, put all the praise psalms together, or all the psalms for the king to use, or all the David psalms. But while there are tendencies along those lines, they're not carried through consistently, and the divisions between the books are pretty random. But the division into five books surely isn't random, because that's the number of books into which the Torah is divided—Genesis, Exodus, Leviticus, Numbers, and Deuteronomy. So there are five books of teaching about how God related to the world and to Israel at the beginning and about God's expectations of Israel, and five books of teaching about praise and prayer. The division of the Psalter into five books thus draws our attention to the reason that the book of Psalms exists. It's to teach us how to praise God and how to pray to God.

I oversimplify slightly. There are about fifteen psalms that are dominated by God's speaking. Psalm 110 is an example; it's an account of promises that God gives to the king. But in the vast majority of psalms human beings are speaking to God. There are four main ways in which they do so:

1. Some psalms are expressions of worship for who God is and for the way God consistently relates to us. Psalm 100 is an example. This psalm also neatly illustrates the two features

3

of a praise psalm of this kind. It begins with an exhortation to praise, then goes on to the reasons for the praise, which is the content of the praise. It's also an example of a feature that appears in other psalms. When it has gone through the praise and the reasons once, it goes through the sequence again, as if just doing it once isn't enough. There are more praise psalms in the second half of the Psalter than in the first half.

2. Some psalms are protests at the fact that God's isn't now relating to us in the way that we would have expected. Psalm 89 is an example. There are fewer of these protest psalms in the second half of the Psalter than in the first half. Psalm 89 is an extreme example of a feature that recurs in these psalms, in that it spends a very long time describing who God is, the way God has acted in the past, and the promises God has made, but all this turns out to be the lead into a complaint that these facts make totally mysterious the way God has been acting more recently.

3. Some psalms are declarations of a trust in God that persists despite such pressures. Psalm 84 is an example. Like a protest psalm, it presupposes the fact that everything may not be wonderful in a person's life. It speaks of having to live in faithless tents—that is, to live in the company of faithless people. It would be much better to be able to live in Jerusalem, in the environs of the temple. But the psalm expresses a kind of contentment with having to live far away from Jerusalem, because God is not confined to the temple and can be the object of trust anywhere.

4. Some psalms are testimonies to or thanksgivings for the way God has acted in response to protests and declarations of trust. Psalm 116 is an example. A thanksgiving or testimony psalm typically gives an account of the danger or trouble a person was in, an account of the way the person prayed, and an account of the way God acted to bring deliverance. It seeks to draw other people into a deeper commitment to God as they realize that this testimony describes not something that has merely been true for one person but something that could be true for them.

One feature that runs through all the types of psalm is the way they are made up of quite short lines that divide into two parts. So the very first line of Psalm 73 is

Indeed, God is good to Israel,
    to the pure in heart.

Typically, the second half of the line restates the first half, though it doesn't simply repeat it. You could get the wrong impression from the first half on its own. It's very important that God is committed to Israel, but the addition of the second half makes clear that it's not enough just to belong to Israel. You have to belong to the pure in heart. A later line in the psalm says,

Indeed, was it for nothing that I had kept my heart clean
    and washed my hands in innocence.

In other words, a proper pure relationship with God and with other people involves what is going on inside us in our intentions and thinking (the heart or mind). It also involves what is going on in our actions, outside us, that our hands are not stained by blood. It's important that our attitude of mind and heart is right, but it's also important for our actions to be right. Another couple of lines later the psalm says,

If I had said I would speak out thus—
    there, I would have betrayed the company of your children.

Here the second half of the line simply completes the first.

Who are the people who express their praise and prayer in the Psalms? It can vary. Sometimes it's the community that speaks as "we." These psalms may be especially instructive if we want to know how to shape the church's praise and prayer. Sometimes it's an individual "I" that speaks. These psalms may be especially instructive if we want to know how to develop our individual praise and prayer. But then there are some "I" psalms that sound as if they deal with the needs of a king or a leader such as Nehemiah, and these may be instructive if we want to know how to pray for our leaders.

We don't know who wrote the Psalms, but we don't really need to know the writers in order to be able to use the psalms, any more than we need to know who wrote a modern hymn or prayer in order to be able to use it. You may think it is obvious who wrote the Psalms—it was surely David? But less than twenty of the psalms we will study in this volume say "David's" in their introduction, so the link with David doesn't help us a great deal. Indeed, a number of these psalms look as if they presuppose a time much later than David—particularly the fall of Jerusalem to the Babylonians and the subsequent transportation of people from Judah to Babylon.

And anyway, it's not at all clear that "David's" means David wrote the psalm. It might mean the psalm was written *for* David, or for a later Davidic king, or it might mean it belongs to one of the collections of psalms that David or the Davidic king sponsored. A few other psalms mention people such as Asaph or the Qorahites, who were people involved in or associated with leading the worship of the temple. Some of the introductions refer to the kind of worship occasion when the psalm was used. Notably, Psalms 120–134 are all "songs of the ascents," which might mean that they were used on pilgrimage up to Jerusalem. Psalms 113–118 became the Hallel Psalms, which were used at major festivals, particularly Passover, though the Psalter itself does not refer to this practice.

PSALM 73

God Redeems Now

Composition. Asaph's.

1. Indeed, God is good to Israel,
   to the pure in heart.
2. But I—my feet all but turned aside,
   my steps were nearly made to slip.
3. Because I was fixated on the exultant,
   on the well-being of the faithless that I can see.

4. Because there are no pressures threatening their death;
   their chest is portly.
5. In human burdens they have no part;
   they are not afflicted with other people.
6. Therefore majesty lies around their neck,
   though a coat consisting of violence wraps around them.
7. Their eye bulges because of hardness;
   the schemes in their mind have overflowed.
8. They scoff and speak of evildoing,
   from their position on high they speak of extortion.
9. They have set their mouth in the heavens,
   and their tongue walks about on the earth.
10. Thus blows come again and again to his people,
    and abundant water is drained by them.
11. But they say, "How does God recognize it?
    Is there recognition with the Most High?"
12. There—these are the faithless people,
    carefree forever, as they have amassed wealth.
13. Indeed, was it for nothing that I had kept my heart clean
    and washed my hands in innocence,
14. when I have come to be afflicted all day long,
    and my reproof happens morning by morning?

15. If I had said I would speak out thus—
    there, I would have betrayed the company of your children.
16. But when I thought about how to understand this,
    it was a burden in my eyes,

¹⁷ until I came to God's great sanctuary,
    so that I might consider their end.
¹⁸ Indeed, you will set them among deceptions;
    you are making them fall to lies.
¹⁹ How they are coming to destruction suddenly;
    they are come to an end, they are finished, through terrors.
²⁰ Like a dream when one wakes up, Lord,
    when one stirs, you will despise their shadow.

²¹ When my mind is embittered,
    and my heart—I am cut through,
²² then I am stupid and I do not understand;
    I became a monster with you.
²³ But I have been continually with you;
    you have held my right hand.
²⁴ By your purpose you lead me,
    and afterward you will take me to honor.
²⁵ Whom do I have in the heavens?—
    and with you, I have not wanted anyone on the earth.
²⁶ When my flesh and my mind are spent,
    God is my mind's crag and my very own forever.
²⁷ Because there—the people who are far from you perish;
    you are terminating everyone who is unfaithful to you.
²⁸ But me—nearness to God is good for me;
    I have made the Lord Yahweh my refuge,
    so as to speak out about all your acts.

Last night we went to a concert by rock-country-bluegrass-folk artist Steve Earle. I first heard him at Nottingham Rock City when he was still fairly fresh out of prison where he had been for drug-related offenses. Twenty years later in a club in Disneyland (!), one of his songs declared that he now believes in prophecy and miracles, and "Yeah, I believe in God, and God ain't me. . . . I believe in God, but God ain't us." Steve Earle was washed up, finished, but he told the audience when introducing another of his songs, "I had my second chance," though he also rejoices in the fact that every day is another second chance. He has been married seven times (twice to the same woman), "but this is the first time sober." When I listen to an addict who is now so full of life, commitment, and creativity referring to how things once were, it can mean I am listening to someone who embodies the miracle of God's reaching into someone's life, and it encourages my faith and hope.

Psalm 73 talks about persecution rather than addiction, but it speaks of that same miracle as an object of faith and hope: "By your purpose you lead me, and afterward you will take me to honor." If the psalmist were an addict, it would be someone who has just come to his or her senses and knows that it is impossible to pull oneself out of the pit of addiction and is beginning to see that there is a higher power with whose help it might be possible to climb out. In the psalmist's case, coming to one's senses means coming to see that this higher power is also bigger than his persecutors.

In terms of the typology I outlined in the introduction, Psalm 73 is a kind of psalm of trust but also a kind of thanksgiving psalm. In *Psalms for Everyone, Part 1,* I noted that the psalms see two stages in God's answering a prayer. Stage one means that God has heard the prayer and made a commitment to doing something concerning what we prayed about. Stage two means God has actually acted. Psalm 73 belongs between stage one and stage two, and it looks back on the process of coming to a conviction that God is going to act. So in accounting for its attitude of trust it tells a story like a thanksgiving.

The beginning sums up the point. The psalmist has reached a point where it is possible to make a positive affirmation of God's goodness to Israel—though the **faithless** people who appear in subsequent verses are quite likely to belong to Israel, so the psalm nuances its point by noting that this affirmation about God's goodness concerns Israelites who are pure in heart, the kind of people who have the right attitude to God and to other people. Affirming the point also reminds the people who listen to this thanksgiving that they need to belong to the company of the pure in heart. After the affirmation indicating the stance the psalmist can now take, the psalm tells the story that lies behind the affirmation. It notes that many people are doing very well in life and are proud of it. They are arrogant in relation to God and thus in relation to other human beings. "Their eye bulges because of hardness"—maybe the phrase is equivalent to being hard-hearted; it suggests looking at other people in a callous way. Further, the reason they are doing so well is that they treat other people so callously. They bring suffering to people and threaten to overwhelm them like a flood.

Western culture often encourages us simply to make it our ambition to join the people who are doing well, and the "prosperity gospel" joins in. What's the point of being a person who is pure in heart and whose hands are not stained by the blood of the innocent? The answer to the question came to the psalmist through going to the sanctuary. The psalmist came to realize once more the truth that many psalms presuppose. The fact that faithless people are doing well now does not mean they will do well forever, and the fact that innocent people are suffering does not mean they will suffer forever. God really is involved in earthly life and will restore the innocent person to honor and see that justice is done to the faithless. While the Old Testament recognizes that things do not always work out that way, it also recognizes that the occasions when it doesn't work out can easily come to dominate our thinking in excessive fashion. At least, that had been the psalmist's experience. But going into the sanctuary reinforced the awareness of God's involvement. After all, the faithless have been pressurizing and causing trouble, but the psalmist is alive to tell the tale: "I have been continually with you; you have held my right hand." And God will continue to do so. So I don't need to look to some other god or for some earthly way of pulling myself out of the hole I am in. No, I am powerless to do anything about my situation. I am not God. But God is God.

It is frustrating that the psalm doesn't tell us what it was about going to the sanctuary that reshaped the psalmist's thinking and attitude. Maybe it was the telling of the story of God's involvement with Israel, especially the **deliverance** from **Egypt** and the putting down of the Egyptians. Maybe it was hearing other people's testimonies to God's acts in their lives. Maybe it was hearing the temple choir sing of God's greatness. Maybe it was simply being in the place where God was present, invisibly enthroned. The psalm's failure to clarify this point for us invites us to infer that the point doesn't lie there. The point is that in some way the psalmist's thinking got reframed (as happened to Steve Earle through a twelve-step program), and God got put back at the center. We are in perpetual need of such reframing, one way or another, so that we stop thinking in a way that leaves out God's involvement with us and resume thinking in a way that puts God's involvement with us at the center.

Some translations give the impression that the psalmist is looking forward to being taken to glory by God after death, but that understanding reads a lot into the text and reads it in a way that would not have occurred to Israelites, who knew that death was death; there was nothing much to follow. (Some Jews did later come to believe there would be resurrection, but there is a basis for believing in resurrection only in light of Jesus' death and resurrection.) The psalm's good news is that we do not have to wait until after death for God to redeem us. God redeems now. The psalm encourages that expectation.

PSALM 74

Enough Punishment Already!

An instruction. Asaph's.

¹ God, why have you rejected us forever,
    [why] does your anger smoke at the flock you pasture?
² Be mindful of your assembly, which you acquired long ago,
    which you restored as your very own clan,
    Mount Zion, where you dwelt.
³ Trace your steps to the perpetual desolations,
    every wrongdoing of the enemy in the sanctuary.

⁴ Your watchful foes roared inside your place of assembly,
    they made their signs into signs.
⁵ It could be recognized as like someone bringing up axes
    against a thicket of trees.
⁶ Now they were smashing its engravings altogether,
    with hatchet and cleavers.
⁷ They gave over your sanctuary to fire, down to the ground;
    they defiled the dwelling of your name.
⁸ They said to themselves, "We will put them down altogether";
    they burnt all God's places of assembly in the country.

11

⁹ We could not see our signs,
     there was no longer a prophet,
     there was no one with us who knew how long.
¹⁰ Until when, God, will the foe blaspheme,
     will the enemy revile your name forever?
¹¹ Why do you hold back your hand,
     withhold your right hand in the midst of your coat?

¹² But God, my king of old,
     the one who effects acts of deliverance in the midst
        of the earth:
¹³ you are the one who parted the sea by your might,
     you smashed the heads of the dragons on the waters.
¹⁴ You are the one who crushed the heads of Leviathan
     so that you could make it food for a company of wildcats.
¹⁵ You are the one who split spring and torrent,
     you are the one who dried up perennial rivers.
¹⁶ Day is yours, night is also yours;
     you are the one who established the light, the sun.
¹⁷ You are the one who put in place all earth's boundaries;
     summer and winter—you are the one who shaped them.

¹⁸ Be mindful of this: the enemy has blasphemed,
     Yahweh, a rogue people has reviled your name.
¹⁹ Do not give the life of your dove to an animal,
     do not ignore forever the life of your lowly ones.
²⁰ Take note of the covenant,
     because the dark places in the country are full of pastures
        of violence.
²¹ The broken must not turn back shamed;
     the lowly and needy should praise your name.
²² Rise, God, contend for your cause,
     be mindful of your reviling by rogues all day long.
²³ Do not ignore the sound of your watchful foes,
     the uproar of the people who rise against you, going
        up continually.

This evening, as I write, will be the beginning of the Jewish
year 5772; in other words, on this reckoning the New Year will
be the 5772nd year since creation. It will be followed by the
Day of Atonement and the Festival of **Sukkot**. Thinking about

creation and about God's **deliverance** of Israel from **Egypt** thus come together at this point in the Jewish year. In the Christian calendar it happens that Christmas is immediately followed by the Western New Year, and the Western method of counting the years also makes a link between ordinary, created life and God's acts of salvation as it begins the count with the date of Jesus' birth. Maybe the collocation is a coincidence, but we could make more of it.

The middle section of Psalm 74 makes the same link, with some subtlety. It describes God's action as king in language that can apply both to creation and to God's deliverance of the people at the **Reed Sea**. Initially, the talk of deliverance would suggest the latter, but by the time it comes to an end, the section is speaking of day and night, summer and winter, and one would rather think of creation. Other Middle Eastern peoples did speak of creation as an act of deliverance, an occasion when God won a great victory over resistant powers such as the sea with its dynamic energy, and the Old Testament can also speak in these terms. So Israelites saying the psalm could as naturally think of creation as of the exodus when they used the middle section of the psalm. One implication would then be that God's act of creation ensured that the universe's tumultuous powers are under God's control; we do not have to be wary of them. Conversely, God's deliverance of Israel at the Reed Sea was an act of the creator God, using the same power that God had showed at creation. Admittedly, God generally declines to use on humanity the force that God used on resistant cosmic powers, perhaps because God is committed to winning our submission rather than forcing it.

The psalm is reminding God and the people who use it that God has power as creator and deliverer, and thus that there is no need for the people's present experience of desolation to continue. The obvious context in which to locate the psalm is the destruction of Jerusalem described at the end of the books of Kings, but these books imply that God would have a snorting answer to the repeated "Why?" question: the city's faithlessness meant it had quite deserved everything it got. Maybe by the time of this psalm, however, decades have passed, and people might reasonably think, "Enough already!"

13

Further, the Prophets have acknowledged that though it's fair in the circumstances for God to act against Israel and to use foreign powers in order to do so, it's also to be expected that God should eventually act against these foreign powers and act to **restore** Jerusalem. That's all the more the case when these peoples' action involves a blasphemous contempt for the God whose **name** was attached to the temple. The psalm implies that the trouble is that the story seems to have gotten stuck. It's time for the people that destroyed the temple to get their redress. And whereas there used to be prophets who spoke to these issues, part of God's abandonment is that God has stopped speaking. Whereas other psalms presuppose that you may receive a response from God when you pour yourself out in your anguish, this psalm testifies to the experience of receiving no response.

Near the end, the psalm appeals to the **covenant**. Some nerve is involved in this appeal because the reason for God's abandoning Israel was the fact that Israel had ignored its covenant obligations. The psalmist again risks a snorting reply: "You dare appeal to the covenant that you broke?" The psalm illustrates that there are no boundaries to the chutzpah that we can show in prayer. God had made a commitment in covenant and cannot escape the obligations of covenant, even though the covenant partner was unfaithful.

PSALM 75

The Promise of a Poisoned Chalice

The leader's. Do not destroy. A composition. Asaph's. A song.

1   We have confessed you, God, we have confessed,
     and when your name drew near, people have declared
     your wonders.
2   "Because I will seize the appointed time
     when I will exercise authority with uprightness.
3   Whereas earth and all its inhabitants are trembling,
     I am the one who ordered its pillars.

14

⁴ I have said to the exultant, 'Do not exult,'
    and to the faithless, 'Do not lift your horn.'
⁵ Do not lift your horn high
    [or] speak with forward neck."

⁶ Because it is not from the east or from the west,
    not from the mountains' pasturage.
⁷ Because God exercises authority;
    this person he puts down, that person he lifts up.
⁸ Because there is a chalice in Yahweh's hand,
    fermented wine, full of spices.
  He is pouring from it, they will indeed drain its dregs;
    all the faithless on the earth will drink.
⁹ But I—I will declare forever,
    I will make music for Jacob's God.
¹⁰ "Whereas I will cut all the horns of the faithless,
    the horns of the faithful person I will lift up."

The news today tells of two men called Abu Elias and Robert who were interviewed as they sat at the bottom of the stairs of the Convent of Our Lady of Saydnaya, a city high in the mountains north of Damascus. It is one of the few communities that still speak Aramaic, the language of Jesus; it is an ancient Christian center whose bishop seems to have attended the council that produced the Nicene Creed in the fourth century; and it has long been a focus for pilgrimage by both Christians and Muslims. Its location in the mountains has protected it from many of the tumults that have affected Middle Eastern life over the centuries. Abu Elias and Robert are there because they are Christian refugees from the conflict in Iraq. But now they are afraid that they may need to be on the run again if current unrest in Syria issues in power passing to a government that will not be interested in providing them with the protection that they have received from President Assad.

Even if they flee again, Abu Elias and Robert, like other Christians (and Jews and Muslims) in dangerous situations, have little alternative but to trust in a dynamic such as the one expressed in Psalm 75. First it looks back. The community recalls the way it has had opportunity to testify to God's action and protection in the past. It has had the experience of God's **name** drawing near—that is, of the coming near of the one whose person is indicated by the name **Yahweh**, which issued in wonders whereby the people had been delivered.

God in person then intervenes in the psalm to confirm that this experience does not belong only to the past. At the crucial moment God will intervene in action, as happens here in words, and will exercise his freedom to act decisively on his people's behalf by doing the upright thing. If the nations are trembling in fear, this fear need not spread to his people, because they know that God is the one who set the earth on secure foundations. Typically, this language refers not merely to the physical creation but also to the structures of its ongoing life. Confronted by people who "exult," people who fancy with a smile that they have power in the world, God puts them on notice.

The second half of the psalm is dominated by a response that affirms and restates what God has said, though it gives more frightening detail on what things look like when God acts against the exultant. Nehemiah's role as cupbearer for the **Persian** king likely included the responsibility of tasting the king's wine before he takes the risk of drinking it. It's quite possible to spike someone's drink, and God intends to do so (these are not the nice-tasting kind of spices) for the overconfident **faithless** people who threaten the community that is praying the psalm. It will mean that this community has the opportunity to make the same kind of confession as that recollected in the psalm's opening line, in respect of what God now does for it. Yes, God will deliver his people.

The antiphonal movement of the psalm (the people and God speak alternately and responsively) concludes with God's final commitment in the closing line.

PSALM 76

Fear or Reverence

The leader's. With strings. A composition. Asaph's. A song.

¹ God caused himself to be acknowledged in Judah,
  in Israel his name is great.

² His shelter came to be in Salem,
 his dwelling in Zion.
³ There he has shattered the bow's flames,
 the shield, the sword, and battle.   *(Rise)*
⁴ You were resplendent,
 glorious on the mountains of prey.
⁵ The stout-hearted let themselves be plundered,
 they fell into a deep sleep,
None of the strong men could lift their hands
⁶ at your blast, God of Jacob.
Both chariot and horse lay stunned;
⁷ you—you were to be held in awe.
Who can stand before you
 in the time of your anger?
⁸ From the heavens you let your decision be heard;
 the earth was in awe and was still,
⁹ when God rose to exercise authority,
 to deliver all the lowly in the land.   *(Rise)*
¹⁰ Because human fury confesses you;
 you gird on the last bit of your great fury.

¹¹ Make promises and fulfill them to Yahweh your God;
 all those around him bring tribute to the one who is
  to be held in awe.
¹² He curbs the spirit of leaders;
 he is to be held in awe by earth's kings.

Last week I was lecturing on the Psalms at a college in Michigan, and I referred to the extraordinary freedom that the Psalms assume we have in our relationship with God. You can say anything to God. In relation to God, we are like children in relation to a parent or a teacher. Of course the image presupposes that you have a good relationship with your parent or teacher; but if that is so, then you can say anything. You can beat on your father or mother's chest, and they will let you do so. In the question time after the lecture, a student at the far back of the auditorium expressed some bewilderment. Didn't we have to fear God?

 The word *fear* is a tricky one. Hebrew has several words equivalent to such English words as *fear*, *dread*, and *awe*, and it uses all of them to denote both a positive sense of reverence and submission and a more negative sense of being afraid or fearful. More often than not, when you read about the fear of God in English Bible translations, you need mentally to substitute a phrase such as "awe before God," "reverence for God," "submission to God," or "obedience to God." When we are in a right relationship with God, then the words for fear have positive connotations. When we have gone wrong in relation to God, then they have negative connotations. In effect, our actions decide which connotation applies.

The most common Hebrew word for fear or reverence comes four times in Psalm 75—I have translated it as *awe* each time. Each time one could understand the word as having either a positive or a negative connotation, so it illustrates how (in this case) the strong men of the earth, the tribute bringers, or the kings decide whether the implications are positive or negative.

The psalm looks back to when God settled in Jerusalem through David's action in taking the city from the Jebusites and making Jerusalem the people's chief sanctuary. It then envisages one of those times when Jerusalem was under attack from people such as the **Assyrians**, but its nature as a hymn of praise that could be used regularly means it's probably a mistake to try to connect it with a particular event. The references to God's blast and to chariot and horse make one think of the **Reed Sea deliverance**, too. They were all events with the same dynamic that established that **Yahweh** needed to be held in awe (if you were willing to submit to God) or to be feared (if you were inclined to oppose God's purpose).

For the last two lines and the last two references to awe, the psalm turns to address Israel. It is an encouragement to us that God acts in such a way as to present that choice before other people. These last two lines make explicit that these events also place the choice before us.

PSALM 77

Has God Changed?

The leader's. On Jeduthun. Asaph's. A composition.

¹ With my voice to God, yes, I will cry out;
  with my voice to God, yes, so that he may give ear to me.

² On the day of my troubles,
 I have sought help from my Lord.
My hand has reached out by night and does not grow numb;
 my heart refuses to find comfort.
³ I shall be mindful of God and complain,
 I shall talk as my spirit faints.
⁴ I have taken hold of the guards on my eyes;
 I have been constrained and I cannot speak.
⁵ I have thought of days of old,
 years of ages past.
⁶ I shall be mindful of my song by night
 as I murmur in my heart, and my spirit has sought hard:
⁷ Is it forever that my Lord will reject,
 and never again show favor?
⁸ Has his commitment ceased to exist permanently,
 his word failed for all generations?
⁹ Has God ignored the showing of grace,
 or shut off his compassion in anger?   (*Rise*)
¹⁰ I said, "That has distressed me:
 the change in the right hand of the One on High."

¹¹ I will make mention of Yah's deeds;
 yes, I shall be mindful of your amazing deeds of old.
¹² I will talk about your every act,
 I will murmur of your deeds.
¹³ God, your way was with holiness;
 who was a god as great as God?
¹⁴ You are the God who performs an amazing deed;
 you made known your might among the peoples.
¹⁵ You restored your people with your arm,
 the children of Jacob and Joseph.   (*Rise*)

¹⁶ Waters saw you, God;
 when waters saw you, they would convulse.
Yes, deeps would tremble;
¹⁷ clouds poured down water.
Skies gave voice;
 yes, your arrows would go about.
¹⁸ The sound of your thunder was in the whirlwind,
 lightning lit up the world.
The earth trembled and shook;

¹⁹   your way was in the sea.
   Your paths were in mighty waters,
      though your steps were not acknowledged.
²⁰ You led your people like a flock
      by the hand of Moses and Aaron.

One of our students came to see me to ask me to meet with another student whose life seemed to be falling apart and who was talking about suicide. The woman had been married for twenty years; her first husband had been "the love of her life." Then he became ill and died. She hated being alone, and more quickly than was wise (one can see with hindsight) she got involved with another man, and they married. Her second husband worked freelance in information technology and at the time they married was doing well, but then the recession came and the bottom fell out of his business. To try to jump-start its growth, they took out a second mortgage on the house that had belonged to her and her first husband, but that attempt failed, and they are now in danger of defaulting on the mortgage and losing the house, and of her having to pull out of school.

Psalm 77 makes me think of this woman. One major aspect of the toughness of her situation is the way things have changed. Five years ago she was happily married, economically secure, and deeply involved in church life. But her problem is not only that things have changed. As the psalm puts it, God has changed.

So she thinks about the contrast between the present and the past. Thinking about the past can be a painful business, but it can also be a constructive one. There are lots of passages in the Bible that talk about God's having a change of mind, and people sometimes get worried about such talk. Does God flip flop? Is God not reliable? Might God say one thing today and another tomorrow? Answer: yes, God might, but God does not change arbitrarily. Most references to God's having a change of mind mean that God doesn't impose a punishment that people have been threatened with, the reason being that people have turned away from their wrongdoing. So in the very act of changing, God is being consistent in showing mercy.

The trouble in this psalm, as for the woman I have been talking about, is twofold. God's change is from blessing to trouble, and there doesn't seem to be a reason for it. Yet the psalm goes on to express a determination to remember how things were in the past. Further, there is then a surprising feature of the remembering. One would expect it to relate to things God had done for this individual who is praying. Instead it relates to things God had done for the whole people. The psalm could then be used by a king or another leader who is praying about a situation when the people as a whole are in trouble. But the opening part made it look more like a psalm for an ordinary person to use. When an ordinary individual used it, the remembering then relates to something bigger than God's past acts in this individual's life. It associates the individual with the great things God did for the people at the exodus and the **Reed Sea**. The equivalent for a Christian would be that we remember what God did for his people in sending Jesus to live and die and rise from death for us.

So what is the point of remembering these events? When I do so, on one hand I am reminding myself of the huge things that God did for all of us, and I am reassuring myself that the reverses of the present cannot be the end. But I am also reminding God of those huge things, and in effect I am saying to God, "You can't stop now." What you are doing now doesn't fit with what you did back then.

Reminding myself that I can remind God about the past then energizes the prayer with which the psalm opens. The psalmist has had no acts of deliverance to look at (the eye guards are the eyelids) and to praise God for (so there are constraints on praise). All one can do in those circumstances is urge God to resume the pattern of acting that God has shown in the past.

PSALM 78:1–37

The Subtle Link between God's Grace and People's Response

An instruction. Asaph's.

¹ Give ear to my teaching, my people;
    bend your ear to the words of my mouth.
² I will open my mouth with a parable,
    pour out mysteries from of old.

³ Things that we have heard and acknowledged,
    that our ancestors have told us,
⁴ we will not hide from their descendants,
    telling the next generation,
the praises of Yahweh and his might,
    the wonders that he did.

⁵ He established a declaration in Jacob,
    laid down teaching in Israel,
which he commanded our ancestors
    to get their descendants to acknowledge,
⁶ so that the next generation might acknowledge them,
    descendants who will be born,
so that they might rise up and tell their descendants
⁷   in order that they might put their confidence in God
and not ignore God's acts
    but keep his commands,
⁸ and not become like their ancestors,
    a rebellious and defiant generation,
a generation that did not make its mind firm,
    and whose spirit was not true to God.

⁹ The Ephraimites, equipped as archers,
    turned back on the day of engagement.
¹⁰ They did not keep God's covenant
    but refused to walk by his teaching.
¹¹ They ignored his deeds,
    the wonders he had let them see.
¹² In the sight of their ancestors he had done a wonder,
    in the country of Egypt, in the region of Zoan.
¹³ He divided the sea and enabled them to pass through it,
    he made the water stand like a mound.
¹⁴ He led them by means of a cloud by day,
    and all through the night by means of a fiery light.
¹⁵ He divided crags in the wilderness,
    and enabled them to drink like the deeps, abundantly.
¹⁶ He brought out streams from a rock,
    and made water flow down like rivers.

¹⁷ But they went on repeatedly offending against him,
    and defying the One on High in the desert.

¹⁸ They tested God with deliberateness,
    in asking food for themselves.
¹⁹ They spoke against God:
    "Is God able to lay a table in the wilderness?
²⁰ Yes, he hit the crag and water flowed,
    torrents gushed.
Can he also give bread,
    or provide meat for his people?"

²¹ Therefore Yahweh listened and raged;
    broke out against Jacob,
    and also anger arose against Israel,
²² because they did not keep faith in God,
    they did not trust in his deliverance.
²³ So he commanded the skies above,
    opened the doors of the heavens.
²⁴ He rained manna on them as food,
    gave them grain from the heavens.
²⁵ Each person ate the food of heroes;
    he sent them provisions to fill them.
²⁶ He would make the east wind move in the
      heavens,
    and he drove the south wind by his might.
²⁷ He rained meat on them like dirt,
    winged birds like the sand at the seas.
²⁸ He made them come down inside his camp,
    around his dwelling.
²⁹ They ate, and they were very full;
    he would bring them their desire.
³⁰ They had not turned aside from their desire,
    their food was still in their mouth,
³¹ when God's anger rose against them,
    he slew some of their sturdiest,
    and put down Israel's youth.

³² For all this they offended again,
    and did not keep faith for all his wonders.
³³ He made their days end in emptiness,
    their years in terror.
³⁴ When he slew them, they would seek help from him,
    turn and search for God.

³⁵ They were mindful that God was their crag,
   God on High their restorer.
³⁶ But they deceived him with their mouth,
   with their tongue they would lie to him.
³⁷ Their mind was not firm with him;
   they did not keep faith with his covenant.

Yesterday in church the Old Testament reading was the giving of the Ten Commandments in Exodus 20, and we followed that reading with some congregational discussion of which of these commands seem most important in our context and whether there were puzzling features about them. One person asked about the warning that God would punish people who made images through to the third and fourth generation; someone else was able to quote God's words that follow not long afterward in Exodus 32, about each individual dying for his or her own sin (I was impressed by her ability to quote that verse). The first contributor apologized later because she thought she might have asked a silly question. I assured her that there are no silly questions and that the questions she was brave enough to ask were often the questions other people wanted to ask but were a bit shy about asking.

One interesting feature of Psalm 78 is its opening assumption that the people of God need to be talking about God's teaching. It does imply that there is a teaching role to be fulfilled by teachers; the psalm begins, "Listen to me." The psalmist assumes the ability to give people a reliable and distinctive account of the "mysteries," the deep truths of Israel's story. Yet the psalm also recognizes that any teacher stands in the midst of an ongoing process. Teaching is possible only if you have listened, and it is effective only if the next generation takes up the telling. Listening and telling involve speaking and not just writing and reading. The **Torah** emphasizes the role of parents in ensuring that children know the story of God's dealings with Israel. It also emphasizes the role of children in asking questions—"What does this mean?" There are no silly questions.

The opening of the psalm makes clear the essential link between God's acts on Israel's behalf and Israel's obeying God and trusting God. There are two traps that it is possible to fall into. One is to assume that because God loves us unconditionally, it doesn't matter how we live; it doesn't affect our relationship with God. The other is to assume that God's love for us is conditional on the lives we live, and that our priority is to gain God's approval of us by living the right kind of life. The opening of the psalm deftly negotiates the space between these two traps. God's relationship with Israel issued from God's acts on its behalf, but it was essential for Israel to respond to God by trusting in God and following in God's way. The passing on and the telling that the psalm speaks of relates both to the acts of God and to the expectations regarding a right response.

The main part of the psalm gives more concrete illustrations of the subtle relationship between God's generous acts and our response. People had declined to keep God's **covenant** (the point about referring specifically to **Ephraim** will become clearer when we get to the end of the psalm), and they had done so despite the fact that God had done such wonders for them. In effect they were testing God. Without realizing it, they were trying to see how far they could push God. One aspect of his response was to provide them with what they explicitly asked for—food from the heavens; bread and meat. But another aspect was to chastise them. The provision illustrated how God would continue to be gracious. The chastisement illustrated the point that nevertheless you will be unwise to think you can mess with God. They would turn back, and God would have them back; but their turning back could never be finally relied on. Yet their disobedience and his chastisement would never be the end of the story.

PSALM 78:38–72

People Who Are Standing Need to Watch Lest They Fall

38 But because he was compassionate, he would
        expiate waywardness
    and not destroy.
  He repeatedly turned his anger;
    he did not stir all his wrath.
39 He was mindful that they were flesh,
    a passing wind that does not return.

40 How much they would defy him in the wilderness,
  pain him in the wasteland.
41 Repeatedly they tested God,
  vexed Israel's Holy One.
42 They were not mindful of his hand,
  the day when he redeemed them from the foe,
43 when he put his signs in Egypt,
  his portents in the region of Zoan.
44 He turned their great river into blood;
  people could not drink from their streams.
45 He would send a swarm against them and it ate them,
  frogs and they devastated them.
46 He gave their produce to the caterpillar,
  their crop to the locust.
47 He slew their vine with hail,
  their sycamore figs with flood.
48 He surrendered their animals to hail,
  their cattle to lightning flashes.
49 He would send among them his angry fury,
  wrath, rage, and trouble,
  a delegation of aides bringing evil
50   that would clear a path for his anger.
  He did not spare their life from death
  but surrendered them to epidemic.
51 He hit every firstborn in Egypt,
  the first issue of vigor in the tents of Ham.
52 He got his people moving like sheep,
  drove them like a flock in the wilderness.
53 He led them in security and they were not fearful,
  but their enemies—the sea covered them.
54 He brought them to his holy territory,
  the mountain that his right hand acquired.
55 He dispossessed nations before them,
  allotted them as a share of their very own;
  he settled the clans of Israel in their tents.

56 But they tested and defied God on High;
  they did not observe his declarations.
57 They went away and were disloyal, like their ancestors;
  they turned like a treacherous bow.
58 They vexed him with their high places,
  aroused him with their images.

26

59 God listened and raged,
    and quite rejected Israel.
60 He abandoned the dwelling at Shiloh,
    the tent where he had dwelt among humanity.
61 He gave his might to captivity,
    his glory to the hand of the foe.
62 He surrendered his people to the sword;
    he raged at his very own.
63 Fire consumed its young men,
    and its girls were not lamented.
64 Its priests fell by the sword;
    its widows could not weep.
65 But the Lord woke up like someone asleep,
    like a warrior shouting because of wine.
66 He beat back his foes,
    gave them permanent reviling.
67 He rejected the tent of Joseph,
    did not choose the clan of Ephraim.
68 He chose the clan of Judah, Mount Zion,
    to which he dedicated himself.
69 He built his sanctuary like the heights,
    like the earth that he established forever.
70 He chose David as his servant
    and took him from the sheep pens.
71 He brought him from following the ewes
    to shepherd Jacob his people,
    Israel his very own.
72 He shepherded them in accordance with the integrity
        of his heart;
    he would lead them by the skillful acts of his hands.

A few months ago one of the members of our church, a lively lady in her nineties who always had something to contribute, suddenly became less consistent in coming to church, and then didn't appear for two or three successive weeks. We then heard that she had died. The odd thing about it was that it was a shock. Last night we went to take Communion to two other ladies in our church, also in their nineties; both have been unable to come to church for the last two Sundays. One is unsteady on her legs; the other has sores on her leg that refuse to heal. We agreed that it looked as if they too were ailing. They have already talked about

27

the kind of funeral they want. (And by the time I am finalizing the editing of this book, one of them has passed, and I will be conducting her funeral this week.) Spending time with such people and watching them become frailer is a solemn experience. Among other things, it makes us think about our own frailty.

One piece of good news in Psalm 78 is that God thinks about our frailty and makes allowance for it; God is mindful that we are flesh, "a passing wind that does not return." When Paul talks about our being flesh, he has in mind that we are morally weak. While this psalm makes clear the Old Testament's recognition that we are morally weak, when it talks about our being flesh, it has in mind the more ordinary physical frailty that is expressed in our mortality. We are like the wind, not in the sense of a genuinely powerful wind but in the sense of a wind that makes a lot of noise but then is gone.

So God makes allowance for our frailty and does not blast us with his own powerful wind in such a way as to destroy us. God holds back out of compassion. Further, God expiates our waywardness. It's an even more remarkable declaration, because by definition expiating sin is what human beings do by making the appropriate offerings. But that process works only because God provides it as a process that will work, and occasions when the Old Testament talks about God's act of expiation bring out the way cleansing and forgiveness always comes about because of God's grace and love.

God has lots of opportunity to exercise self-restraint and compassion. The psalm goes on to review the story of God's involvement with Israel. It starts with a long reminder of what God did in **Egypt** to try to lean on its people to let the Israelites leave their country. It recalls God's providing for the Israelites on their journey to **Canaan** and giving them their new home there. This involvement might have been expected to arouse a response of gratitude and commitment, but all it aroused was defiance, vexation, and pain. So God responded with rage, rejection, and abandonment. Three times the psalm refers to the people's "testing" God to see how far they can push him. Can they get him finally to abandon them? Answer: No, they can't. When it looks as if they have done so and as if God has gone to sleep on them, he wakes up and acts.

At the beginning of the psalm, there was a puzzling reference to **Ephraim**; the significance of that reference emerges near the end of the psalm. One of the ways that God seeks to handle the necessity both to be faithful to his people and to take its waywardness seriously is to cast off part of the people but keep another part of it in existence. Ephraim is bigger than **Judah** and would have made the more obvious political and religious center for Israel, but instead God makes Judah the center. The historical books see this simply as David's action; the psalm is prepared to see God behind David's action. David became the people's skillful shepherd.

If you belonged to Judah, you could be tempted to feel rather superior when you get to the end of the psalm. You are the people God chose, rather than those Ephraimites to the north! But then you might notice the dynamic of the story as the psalm tells it. When God exercises some choice or shows some grace, the question is how the beneficiaries respond. The fate of earlier generations of Israel and of Ephraim in particular needs to be a warning to you, otherwise you could go the same way— which is in fact exactly what happened. There is an equivalent dynamic to a Christian reading of the psalm and of the Old Testament in general. If we think that God cast off the Jewish people, Paul points out in 1 Corinthians 10 that we had better watch it because God could also cast us off.

PSALM 79

One Way to Evade Compassion Fatigue

A composition. Asaph's.

¹ God, nations came into your own possession,
      defiled your holy palace,
      made Jerusalem into ruins.
² They gave your servants' corpses as food
      to the birds of the heavens,
   the flesh of the people committed to you
      to the creatures of the earth.
³ They poured out their blood like water
      around Jerusalem, with no one to bury them.

29

⁴ We became an object of reviling to our neighbors,
 of scorn and derision to the people around us.
⁵ How long, Yahweh—will you be angry forever,
 will your passion blaze like fire?
⁶ Pour out your wrath on the nations,
 which have not acknowledged you,
on the kingdoms,
 which have not called on your name.
⁷ Because they have consumed Jacob,
 and desolated his abode.

⁸ Do not keep in mind in respect of us
 the wayward acts of the past.
May your compassion meet us quickly,
 because we have got very low.
⁹ Help us, God our deliverer,
 for the sake of the honor of your name.
Rescue us, make expiation for our offenses,
 for the sake of your name.
¹⁰ Why should the nations say,
 "Where is their God?"
May redress for your servants' blood that was poured out
 be acknowledged among the nations before our eyes.
¹¹ May the captive's groan come before you;
 in accordance with the greatness of your might
 preserve the people about to die.
¹² Give back to our neighbors sevenfold, into their bosom,
 their reviling with which they have reviled you, Lord.
¹³ But we will be your people,
 the flock you shepherd.
We will confess you forever;
 to all generations we will tell your praise.

The expression "compassion fatigue" has been around for a while. The nature of modern communications media means that we become instantly aware of suffering in different parts of the world, but we cannot deal with all that suffering or live with that awareness, and we have to turn off. When I was caring for my first wife through the years she was ill, I had to live with the temptation to feel guilty that I couldn't be a good husband because I couldn't "solve" her illness. People who are a step further away from someone who is ill are often inclined to stay one step away because coming close means becoming involved in the sense of helplessness and guilt. If that experience is a reality in connection with individuals, how much bigger a reality it is in connection with the suffering of communities and nations. A recent newspaper article noted how it applies to the problems of joblessness, house foreclosures, and starvation. It can seem that we pump millions from state money or individual generosity and the problem in question refuses to go away (indeed, we hear that the money has been siphoned off by profiteers).

A prayer such as Psalm 79 at least provides us with a way of praying for cities, nations, and communities. Presumably in its origin it was a prayer that the people of Jerusalem prayed for themselves, but for most people in the West reading this psalm, it becomes a means of entering into the pain and anger of a suffering community and joining that community in bringing its pain and anger to God.

First, in the common fashion of such protest psalms, we describe the situation in concrete detail to God. We rehearse the story of what has happened: destruction, defilement, death dealing, and dishonor. We ask God sharp questions—how long are you going to let this go on? We challenge God about whether it is not more appropriate to bring such trouble on the people who cause this suffering rather than leave the sufferers with it. We urge God to recognize the discredit that affects God himself when he gives the impression that people can do what they like to others and get away with it. We appeal to God's compassion; if compassion fatigue is a reality for human beings, then we need God to resist its effect. We urge God to take redress not for ourselves but for other people and not for our attackers' reviling of us but for their reviling of him.

It doesn't come naturally to us to pray this way, which is presumably part of the reason that a psalm such as this one is important. If God doesn't care to take redress of people for their reviling, then that is his business. If we aren't incensed at people's reviling of God and thus desirous that God should do so, it raises questions about us. In our world, it may well come more naturally to people who are going through that kind of experience to protest in this way. If we can't come to join in their protest, then such inability also raises questions about us.

In this psalm the people of God who are praying make no claim to be undeserving of the trouble that has come upon them. Maybe the psalm presupposes a situation such as a time when the fall of Jerusalem in 587 is now some decades past, as may be the case with Psalm 74. People know they can do nothing to put their past right. They make two bold requests in respect of that past. One is for God to put it out of mind, to forget. The psalms assume that God has control of his memory and can choose not to remember things. The other request restates that first one. Like Psalm 78, it speaks of God's expiating our offenses, the act that (by definition) we are responsible for but that God can be urged to undertake as an expression of compassion. This psalm nuances the point by speaking of God's so acting "for the sake of your **name**." In other words, it says, "That's the kind of person you are, so act with mercy and forgiveness in this way in order to be yourself."

PSALM 80

Bring Back! Come Back!

The leader's. For lilies. A declaration. Asaph's. A composition.

¹ You who shepherd Israel, give ear,
      you who drive Joseph like a flock.
   You who sit on the cherubs, shine out
²   before Ephraim, Benjamin, and Manasseh.
   Stir your might,
      come as deliverance for us.
³ God, bring us back,
      shine your face so that we may find deliverance.

⁴ Yahweh, God Armies,
      how long have you fumed at your people's plea?
⁵ You have fed them weeping as food,
      made them drink tears by measure.
⁶ You have set us at contention with our neighbors;
      our enemies mock us at will.

[7] God Armies, bring us back,
    shine your face so that we may find deliverance.
[8] You moved a vine from Egypt,
    dispossessed nations and planted it.
[9] You cleared a way before it,
    it put its roots down and filled the country.
[10] Mountains were covered by its shade,
    mighty cedars by its branches.
[11] It put out its boughs as far as the sea,
    its shoots to the river.
[12] Why have you broken open its walls,
    so that all the people who pass by pluck it?
[13] The boar from the forest tears at it,
    the creature of the wild feeds on it.

[14] God Armies, will you come back,
    take note from the heavens and see,
    attend to this vine,
[15] the stock that your right hand planted,
    and over the offspring you took hold of for yourself.
[16] Burned in fire, cut,
    at the blast from your face they perish.
[17] May your hand be upon the one at your right hand,
    on the man you took hold of for yourself.
[18] We will not turn aside from you;
    give us life, and we will call on your name.

[19] Yahweh, God Armies, bring us back,
    shine your face so that we may find deliverance.

It's nearly three hundred years since the First Great Awakening, a revival of religious life in Britain and even more in the British colonies in America a few decades before the War of Independence. This First Great Awakening was mostly a movement within the church. The Second Great Awakening in the United States at the beginning of the nineteenth century took the form of successful evangelistic efforts to bring people to faith in Christ, and, as a result, in American English the word *revival* came to denote an evangelistic campaign. But the original meaning of the word suggests a renewing of religious life like the First Great Awakening rather than the finding of religious life for the first time.

In preaching about and praying for revival in the First Great Awakening sense, Psalm 80 has been a favorite text. In many translations, the next-to-last line pleads, "Revive us, and we will call on your **name**." In Britain and the United States in the twenty-first century, one can see how this prayer would be appropriate.

The prayer would fit **Ephraim** at various points—in the latter years of its existence as a nation (this understanding would fit the apparent reference to the king near the end of the psalm), in the aftermath of its conquest by **Assyria**, or in subsequent centuries. It is like a vineyard on which its owner had expended considerable effort. And Ephraim has indeed flourished in the past, like the church in Britain and in the United States, exercising power and influence. But God, the vineyard owner, has then neglected it—indeed, has personally ravaged it. Such treatment of Ephraim corresponds to warnings to **Judah** in Isaiah 5 about how things will be when the vine does not produce good grapes, yet this prayer evidently does not think the people's own waywardness explains its fate. (Of course, like any prayer, in some situations it may earn a snorting response from God in this connection; but then at least you know what you have to do next—that is, repent.) Perhaps it parallels Psalms 74 and 79 in thinking that whatever chastisement was appropriate at some stage, the present generation has not earned the affliction it experiences. The psalm actually begins with the other classic image for the people of God: as well as being a vineyard, Ephraim is a flock that has had **Yahweh** as its shepherd and driver. So why is the shepherd neglecting it—neglecting us?

As well as being the shepherd, Yahweh is the king, the one who sits enthroned on the **cherubs**. The psalm keeps repeating variants on the kingly title **Yahweh Armies**. One aspect of a king's responsibility is to be responsive to pleas from his subjects when they are in need and/or when they are under attack and to **deliver** them. Why is God not acting like a king? Why does he behave as if he is angry with the people's pleas rather than sympathetic to them? Why does he make them look stupid in the face of the rest of the world?

They need God to bring them back, to restore them, to bring them back to life. But the reason that they need restoration and the key to that restoration is that they need God to come back. The two appeals "Bring back" and "Come back" are related in Hebrew and in English, and the use of the two variants on the same words brings out the fundamental nature of the problem. God has gone away. If there is to be restoration of the people, it must be by restoration of God's presence. Currently the people experience a blast from Yahweh's face ("face" is the Hebrew word for "presence"). They need instead to experience God's face shining, smiling, because that signifies both personal warmth and the deliverance and blessing that naturally issue from personal warmth.

Perhaps the most remarkable feature of the psalm is that those things it says about God's neglecting and ravaging don't stop people from coming to God about what has happened. Indeed, they make people do so.

PSALM 81
On the Relationship between Worship and Sermon

The leader's. On the Gittite [a tune?]. Asaph's.

1. Resound for God our strength,
    shout for Jacob's God.
2. Raise the music, strike the tambourine,
    the melodious guitar with the harp.
3. Blow the horn at the new moon,
    at the full moon for our festival day.
4. Because it is a law of Israel,
    a decision of Jacob's God,
5. a declaration he laid on Joseph,
    when he went out over the country of Egypt.

   I listen to a lip I had not acknowledged:
6. "I removed his shoulder from the burden;
    his hands moved away from the basket.
7. In trouble you called and I rescued you,
    I answered you in the secret place of thunder.
   I tested you at the waters of Contention:

⁸ 'Listen, my people, and I will testify to you;
    Israel, if you listen to me . . .
⁹ There will not be for you a foreign god,
    you will not bow down to an alien god.
¹⁰ I Yahweh am your God,
    the one who brought you up from the country of Egypt;
    open your mouth wide and I will fill it.'
¹¹ But my people did not listen to my voice;
    Israel was unwilling in relation to me.
¹² So I sent them off in the stubbornness of their mind,
    so that they might walk by their own plans.
¹³ If only my people were listening to me,
    if only Israel would walk on in my ways.
¹⁴ I would quickly put down their enemies,
    turn my hand against their foes."
¹⁵ Yahweh's opponents would wither at him,
    and their fate would be forever.
¹⁶ He enabled them to eat of the best of wheat;
    "From the crag I filled you with honey."

We went to the first regular seminary chapel service of the quarter yesterday, and there was lots of resounding singing, (tuneful) shouting, and melodious guitar and piano (equivalent to the harp?). There were no horns this time, but I expect they will feature next week. The service was followed by a sermon that happened to be based on the story in Exodus 17 about the confrontation between the Israelites and Moses and God, to which Psalm 81 refers. In the United States it is common for worship services to comprise a simple liturgical sequence of (a) a lot of music and singing and (b) a sermon. As someone from the Church of England, I still find it a bit plain and basic, though at least it is consistent with the nature of a sandwich in the United States (a huge amount of bread wrapped around a huge amount of meat).

Psalm 81 rebukes me for my narrow-minded Britishness, because it more or less follows that simple sequence. In a formal sense it also follows the regular formal sequence of a psalm of praise. First, people address one another—one can imagine a minister addressing the opening lines to the choir or the congregation as a whole. The reference to the new moon and the full moon suggests that the psalm belongs to the month of Tishri in the fall, which starts with the New Year and has the festival of **Sukkot** at its midpoint. This chronology fits with the fact that Sukkot reminds people of the giving of Moses' **Torah**, to which the main part of the psalm will refer.

The psalm then follows the exhortation to worship with the reasons for worship. But here the psalm begins to tread a distinctive path. Usually the reasons for worship are also the content of the worship. Here they are more the explanation for it, the fact that God laid down these worship expectations in connection with "going out over **Egypt**"—that is, taking action to rescue the Israelites from Egypt.

The main part of the psalm begins with the minister beginning to preach a sermon about the expectation that he now realizes he had to heed from God, and he implies that the whole people have to heed it. God always has to remind his people of the need for a link between what he has done for them and the way they respond to him. The Israelites had to labor carrying bricks for the Egyptians; **Yahweh** relieved them. They were in trouble at the **Reed Sea**; Yahweh rescued them, coming from his secret place in the heavens. Thunder regularly comes from there, and it can be a metaphor for Yahweh's thunderous arrival to intervene on earth. The people "contended" with Moses about having no water in the wilderness, and Yahweh made water flow out of a cliff face. But in connection with those experiences in the wilderness on the way to **Canaan**, Yahweh pointed out that in response to how he had acted as their God, he expected them to live as his people. Further, that sequence would then also be the pattern for the future. He was committed to providing for them in the future on an ongoing basis, and he did so, for when the psalm goes on to talk about the wheat and the honey, it is evidently referring to life in the promised land and about God's fulfilling promises made in Deuteronomy 32.

But they never really gave Yahweh the response that went along with being his people. The word "listen" recurs in the psalm, but listening itself did not recur much. God is apparently powerless to change that aspect of the situation; all he can do is say, "If only." All God can do is let people exercise their freedom, make their own decisions, and live with the consequences.

We so love to make our plans (plans for a family, career plans, retirement plans . . .), to control our futures, our destinies. It is a frightening situation when God surrenders us to our own willfulness, to our own plans. The psalm closes with a final recollection of the way God has provided for the people, and it thereby puts the congregation on the spot. Are you going to continue that pattern from the past? The ball is in your court.

It turns out that the relationship between worship and sermon is less comfortable than is usually the case in our worship.

PSALM 82

On Challenging the Gods and God

A composition. Asaph's.

¹ God is standing in the divine assembly;
    in the midst of the gods he exercises authority.
² How long will you [gods] exercise authority for wickedness,
    lift up the faithless?   (*Rise*)
³ Exercise authority for the poor and orphan,
    show faithfulness to the lowly and destitute.
⁴ Rescue the poor and needy,
    save them from the hand of the faithless.
⁵ They do not acknowledge,
    they do not consider.
As they walk about in darkness,
    all earth's foundations fall down.

⁶ I myself said, "You are gods,
    all of you are offspring of the One on High.
⁷ Therefore you will die like human beings,
    fall like one of the leaders."
⁸ Arise, God, exercise authority for the earth,
    because you possess all the nations as your own.

Two friends who live in the Philippines had lunch with us a week or so ago while on a visit home in the United States. One of them, a Chinese American, told us that in the Philippines he had a sense of the presence of evil spirits that he did not have in the United States. It reminded me of the comment of a former colleague when she came back from a time in India, where she had the same experience. I do not infer that countries such as India and the Philippines are more affected by evil spirits than the United States or Britain; my wife's comment was that there is so much evil in our Western countries that evil spirits do not have to bother with us very much. To put it another way and adapt a comment from C. S. Lewis's *The Screwtape Letters*, the devil is sometimes clever enough not to make his activity so obvious that we forget that he exists.

Psalm 82 assumes that there are indeed supernatural entities involved in the government of the world. Although the Old Testament assumes that there is one God, it also assumes that there are lots of gods—they are the figures who can also be referred to as **aides** (angels) or as leaders (the word that comes near the end of the psalm). In English we usefully have the convention of being able to distinguish between the word *God* and the word *god* by using a capital letter for the former. Oddly, you might think, the word for *God* and the word for *gods* in the first line of the psalm is the same in Hebrew. So there is occasionally ambiguity about whether a passage refers to God or gods, but the context nearly always makes clear which sense of the word is right, and so it is here. The picture is of God as president over the assembly of divine beings. One might have expected God to be sitting, not standing, but standing is the posture the president of an assembly would take when giving a decision and when initiating action.

The psalm later alludes to one difference between God and the gods: the gods can die. They come into being, and they can expire. God's being exists forever backward and forever forward. But the psalm first concerns itself with another difference: God is the supreme authority; the gods are God's underlings. God exercises **authority** in the assembly, but the gods exercise authority in the world, a derived authority given them by God. Elsewhere the Old Testament implies that there is one god for each of the nations—for instance, Chemosh is the god of the Moabites—and here the psalm makes that assumption and may be concerned about the gods' exercise of authority over their individual areas of responsibility in the world as a whole. The psalm's closing reference to all the nations as belonging to God would support the idea that the psalm refers to the gods' being in authority over different nations. On the other hand, the talk about exercising authority for the poor and vulnerable parallels the way the Prophets speak to people who hold human power in Israel, and the psalm may have the same focus. The gods are supposed to be concerned about exercising authority on behalf of the needy.

Certainly the gods are behaving in the same way as people with human power in Israel. The idea of leadership is that one should use it in order to keep the powerful and wealthy people in check and protect the weak and vulnerable, but leaders usually use their power to benefit themselves and impoverish ordinary people. Behind this activity by human leaders the psalm sees the influence of divine beings. They exalt the wicked and **faithless** people and fail to act **faithfully** by rescuing the vulnerable. So the faithless people are able to avoid thinking about what they should be doing and about the moral implications of their acts. They are free to go about in the dark concerning what their exercise of power and influence should be like. They thus undermine the foundations of human life in society.

Through most of the psalm it's not clear who is issuing the rebuke to the gods, and you could infer that the reason God is standing is to do so. But in a psalm, the speaker is usually a human being, and this is certainly the case at the end of the psalm when the speaker goes on to issue a challenge to God. The implication of the closing line is that God has that notice on his desk that says, "The buck stops here." Why are the troubles in the world what they are? If one factor is the way the gods exercise their authority, God cannot make that a basis for saying, "It's not my fault." The gods are his underlings. He needs to do something about them.

How brave prayer can be!

PSALM 83

Choose Your Fate

A song. A composition. Asaph's.

¹ God, do not keep your silence,
   do not be mute, do not be quiet, God.

2 Because there—your enemies rage,
  your opponents have reared their head.
3 They devise a plan against your people,
  they engage in consultation against the people you cherish.
4 They have said, "Come on, let's wipe them out from being
      a nation,
  so that Israel's name will be brought to mind no more."
5 Because they have consulted together with one mind;
  against you they have sealed a covenant—
6 the tents of Edom and the Ishmaelites,
  Moab and the Hagrites,
7 Gebal, Ammon, and Amalek,
  Philistia with the inhabitants of Tyre.
8 Assyria, too, has joined with them;
  they have become the strength of the descendants
      of Lot.   (*Rise*)

9 Act toward them like Midian,
  like Sisera, like Jabin, at the Qishon Wash,
10 who were destroyed at En-dor,
  became manure for the ground.
11 Treat them—their nobles like Oreb and like Ze'eb,
  all their leaders like Zebah and Salmunna,
12 people who said, "Let's take possession
  of God's pastures for ourselves."
13 My God, make them like a whirl,
  like stubble before the wind.
14 Like fire that burns a forest,
  like a flame that sets mountains ablaze,
15 so will you chase them with your tempest,
  terrify them with your storm.
16 Fill their faces with humiliation
  so that they seek help from your name, Yahweh.
17 May they be shamed and terrified forever,
  may they be disgraced and may they perish.
18 May they acknowledge that you,
  whose name is Yahweh alone,
  are the One on High over all the earth.

Biblical scholar Michael V. Fox has what you might call a typical
Jewish background. At the beginning of the twentieth century

his grandfather had a narrow escape from pogroms in Russia, when hundreds of Jews were killed and thousands raped, mutilated, and despoiled. He has described how he happened to be born outside of the reach of Nazi power and thus escaped the Holocaust, and in a study titled *Character and Ideology in the Book of Esther* ([Grand Rapids: Wm. B. Eerdmans Publishing Co., 2001], 12) Fox writes of what the book of Esther means to him in light of the history of his family and people. He comments on the way that God seems to be hidden in the Esther story, "as he has been so often, so inexplicably, so unforgivably, throughout history."

Psalm 83 presupposes such hiddenness. God is silent, mute, quiet, inactive, and hidden at a moment when his people are under horrendous pressure. The psalm wants the people in its day who are playing the role of would-be destroyers to be destroyed themselves, and it suggests various images for that destruction. Some come from the biblical story in the book of Judges, which shows that there is nothing outlandish about the request—it is in keeping with the way God has acted previously. So there is encouragement in these stories for the victims of current atrocities. Silence may not be God's last word. God has shown in the past a willingness to act against people who have collaborated in seeking to wipe out Israel, so there could be hope that God would do so again. Further, referring to these earlier events in a prayer implies that they should also be significant for God. In effect, they say, "You acted that way before—we need you to do so again." At the moment God is silent, as God often is.

Maybe God has good reason; maybe God is giving the oppressors a chance to repent. Maybe that is why God often seems silent in the Western church in our own day. The second way the psalm speaks of God's action is in terms of a fire that chases people. But sometimes people flee from a fire and succeed in getting away from it. It terrifies them, but it terrifies them into escaping. Then the psalm speaks of God's humiliating the attackers in such a way that they turn to God for help. Translations commonly speak of them "seeking God's **name**," but this translation does not make clear what is implied by "seeking." It means having recourse to someone, looking to someone for guidance or support. We may think of confidence as a positive attitude, but when the confidence is falsely placed (for instance, in our own resources when we are opposing God's purpose), humiliation, shame, or disgrace is the positive experience; it makes you turn to God. It makes you acknowledge God.

Or rather, in the psalm, it makes you acknowledge **Yahweh**. The psalm's prayer concerns attacks by other peoples, and it is quite plausible to imagine these peoples disparaging the God of the people they are attacking, as the **Assyrians** explicitly do in the story in Isaiah 36–37. The psalm thus suggests a number of possibilities for the destiny of Israel's attackers, not all mutually compatible. It could be death and/or escape and/or humiliation and/or submission and/or recognition of Yahweh. The nations' decision decides their fate.

Interpreted literally, to say that Yahweh is the only God whose name is Yahweh is to say the obvious. But the statement is a compressed one that presupposes that Yahweh is the only God, and thus that Yahweh is the God who is on high over all the earth. It is apt that Psalm 83 begins with its double address of "God" and ends up with its double reference to Yahweh. Psalms 42–83 are more sparing in their use of the name Yahweh than other psalms; Psalm 84 marks a reversion to the more familiar frequent usage of the name.

PSALM 84

The One Day and the Thousand Days

The leader's. On the Gittite [a tune?]. The Qorahites'. A composition.

¹ How much loved is your fine dwelling,
      Yahweh Armies.
² My whole being yearned,
      it is spent [with looking] for Yahweh's courtyards
   so that my heart and my body might resound
      for the living God.
³ Yes, a bird—it found a home,
      a pigeon [found] itself a nest,
      where it has put its young—

your great altar, Yahweh Armies,
    my King and my God.
4 The blessings of the people who live in your house,
    who can still praise you!   (*Rise*)

5 The blessings of the person whose strength comes
        through you,
    with the highways in their mind!
6 The people who pass through Balsam Vale
    will make it a spring.
Yes, the first rain will cover it with blessings;
7   they will walk from rampart to rampart.
The God of gods will appear in Zion,
8   Yahweh God Armies.
Listen to my plea,
    give ear, God of Jacob.   (*Rise*)
9 Look at our shield, God,
    look at the face of your anointed.
10 Because a day in your courtyards is better than a thousand,
    I would choose being at the threshold of my God's house,
    rather than dwelling in the tents of the faithless person,
11   because Yahweh God is sun and shield.
Yahweh gives favor and honor;
    he does not withhold good for people
    who walk with integrity.
12 Yahweh Armies,
    the blessings of the person who trusts in you!

Each of the churches to which I belonged as a minister in England used to have something like a retreat each year—not a business-focused retreat (the connotation that often attaches to the word *retreat* in the United States) but a weekend or a week in which the community focused on its relationship with God. Obviously the congregation focused on God and on its relationship with God for an hour or so each Sunday, but these retreats gave people extended time to do so outside their everyday work and life concerns. There were often times when the congregation as a whole moved forward in their understanding and commitment, and times when individuals moved forward. There would be a sobriety, even a sadness, in the air as people packed their bags and climbed into their cars to go home, for they knew (or at least felt) that the sense of God's involvement with us that they had while they were away could not be maintained when they returned to work and life concerns.

Psalm 84 reflects that dynamic and speaks to that sense of sadness or sobriety. Whereas people who lived in Jerusalem could visit the temple frequently, most Israelites were likely to be able to do so only once a year, if they were lucky, for a festival such as **Sukkot**. One can imagine then the sense of anticipation as they made this pilgrimage. They have the highways, the roads that lead up to Jerusalem, in their minds. We don't know of a place called "Balsam Vale," but the word for balsam (a plant or tree) sounds the same as the word for weeping—hence the expression "vale of tears." So the idea is that people who come in sadness or pass through sadness are able to find refreshment. If they are making their pilgrimage at Sukkot in September/ October, then it is the end of the dry season when people know they need the rain to come soon to begin the new farming year, and that need will be one of the subjects of their prayer when they get to Jerusalem—hence the reference to the first rain and the blessing it is. In Jerusalem they will walk around the city's walls rejoicing to be in the city of **Zion,** whose strength comes from the protection of **Yahweh Armies,** and they will pray for the king as the earthly leader through whom God works.

At last they will be able to sit in the courtyards of the temple, like guests visiting friends and sitting in their courtyard having dinner. I have a photograph of a pigeon sitting in a cleft of the stones of the temple wall—the psalmist feels like a bird able to make its home there. The bird might seem insignificant, and the pilgrims feel insignificant, but they have this freedom to relax in the safety and privilege of the temple courtyards, the place where God lives. No wonder they see one day in these courtyards, one day on **Yahweh's** doorstep, as better than a thousand ordinary days spent in their home town with people who do not honor Yahweh properly or do not honor Yahweh at all. (Maybe the reference to a thousand days suggests they might be able to expect to go to the festival only once every three years.)

Yet they also point to a paradox that the churches to which I have belonged sought to get people to see. If the God people met on a church retreat is real, then that God is real in their factory or store or school as well. If God is not real in everyday life, God is not truly real at all. The psalm speaks of the good fortune of the people who live in Jerusalem and can be in the temple every day, like Simeon and Anna in the story in Luke 2. It also speaks of the good fortune of the people who find their strength through Yahweh, which might mean Yahweh gives them the energy to make the long journey, but it might also mean Yahweh gives them the strength to live their everyday lives with their challenges, demands, and temptations. It speaks, too, of the good fortune of the people who trust in Yahweh, and there is no doubt that this description relates to the thousand days and not just to the one day. The joy and encouragement of the one day in Yahweh's house thus function to build up trust in Yahweh and make it possible to live the thousand days in integrity and hope.

PSALM 85

Restore Us Again

The leader's. The Qorahites. A composition.

¹ Yahweh, you favored your country,
   you renewed Jacob's fortunes.
² You carried your people's waywardness,
   you covered all their offenses.
³ You withdrew all your fury,
   you turned from your angry burning.

⁴ Renew us, God our deliverer,
   call off your vexation with us.
⁵ Will you be angry at us forever,
   prolong your anger generation after generation?
⁶ Will you yourself not again bring us to life,
   so that your people may celebrate you?
⁷ Yahweh, let us see your commitment,
   give us your deliverance.

46

⁸ I will listen to what Yahweh God will speak,
    because he will speak of well-being
  to his people and to those committed to him,
    those who must not turn to folly.
⁹ Yes, his deliverance is near for people who are in awe
    of him,
    so that his honor may settle in our country.
¹⁰ Commitment and truthfulness—they have met;
    faithfulness and well-being—they have embraced.
¹¹ Truthfulness—it springs up from the earth;
    faithfulness—it has looked down from the heavens.
¹² Yes, Yahweh—he will give good things;
    our land—it will give its increase.
¹³ Faithfulness—it will walk before him
    as he sets his feet on the path.

It is easy for me as a Brit to be resentful of the U.S. media's critiques of Britain and Europe. "Why do they think it's their business to criticize when the United States can't solve its own problems?" I wonder. "Are the British media so critical of the United States?" But then I remind myself that the U.S. media are also critical of the United States. At present there is a sense of the United States no longer being number one, as it once was—in education, economics, healthcare, transportation, and so on. The media commentators seem to be saying, "We are Americans, and the rest of the world looks best when framed in our rearview mirror. So we need to ask searching questions about how we lost our leading position and what can be done about it and about what our goals and hopes should be."

You could almost hear the opening of this psalm on the lips of people who see the United States as God's chosen people. Israel was hardly ever number one in the Middle East, but Israelites did know what it was like to experience good fortune, life, **well-being**, and increase. Much of the time, their life was certainly "good enough." Like people in the United States looking back to the Great Depression, they could look back to times that had been worse and then to times when things had gotten much better. The psalm speaks for people who now experience another reversal.

The psalm begins by recalling a restoration in the past that sounds like the restoration of the community after the **exile**. That time was indeed one when **Yahweh** carried the people's waywardness, gave up being angry with them, and made it possible for them to rebuild the temple and rebuild Jerusalem and their community. If we want a present context against which to imagine the psalm being used, then Calvin suggests an illuminating one. He imagines the psalm being prayed three or four centuries later, in the 160s BC, when the relatively benign authority of the **Persians** has been succeeded by Alexander the Great and then by the more oppressive authority of a **Greek** empire centered in Syria (it is the oppression reflected in the visions in Daniel). Worship of Yahweh in accordance with the **Torah** was forbidden, and people in Jerusalem who insisted on staying faithful to Yahweh met with martyrdom. So does it turn out that Yahweh is angry with them again, and is there reason for that attitude?

The psalm goes on to ask a question along those lines, but it seems to be a rhetorical one that in some situations (at least) would be worrying. People need to take seriously the possibility that there is a good reason for God's displeasure. But the speaker, presumably a worship leader, reckons actually to know the answer to the question. It's surely an uncontroversial one. If people are **committed** to Yahweh and hold Yahweh in awe, as opposed to turning to folly (that is, becoming committed to other deities), then surely Yahweh will undertake the **deliverance** that the people need in the first instance, restore his honor to the land, and then make it possible for them to experience well-being. To put it another way, when human truthfulness springs up from the earth, divine **faithfulness** will look down from the heavens.

The psalm makes that assertion by faith against the evidence of present experience. It stands boldly before God, daring God not to live by the faith it has declared. The worship leader also stands boldly before the people, daring them to believe that God will vindicate the declarations the psalm makes. If we again imagine people praying the psalm in the context of the oppressive rule of the Syrian empire in the 160s, then we know that its statement of faith was vindicated. God indeed restored the people's freedom to worship him in the way the Torah said—though in due course there came the oppressive rule of the Romans that is the background to the New Testament. Thus in New Testament times people could be praying this way again.

I don't see any reason that people in the United States or Britain shouldn't claim the psalm's perspective and seek for God to bless them once again. But its language about "bringing to life" has also made it a favorite with people who think and pray about revival in the church, like Psalm 80. I also don't see any reason that we shouldn't claim its perspective in that connection as well.

PSALM 86

A Servant Leans on His Master

A plea. David's.

¹ Bend your ear, Yahweh,
    answer, because I am lowly and needy.
² Watch over my life, because I am committed;
    deliver your servant—you are my God.
  As one who trusts in you, ³be gracious to me,
    because to you I call all day long.
⁴ Make your servant's soul rejoice,
    because to you, my Lord, I lift up my soul.
⁵ Because you, my Lord, are good and forgiving,
    big in commitment to everyone who calls you.
⁶ Give ear to my plea, Yahweh,
    heed the sound of my prayers for grace.
⁷ On the day of my trouble I call you,
    because you answer me.

⁸ There is no one like you among the gods, my Lord,
    and there are no acts like yours.
⁹ All the nations that you have made will come
    and bow low before you, my Lord.
  They will honor your name,
¹⁰   because you are great, one who does wonders.

You are God alone;
¹¹   teach me your way, Yahweh.
I will walk by your truthfulness;
     may my heart be one, in awe before your name.
¹² I will confess you, my Lord, my God, with all my heart;
     I will honor your name forever.
¹³ Because your commitment is great over me;
     you will rescue my life from deepest Sheol.

¹⁴ God, willful people have arisen against me,
     a group of terrifying people has sought my life.
Whereas they have not put you before their eyes,
¹⁵   you are my Lord,
the compassionate and gracious God,
     long-tempered and big in commitment and truthfulness.
¹⁶ Turn to me and be gracious to me,
     give your strength to your servant.
Deliver the son of your maid,
¹⁷   give me a sign for good,
so that the people who are against me may see and
          be shamed,
     because you, Yahweh, have helped me and comforted me.

The media report that two days ago Christians in Egypt undertook a demonstration related to obstacles put in the way of
building a church. The demonstration then became an expression of dissatisfaction with military rule in Egypt, so Muslims
joined with Christians in the demonstrations. The police and
the army attempted to dispel the demonstrators; things became
violent; military vehicles drove into the demonstrators; and
more than twenty people were crushed or shot to death. A
priest protested that it amounted to persecution of Christians,
but Muslims also described it as a betrayal of the political revolution that Egypt had seen earlier in the year. Today's front page
shows a picture of a woman mourning over a relative's coffin.

As Psalm 86 describes willful, terrifying attackers ignoring
God, seeking the lives of people, and thus threatening them
with a descent into **Sheol** before their time, it is the kind of
psalm we could use in praying for our fellow believers in such
a context. Such prayer is pressing, persistent, and urgent as it

seeks God's attention. It is based on the great need of the people who pray—they are lowly and disadvantaged, people without power and influence or tanks and machine guns. It is also based on their relationship with God: they are people who are **committed** to God, people who trust in God and not in other gods or in their own resources, and people committed to walking by God's truthfulness—that is, to living truthful, honest, steadfast lives and to being single-hearted.

Such prayer is based on who God is: good, forgiving, and long-tempered. These are not people who pretend they are sinless, but they know that God does not hold our sins against us when we face up to them before him. It is part of the nature of God's own big commitment, to which our commitment is a response. They know that there is no God like **Yahweh**, so that there is actually no real God but Yahweh. The description of God's characteristics follows God's own self-description in Exodus 34, so the prayer implicitly points out to God that he has little alternative but to respond to the prayer. He has to be himself.

Yahweh is one who does wondrous, extraordinary deeds, the kind that began at the exodus and that the people who pray this psalm need to see continued in their own lives. Those acts inspire awe on the part of the people praying, an awe that expresses itself in submission and obedience. It will also overflow in confessing faith in this God and honoring this God before other believers and before the attackers who are confounded by God's acts.

Interwoven with the psalm's twofold understanding of wonder and awe, and its threefold reference to commitment (ours and God's), are four variants of the word *grace*. The idea of grace or favor is that we are not claiming that we have any rights in a situation or that God owes us anything. All we can do is cast ourselves on God's mercy and love. So the psalm appeals, "Be gracious to me." Our prayers are "prayers for grace." The very nature of prayer is to appeal for something that God is not bound to give but still gives freely. You might think that there is some tension with the implication that God is really obliged to respond to this prayer because of who God is, but maybe appealing to God's grace is simply another way of making the same point. While in one sense God is not bound to respond to us, in another sense God is bound to do so because it is God's character, and God has to be true to himself. Yahweh is "the gracious God." So once again near the end of the psalm it appeals, "Be gracious to me." It's odd that people sometimes assume that the Old Testament is based on law and that only the New Testament is based on grace.

In another slight paradox, however, alongside the appeal to grace is a sixfold appeal to the fact that Yahweh is "Lord." The word LORD (in capitals) recurs in English translations because they usually replace the name Yahweh with that word, but in Psalm 86 the Hebrew word for *Lord* itself comes six times. Its implication is that we pray as the servants of this master, and masters have obligations to servants as servants have obligations to masters. It is another basis for leaning on God on our own behalf or on other people's behalf.

PSALM 87

Glorious Things of Thee Are Spoken, Zion

The Qorahites'. A composition. A song.

¹ Founded by him among the holy mountains,
   Yahweh gives himself to the gates of Zion
   more than all the dwellings in Jacob.
² Honorable things are spoken in you,
   God's city.   (*Rise*)
³ I will make mention of Rahab and Babylon
   to the people who acknowledge me.
There are Philistia, Tyre, with Sudan—
   each was born there.
⁴ To Zion it will be said,
   "Each and every one was born in it."
He will establish it, the One on High;
⁵   Yahweh will record, in writing down the peoples,
   "Each was born there."   (*Rise*)
⁶ They sing as they dance,
   "All my fountains are in you."

A few weeks ago, we had a visit from friends in London who told us exciting tales about developments in their parish, where they have a rector who is full of ideas for reaching out into the community and a church that is growing. Like many churches in our area, the church of which I am honorary minister is shrinking, and I don't know what to do about it (I am only an Old Testament professor, after all; I don't have that London rector's instincts and ideas). A lively and outspoken lady on the church council declared last month, "We have to find ways of reaching out to the community; otherwise we'll soon be dead." In the past, it's been easy for churches in the West to assume that if they just carry on as they always have, they will be able to continue maintaining themselves—which is no longer so in the United States, any more than it is in Britain.

What Psalm 87 offers is a promise that God still has a vision for his people—that it should embrace the whole world, not shrivel into nothingness. For much of Israel's history it would be tempting to assume that such shriveling was Jerusalem's destiny. After it reached its highpoint of political importance in the time of David and Solomon, things were pretty much downhill through Old Testament times. So in almost any period when one imagines this psalm being used, its vision would seem crazy (in the terms of an analogy used by my wife's former pastor, it's like the Hopi nation thinking it will rise up and rule North America). Maybe that's why it looks less like a regular psalm designed for the temple choir to sing and more like the word of a prophet, like some other psalms, such as Psalm 110.

First, the declaration reminds people that **Yahweh** founded **Zion**, so it belongs to him, and he gives himself to it; he is dedicated to it (the word is often used for "love"). Often Jerusalem got attacked and sometimes taken, but evidently Yahweh would not tolerate its capture as a long-term reality. He founded it among the holy mountains—that is, in the holy land—and he is more committed to Zion than to all the other cities in Israel (and the other cities did get taken more often than Jerusalem did). It is honored by him as his city, the place where he deigns to dwell.

After the expression of such enthusiasm for Israel's capital, it might be surprising to find Yahweh moving to talk about its potential importance to other people. Evidently Israel is not to ignore them. God speaks to the people who acknowledge him (that is, to Israel) about peoples who don't, but not in order to dismiss the latter. God speaks about **Egypt**, the great oppressor to the south. *Rahab* is a term for Egypt (it is spelled differently in Hebrew from the Rahab in Joshua); it is a term for a sea monster that epitomizes opposition to God. God speaks about **Babylon**, the great oppressor to the north who destroyed Jerusalem and took many of its people into **exile**. God speaks of **Philistia, Judah's** traditional local foe, and of Tyre, a significant power to the northwest of **Ephraim**, and of Sudan, often associated with Egypt. "Each was born there," Yahweh says. The statement recurs three times, and the psalm adds that Yahweh will record these peoples' names in this connection. They were not literally born in Zion, but they will come to be counted as peoples who were born there. They are going to become adopted citizens of Zion (the verb "born" can be used to mean "adopted").

The psalm thus makes the same statement as the Prophets do, though it uses different imagery. The nations are going to come to Jerusalem to acknowledge its importance because they will acknowledge that the real God is there; they will be welcomed as its true citizens; and there they will sing and dance as they rejoice in the city's importance to them. It gives Israel a basis for expectation that God will fulfill his purpose of gaining the world's acknowledgment through Zion (oddly, the hymn "Glorious Things of Thee Are Spoken," based in part on this psalm, does not include this hope). Yes, God has a vision for his people to embrace the whole world, not to shrivel into nothingness.

PSALM 88

A Cry from the Grave

A song. A composition. The Qorahites'. The leader's. On "Pipe" [a tune?]. For affliction. An instruction. Heman the Ezrahite's.

¹ Yahweh, my God who delivers,
   by day I have cried out, by night before you.

² May my plea come to your attention;
  bend your ear to my shout.

³ Because my whole person is full of trouble;
  my life has arrived at Sheol.
⁴ I have come to count with the people who go down to the Pit,
  I have become like a man without strength,
⁵ an outcast among the dead,
  like people slaughtered, lying in the grave,
 of whom you have been mindful no more,
  when they are cut off from your hand.
⁶ You have put me in the deepest Pit,
  in dark places, in the depths.
⁷ Upon me your fury has pressed down;
  with all your breakers you have afflicted me.

⁸ You have distanced my acquaintances from me,
  made me a great abomination to them.
 I am confined so that I cannot go out,
⁹ my eye has become dim through affliction.
 I have called you, Yahweh, each day,
  I have stretched out my hands to you.
¹⁰ Do you work a wonder for the dead,
  do ghosts rise to confess you?
¹¹ Is your commitment announced in the grave,
  your truthfulness in Abaddon?
¹² Is your wondrous act made known in the darkness,
  your faithfulness in the land of forgetting?

¹³ But I, Yahweh, I have cried to you for help,
  in the morning my plea meets you.
¹⁴ Yahweh, why do you reject me,
  hide your face from me?
¹⁵ I am afflicted, dying since youth;
  I have borne your terrors, I despair.
¹⁶ Your acts of fury have overwhelmed me,
  your acts of terror have destroyed me.
¹⁷ They are around me like water all day long,
  they have surrounded me altogether.
¹⁸ You have distanced friend and neighbor from me,
  my acquaintances—darkness.

Last night we watched a movie called *Incendies* about a family caught in an intracommunity conflict in Lebanon in the 1970s and 1980s. It was a fictional movie, but much of the story could be replicated in factual accounts of what happened to people during those decades. The central figure in the story is a Christian woman who had to watch members of another community murder the Muslim father of her unborn child. She was then cast out of her own community and had to give up the child. She later discovered the orphanage where her child had been taken, but it had been destroyed in the conflict, and the woman was subsequently taken captive and repeatedly raped and impregnated. One thing that infuriated her captors was the fact that she would keep singing; she became known simply as "the woman who sings."

Not knowing Arabic, I couldn't tell what she sang, but Psalm 88 would make an appropriate lament for her. She had indeed been dying since youth, and I shall think of the person praying this psalm as a woman. Among the psalms that appeal to God, which occupy so much space in the Psalter, Psalm 88 is the most extreme. Its introduction has the longest string of epithets of all the psalms; I wonder if that fact means it appeared in a number of the collections of psalms from which the Psalter was compiled, and whether it was therefore especially well-known and much used. (Heman was another of the temple worship leaders, like **Asaph;** he is mentioned in 1 Chronicles 6.)

In general, such prayer psalms have a number of regular features: they address God; they describe someone's suffering; they urge God to listen and act; they testify to their commitment to God's ways; they affirm their trust in God; they declare their expectation that God will **deliver;** and they look forward to returning to worship to witness to God's having done so. While not all these features appear in every prayer psalm, a number of them consistently do so. But it is not the case with Psalm 88. It begins with an invocation of **Yahweh,** God as known to Israel; it addresses Yahweh as "my God"; and it pointedly calls this God the one who delivers. The invocation thus comprises a series of basic theological statements that underlie the content of the psalm. It then goes on to urge God to listen. But that is the only actual prayer in the psalm, and it presages what will follow by the urgency of its plea, not least in its use of the closing word "shout." Listen to the noise I make, it implores.

After the first two lines, the entirety of the psalm is occupied by a pained description of suffering and fear along with a series of protests about it in the form of questions. An immediate feature is the way the speaker describes herself in terms of being as good as dead. She does not trouble to be too logical about the way she describes her position. She is at the gates of **Sheol**. Or she is like someone who has actually gone down to the Pit, which is another way to describe the home of dead people, deriving from the fact that people may be buried in a grave pit. Indeed, she has been thrown into the depths of such a pit, and thus into the deepest of darkness. Or she is like a warrior who is so exhausted by the battle that he lacks the strength to carry on living or like someone who has not had a proper burial, whose body lies there on the battlefield. Because our bodies are intrinsic parts of us, we can hardly be at rest if they are simply thrown aside and abandoned in that way.

The trouble with being in the realm of death is that it is a realm from which God is absent. Indeed, perhaps the logic of her lament works in the opposite direction— she knows she is in a realm from which God is absent, so it must be the realm of death. God and death are antithetical; Yahweh is the God of life, and there is no other god who could be portrayed as the god of death, as other peoples thought. God does not work wonders in the realm of death; once you are in Sheol, you are there permanently. There is no celebrating of God's **commitment** and **faithfulness** there, because God does not act there; ghosts do not stand up to testify to what God has done for them. (Of course God will eventually act in Sheol, reaching in to raise Jesus from death, but this has not happened yet. And if a woman in our own time goes through the kind of experience that the psalm describes, it is as if Jesus has not yet died and risen from death.) God is not mindful of people in Sheol; it is the land put out of mind, the forgotten country.

The psalm ends in incoherence; the Hebrew words are an appropriate expression of an experience that does not make sense. The psalm as a whole is the Psalter's most extraordinary gift from God to the person whose experience makes him or her need to pray in this way.

PSALM 89:1–37

Is Anything Stable?

An instruction. Ethan the Ezrahite's.

¹ Of Yahweh's acts of commitment I will sing forever,
      for all generations I will cause his truthfulness to be
         acknowledged with my mouth.
² Because I have said, "Your commitment is built up forever;
      the heavens—you establish your truthfulness in them."
³ "I sealed a covenant for my chosen,
      I swore to David my servant:
⁴ 'I will establish your offspring forever,
      I will build your throne for all generations.'"

⁵ In the heavens they confess your wondrous act, Yahweh,
      your truthfulness, too, in the congregation of the holy.
⁶ Because who in the sky can equal Yahweh,
      can compare with Yahweh among the divine beings,
⁷ the God inspiring great veneration in the council of the holy,
      inspiring awe above all those surrounding him?
⁸ Yahweh, God of Armies,
      who is like you, mighty Yah,
      with your truthfulness surrounding you?
⁹ You rule over the rising of the sea;
      when it lifts its waves, you are the one who can still them.
¹⁰ You are the one who crushed Rahab, like a corpse;
      with your powerful arm you scattered your enemies.
¹¹ The heavens are yours, the earth is yours, too,
      the world and what fills it: you are the one who
         founded them.
¹² North and south—you are the one who created them;
      Tabor and Hermon—they resound at your name.
¹³ To you belongs an arm with strength;
      your hand is powerful, your right hand stands high.

¹⁴ Faithfulness in the exercise of authority is the stability
     of your throne;
    commitment and truthfulness come to meet your face.
¹⁵ The blessings of the people that acknowledges the shout,
    that walks about in the light of your face, Yahweh!
¹⁶ In your name they celebrate all day long,
    in your faithfulness they stand high.
¹⁷ Because you are their powerful glory;
    through your favor our horn stands high.
¹⁸ Because our shield belongs to Yahweh,
    our king to Israel's Holy One.

¹⁹ Then you spoke in a vision to the people committed to you.
    You said, "I put help on a warrior,
    I raised high one chosen from the people.
²⁰ I found David, my servant,
    with my holy oil I anointed him,
²¹ the one with whom my hand will stand firm;
    yes, my arm will strengthen him.
²² No enemy will extort from him,
    or wrongdoer afflict him.
²³ I will crush his foes before him,
    strike down the people who are against him.
²⁴ My truthfulness and commitment will be with him,
    and in my name his horn will stand high.
²⁵ I will set his hand on the sea,
    his right hand on the great river.
²⁶ This man will call me, 'You are my father,
    my God, the crag that delivers me.'
²⁷ Yes, I myself will make him my firstborn,
    on high in relation to earth's kings.
²⁸ Forever will I keep my commitment to him;
    my covenant will be true for him.
²⁹ I will set his offspring evermore,
    his throne like the days of the heavens.
³⁰ If his sons abandon my teaching
    and do not walk about by my decisions,
³¹ if they profane my laws
    and do not keep my commands,
³² I will attend to their rebellion with a stick,
    their waywardness with blows,

³³ but my commitment I will not annul from him;
    I will not be false to my truthfulness.
³⁴ I will not profane my covenant;
    what has come out of my lips I will not change.
³⁵ Once and for all I have sworn by my holiness:
    'If I lie to David. . . .'
³⁶ His offspring will continue forever,
    his throne like the sun before me,
³⁷ like the moon, which will stand firm forever,
    a witness in the sky that is truthful."   (*Rise*)

My wife once lived in a house on the side of a canyon in California that seemed capable of tumbling into the ocean if there was an earthquake, and after one worrying quake not far away she took to checking the weekly earthquake reports. Apparently California has five hundred earthquakes a week; almost all of them are undetectable on the surface. She half agreed that checking on what was going on was a bit pointless because it could not reveal what might happen in the future. But (she pointed out) if there are lots of little earthquakes, it is good news because it is a sign that the tensions in the earth are finding expression. It is when there is no shifting of the earth and tension builds up that there is danger of a serious quake. Me, I am more freaked out by the signs that have sprouted by the ocean announcing that you are entering a tsunami hazard zone and/or that give you implausible instructions about which direction to run in the event of a tsunami.

I am therefore encouraged by psalms such as Psalm 89 that draw attention to the fact that the world's security rests on God's having constructed it securely. The heavens and the earth witness to God's truthfulness—the word comes eight times in verses 1–37. It denotes God's steadfastness, reliability, or trustworthiness. So associating the creation with this aspect of God makes a strong statement. God has written his own truthfulness into the world he created. It naturally follows that the creation also embodies and reflects God's **commitment**; that word comes seven times. The world is securely built up and established. The powers of the heavens recognize that this is so and that **Yahweh** is the only one who made it so. When earth heaves or oceans rise, Yahweh can still them. The act of creation involved doing so when God put in their place self-assertive forces such as the sea monster Rahab (not the Rahab in Joshua, whose name is spelled differently in Hebrew, but the Rahab also mentioned in Psalm 87). The shout that people acknowledge will be the acclamation that Yahweh is indeed the great creator.

The first pair of references to God's truthfulness and commitment come in the psalm's first two lines, but then the psalm makes a sudden transition to speaking of God's sworn **covenant** to David, which is also securely built up and established. Similarly, the long section referring to creation's stability makes an unexpected transition to speaking of Israel's king, and verses 19–37 then focus on God's covenant to David. There is a father-son relationship between God and the Davidic king. The point about that image is twofold. It implies mutual commitment and also the father's disciplining the son. But the father will never cast the son off. Husbands and wives can divorce each other; you can stop being someone's spouse, but you can't stop being someone's father or son, even if you want to.

So there's a link and a consistency between God's acts in creation and God's acts in Israel's history. Well, of course there is. How could God not be consistent in his actions in different spheres? An implication is that one's conviction about one of the spheres can reinforce one's conviction about the other. Suppose creation looks unstable; reflecting on the truthfulness of God's acts in Israel's story, in Jesus, and in the Spirit helps to reinforce one's conviction about the stability of creation. Or suppose we can't see God's actions in history, in Jesus, and in the Spirit; reflecting on the reliability of God's work in creation helps reinforce our conviction about God's involvement in history.

The Ethan mentioned in the introduction is presumably another of the temple worship leaders (like **Asaph**), the one mentioned in 1 Chronicles 6.

PSALM 89:38–51

Facing the Other Set of Facts

[38] But you yourself have rejected, spurned,
raged with your anointed.

³⁹ You have renounced your servant's covenant,
    profaned his diadem to the earth.
⁴⁰ You have breached all his walls,
    made his strongholds a ruin.
⁴¹ All the people who pass his way have plundered him;
    he has become an object of reviling to his neighbors.
⁴² You have lifted high his foes' right hand,
    you have let all his enemies celebrate.
⁴³ You have also turned back his sword's blade,
    not enabled him to stand in battle.
⁴⁴ You have ended his purity;
    his throne you have hurled to the earth.
⁴⁵ You have cut short the days of his youth,
    clothed him in shame.   (*Rise*)

⁴⁶ How long, Yahweh—will you hide forever,
    will your fury burn like fire?
⁴⁷ Be mindful—I, what short span of life,
    for what emptiness you have created all human beings.
⁴⁸ Who is the man who can live on and not see death,
    can rescue himself from the hand of Sheol?   (*Rise*)
⁴⁹ Where are your former acts of commitment, my Lord,
    which you swore to David in your truthfulness?
⁵⁰ Be mindful, my Lord, of your servant's reviling,
    which I have carried in my heart, of all the many peoples
⁵¹ who have reviled, of your enemies, Yahweh,
    those who have reviled the steps of your anointed.

Here's a strange thing. In Episcopal worship, we use the Psalms in all our Sunday services and on special days. We use the first part of Psalm 89 on Christmas Eve and on other occasions during the Christmas season, and we use it on Saint Joseph's Day, and sometimes we use it again on a Sunday in June. Given its account of God's promise to David and his successors, you can see why we would use it in connection with Jesus' birth. What is strange is that we never use the last part of the psalm (except when it comes up in a separate daily cycle that includes all the psalms). We prefer the first part.

The irony is that you don't really get the point of the first part until you reach this last part, which constitutes an extraordinary transition after the earlier celebration of God's

covenant, truthfulness, and **commitment**. This last part asks, "What has happened to that covenant and truthfulness and commitment, then?"

The move is so abrupt that one might ask whether the last part is a later addition to the psalm. In principle there is no reason that this should not have been the case. Overlaps between different psalms indicate that later psalmists could take earlier psalms and rework them, or take up their own earlier psalms and rework them—the same thing happens to Christian hymns. Thus Psalm 108 reuses material from Psalms 57 and 60. But there is no concrete indication of this process in the case of Psalm 89, and the complete version is the form that Israel put in its own hymnbook. Further, the way the last part picks up words such as *covenant, truthfulness,* and *commitment* from the earlier part shows that it was designed to follow the first part. And with hindsight, the very length of the celebration in the first part adds to the impact of the questioning in the last part. The longer the celebration goes on, the more forceful is the protest that says, "So what on earth is going on?" (Only Psalms 78 and 119 are longer than Psalm 89.)

A number of the protest psalms have as part of their genius their resolute insistence on facing two sets of facts. Psalm 22 is the most intricate example, but Psalm 89 is the sneakiest. God's ensuring the stability of creation and of the Davidic throne is one set of facts. God's allowing the Davidic king to be defeated and reviled and his capital city to be devastated is another set. The reference to ending his purity perhaps takes up the fact that his being anointed put him in the same position as a priest (priests were also anointed). The reference to creation in the last part takes up the other side to the theme of the first part of the psalm, the theme of creation alongside the theme of God's commitment to David. The glory of creation is compromised by the ease with which people can be prevented by war from living out their full lifespans.

We do not know to what particular defeat and devastation the psalm refers, though in any case its presence in the Psalter as usual indicates that the psalm does not just relate to one such event; it could be used on other comparable occasions. God has put himself into a bind by making the kind of commitments the first part of the psalm relates. He has left himself wiggle room for inflicting minor defeats as a consequence of the king's disobedience to God's teaching, but the psalm assumes that the defeat and humiliation that God has inflicted go beyond anything God had allowed for. The last part of the psalm challenges God about how it is now possible to make sense of the first part; it thus challenges God to act in fulfillment of those commitments.

PSALM 89:52

Amen Anyway

⁵² Yahweh be worshiped forever.
   Amen, amen.

There is a play by Elie Wiesel called *The Trial of God*, set in a concentration camp and based on something the author witnessed. At the end of the trial, God is found guilty of crimes against creation and humankind. After a period of silence, a Talmudic scholar who had taken part in the trial looks at the sky and says, "It's time for evening prayers," and the members of the tribunal recite the synagogue evening service.

This line at the end of Psalm 89 has something in common with that dynamic. I noted previously, in the introduction to this volume, that the Psalter divides into five "books" and that Psalm 89 marks the end of Book Three. This line marks that we have reached that point—you can see a similar line at the end of Psalm 106, marking the end of Book Four. So it is not actually part of Psalm 89, yet it makes a noteworthy statement of faith when juxtaposed by it. Psalm 89 ended with protests that receive no response. This additional line boldly declares that we worship God nevertheless, and say, "Amen" to all that has preceded (which includes the last part of Psalm 89).

PSALM 90

God's Time and Our Time

A plea. Moses', God's man.

¹ My Lord, you were a shelter for us,
   generation after generation.

2 Before mountains were birthed
       and you labored with the earth and the world,
    from age to age,
       you were God
3 You would turn mortals to crushing;
       you said, "Turn, people!"
4 Because a thousand years in your eyes were like a day,
       yesterday when it passes, or a watch in the night.
5 You swept them away in sleep,
       though in the morning they would be like grass that
          grows fresh.
6 In the morning it can flourish and grow fresh;
       by evening it dries up and withers.

7 Because we are spent through your anger,
       through your fury we have been overwhelmed.
8 You have set our wayward acts in front of you,
       our youthful deeds in the light of your face.
9 Because all our days have passed away in your wrath;
       we have spent our years as moaning.
10 The days of our years in themselves are seventy years,
       or—with strength—eighty years.
    But their energy has been trouble and toil,
       because it has passed by speedily and we have flown away.
11 Who acknowledges the force of your anger,
       and your wrath in accordance with awe for you?
12 In counting our days, so make us acknowledge it,
       in order that we may get a wise mind.

13 Turn, Yahweh, how long?—
       relent about your servants.
14 Fill us in the morning with your commitment,
       and we will resound and celebrate all our days.
15 Enable us to celebrate in accordance with the days of
          your afflicting us,
       the years we have seen evil.
16 May your act appear to your servants,
       your majesty for their descendants.
17 May my Lord's wish come about,
       our God for us.
    Establish the deed of our hands for us;
       yes, the deed of our hands—establish it.

My first mother-in-law used to say that time went faster the older you got, and I used to tell myself that really she was simply afraid of the approach of death. As I have gotten older, I have realized that she was right, and I see that my realization does not merely indicate that I fear the approach of death. There is a reason we have this impression. Today in church we celebrated the birthdays of a thirteen-year-old and of a ninety-two-year-old. When you are thirteen, the previous year is one thirteenth of your life, so it's a long time as a proportion of your life and of what you have experienced. But when you are ninety-two, the previous year is only one ninety-second of your life, and the length of experience of life that you have can make it seem to have gone very quickly. I have one surviving aunt, and I remember now that at ninety-two she warned me that after you reach eighty, time goes very quickly. Even if time is something objective, our experience of it is subjective.

Psalm 90 reminds us at any age to set our experience of time into the context not only of our own lives but in light of God's "age." It doesn't quite say that God is ageless, though I dare say that Israelites would have assumed that this is so. Rather, it declares that God's "age" goes back to the time before the world came into existence (unusually, it describes God's act of creation as an act of going into labor and giving birth) and that it will go on for an equivalent period—it lasts "from age to age." A human seventy, eighty, or ninety years is insignificant in comparison. The thirteen-year-old whom I mentioned illustrates how, in the morning, life flourishes and grows fresh; in this connection, I don't want to think about the way by evening life dries up and withers, but there was another young man for whose family we prayed today, a man who was diagnosed with cancer when he was sixteen and who had just died at twenty-six. And while another of our ninety-plus-year-olds is just skin and bones now, as her body does not seem to be replenishing or repairing itself, she remains a person full of spark, vitality, humor, and love.

Psalm 90 has traditionally been used at funerals, and in that context it solemnly reminds people that no matter how flourishing we are, our vitality will dry up and wither. It's not a fact to paralyze us or depress us but one to give us a true perspective on life. When we have a true perspective, we can live as people who have nothing to hide from and nothing to lose.

But the psalm is at least as concerned about the community's relationship with God over the ages. In the Old Testament, seventy years is not a figure for a human lifetime (most people died way before reaching seventy) but a figure for the time Israel may stay under God's judgment. The idea that it might last eighty years makes the point even more solemn. The psalm looks back on the long periods when Israel knew God's blessings and knew God's protection from its attackers, who just got swept away. If sometimes its oppressors seemed to triumph forever—well, that is when Israel needs to remember that what seems like forever to us (a thousand years) is only a day to God, or only a watch in the night (a few hours). Further, if judgment lasts for seventy or eighty years, maybe there will still be one or two people alive who remember life under God's blessing—or at least there will be people whose parents or grandparents had this experience and told them about it.

That experience of blessing and protection contrasts with the community's more recent experience of being dried up and withered, as those attackers used to be. It's as if God can't stop looking at its wrongdoing. The way the psalm prays corresponds to the way the community was feeling as the **exile** wore on—the exile was often pictured as lasting seventy years. It is as if God is still stuck in the waywardness that led to the exile. But in this connection, too, the psalm asks to be enabled to face the facts about time so that it can learn what it needs to learn from its experience of God's chastisement. Then finally it asks, "Couldn't enough be enough?"

PSALM 91

Shadow of the Almighty

1   As someone who lives in the shelter of the One on High,
        who stays in the shade of Shadday,
2   I say of Yahweh, "My refuge, my stronghold,
        my God in whom I trust."

67

³ Because he is the one who will rescue you from the
      trapper's snare,
    from the devastating epidemic.
⁴ With his pinion he will cover you,
    and under his wings you will find refuge;
    his truthfulness will be a body-shield, a rampart.
⁵ You need not be afraid of a terror by night,
    of an arrow that flies by day.
⁶ of an epidemic that walks in the dark,
    of a scourge that destroys at noon.
⁷ A thousand may fall at your side,
    ten thousand at your right hand—
    it will not reach to you.
⁸ You will just look with your eyes
    and see the recompense of the faithless.
⁹ Because you are one who has made Yahweh "my refuge,"
    the One on High your shelter.
¹⁰ No evil will be given access to you,
    no harm will approach your tent.
¹¹ Because he will command his aides
    to guard you in all your ways.
¹² They will carry you on their hands
    so that your foot does not crash into a stone.
¹³ You will tread on cub and viper,
    you will trample on lion and serpent.

¹⁴ "Because he is devoted to me, I will rescue him;
    I will lift him to safety, because he has acknowledged
      my name.
¹⁵ He will call me and I will answer,
    I will be with him in trouble,
    I will save him and honor him.
¹⁶ I will fill him with long days
    and show him my deliverance."

I have a vivid memory from when I was a teenager of watching a filmstrip (a prehistoric antecedent of DVDs) that told the story of five young men from the United States who went to a rainforest in Ecuador to seek to bring the gospel of Christ to the Auca people there. The tribe was known for its violence, and its members killed the five men. Some years later, Elisabeth

Elliot, the wife of one of the young men, wrote a profile of her husband, Jim, which she called *Shadow of the Almighty*. The profile was based in part on her husband's diaries, which included the much-quoted line "He is no fool who gives what he cannot keep to gain what he cannot lose." But the title of the book came from the opening line of Psalm 91, in the King James Version.

To take up that phrase was an act of great boldness, because it might seem that if there was anyone whose life raised a question about the truth of Psalm 91, it was Jim Elliot. The psalm is a declaration of trust in **Yahweh** that one person gives to another as an invitation to take the same stance. It wouldn't be surprising if the person to whom the declaration of trust is given is a leader such as a king, the kind of person who has to lead his people in battle and who is then the object of the enemy's special attention. He is the person who is in the most danger. The one who speaks and tells us that he has made these promises the basis of his own life might then be a priest, and it will then be he who also mediates the direct promise from God in the closing lines. But there is nothing in the psalm to limit its promises to a person such as the king. And whether you are a king or an ordinary person, you would be familiar with examples of people like you who no more experienced the fulfillment of the psalm's promises than Jim Elliot did.

An odd feature of Western Christian attitudes is the way such examples trouble us so much that it is hard for us to hear the promises. The Psalms make clear that people did notice the occasions when the promises did not find fulfillment, yet this awareness didn't have that effect. Maybe it's another facet of what I called "facing two sets of facts," in connection with the last part of Psalm 89.

One can't always explain why God doesn't fulfill his promises, though one can sometimes see what God brings out of such failures. I wasn't the only person deeply affected by the story of the death of those five U.S. missionaries. The event had a galvanizing effect on Christians in the United States, inspiring people to be willing to give their lives to take the story of Christ to people who did not know about it, and inspiring others to provide the finances to make that possible. Much more ironic and paradoxical is the aftermath of Satan's quoting these promises to Jesus (see Matthew 4). On the assumption that they were originally promises to the king, then applying them to Jesus would be a clever move if Jesus has any claim to being the messianic king. Jesus perhaps perceives that Satan misuses them in attempting to make them the basis for Jesus' jumping off the temple to prove that God would look after him (and Christians can fall into the trap of taking a risk for God's sake that God hasn't called us to, and then expecting God to take care of us). But Jesus' own death then constitutes the greatest example of the promises failing to come true. Yet his death bears strange fruit, and this development makes the promises' failure seem insignificant.

Given that such can be the aftermath of the promises' failure, we are emboldened to meditate on the promises in such a way as to base our lives on them and not to lose their impact through fretting about the occasions when they fail.

PSALM 92

What Sabbath Worship Looks Like?

A composition. A song. For the Sabbath day.

¹ It's good to confess Yahweh,
    to make music for your name, you who are the One
        on High,
² to tell of your commitment in the morning
    and of your truthfulness each night
³ with the ten-string and with the harp,
    with recitation, on the guitar.
⁴ Because you have made me joyful, Yahweh, by your act;
    at the deeds of your hands I resound.
⁵ How great your deeds have been, Yahweh;
    your plans were very deep.
⁶ The brutish person—he does not acknowledge,
    the stupid—he does not understand this:
⁷ when the faithless flourish like grass,
    and all the wicked people thrive,

it is to be destroyed for all time,
8   whereas you are up on high forever, Yahweh.
9 Because there—your enemies, Yahweh,
       because there—your enemies perish;
       all wrongdoers scatter.
10 But you have raised up my horn like a buffalo,
       my exhaustion with refreshing oil.
11 My eye has looked at my watchful foes;
       the people who rose against me, acting wickedly—
       my ears can listen to them.

12 The faithful person is like a date palm that flourishes,
       like a Lebanese cedar that grows great,
13 planted in Yahweh's house,
       which flourish in our God's courtyards.
14 They still fruit in old age,
       they become rich and fresh,
15 proclaiming that Yahweh is upright,
       my crag in whom there is no wrongdoing.

If I am preaching on Sunday, instead of giving a ten- to fifteen-minute sermon after the Scripture readings (Episcopalians are not used to long sermons), I have gotten into the habit of talking for a few minutes after each of the three readings that come from the Old Testament, the Epistles, and the Gospels. I assumed that breaking up the sermon might make it easier for people to listen and to assimilate its message, and I have been encouraged at people's unsolicited response that it did have that effect. However, I was also encouraged by someone's comment that she felt she was thereby getting a wider range of teaching—otherwise, she said, the readings just float past people. The main reason for preaching is to get people to change in some way, not merely to learn something—but if they are learning, I am not going to complain.

Psalm 92 is the only psalm that mentions the Sabbath. This may seem odd, for we are inclined to assume that the Sabbath would be the main day for worship in the temple as Sunday is the main day for church worship, but the parallel does not really hold. Worship was being offered in the temple every day, and there was not much difference about the worship offered on the Sabbath. The main point about the Sabbath was that it be a day of stopping work, and of course nearly all Israelites lived too far away from the temple to be able to go there each week. They would take part in worship in the temple and come across the psalms there only on festivals and special occasions. But when they worshiped at home on the Sabbath, it wouldn't be surprising if they also used this time to learn about the faith that the **Torah** also expected of people.

There is a teaching aspect to Psalm 92, and the way Sabbath and teaching come together in the psalm is suggestive. Much of the opening lines suggests it's going to be a thanksgiving or testimony psalm, one that rejoices in what God has recently done for an individual or the community, but it does not go on to focus on the specifics of such an experience in the way such a psalm usually does. Further, the nature of such a psalm is to have a teaching aspect, and the actual opening words "It's good to confess **Yahweh**" already underline that didactic intent, in that the psalm is designed to get people to confess Yahweh. The teaching concern comes out further in the general statements about what the brutish or morally stupid person won't recognize and then in the statements about what God does for the person who is **faithful**. In effect they are statements of praise. So the psalm suggestively combines praise for what God always does, testimony to what God has done for this person, and teaching about what people need to learn from all this. That is not the whole of what Sunday worship might comprise (prayer is the main further feature), but it gets at key features of it.

PSALM 93

Is the Earth Vulnerable?

1. Yahweh began to reign, put on majesty;
      Yahweh put on, girded on might.
   Further, the world stands firm, it does not collapse;
2.   your throne is standing firm since long ago—
      you are from of old.

³ Rivers lifted up, Yahweh,
  rivers lifted up their voice,
  rivers lift up their crushing.
⁴ Above the voices of many waters,
  majestic, the breakers of the sea,
  Yahweh was majestic on high.

⁵ Your decisions have been very truthful,
  your holiness has adorned your house,
  Yahweh, for long days.

I just saw a fabulous picture of the earth taken from above the North Pole. I know in theory that Canada, Greenland, Russia, Norway, and Alaska almost meet in the Arctic, but I am so used to the regular Mercator Projection world map that I don't usually think in those terms. It was a fabulous picture but also a worrying one because it showed how much the Arctic ice pack has shrunk over the last decade. It opens up whole new possibilities in connection with oil drilling and fishing. But of course the bad news is that it is another sign of how fast the earth is warming and of how the shores of many countries all over the world may soon be taken over by the ocean. Is the earth secure?

This psalm declares that creation was the moment when Yahweh began to reign; therefore the earth is securely founded. The psalm doesn't imply that someone else was reigning before this moment but that Yahweh asserted **authority** in the cosmos at the time of creation and declared that it was going to stand firm because he stands firm. There were forces that sought to resist Yahweh's sovereignty or could have done so—forces that had a dynamic power of their own, epitomized in the terrifying force of churning oceans and flooding rivers—but Yahweh insisted on asserting authority over them. And Yahweh did so in a way that has been truthful and reliable over the millennia and has ensured that Yahweh's holiness has been acknowledged in his palace in the heavens by all other would-be powers.

Yes, the world is secure; it will not be vulnerable to other supernatural powers because Yahweh has determined to force their submission. Of course Yahweh is not so inclined to force the submission of human powers. It seems that we have a different kind of free will. So we dare not assume we could not destroy the planet.

PSALM 94

The God of Redress

1 God of redress, Yahweh,
    God of redress, shine forth.
2 Rise up as the one who exercises authority over the earth,
    give their recompense to the eminent people.
3 How long will the faithless, Yahweh,
    how long will the faithless exult,
4 will they pour out, speak assertively,
    will all the wrongdoers hold forth?
5 They crush your people, Yahweh,
    they put down your very own.
6 They slay the widow and alien,
    they murder the orphan.
7 They say, "Yah does not see,
    Jacob's God does not take note."

8 Take note, you brutes among the people,
    you fools, when will you show some insight?
9 The one who plants the ear—does he not listen;
    the one who shapes the eye—does he not look?
10 The one who disciplines nations—does he not reprove,
    the one who instructs humanity about knowledge?
11 Yahweh knows about humanity's plans—
    they are empty.

12 The blessings of the man whom you discipline, Yah,
    and instruct from your teaching,
13 to give him rest from bad times
    until a pit is dug for the faithless person!
14 Because Yahweh does not forsake his people,
    does not abandon his very own.
15 Because authority will return to [basing itself] on doing
        what is faithful,
    and all those who are upright in mind will go after it.

¹⁶ Who rises up for me with the evildoers,
  who takes a stand for me with the wrongdoers?
¹⁷ Were Yahweh not a help for me,
  soon I myself would have dwelt in silence.
¹⁸ If I said, "My foot has slipped,"
  your commitment, Yahweh, holds me up.
¹⁹ When anxieties multiply inside me,
  your comforts rejoice my being.
²⁰ Can the throne that brings destruction ally with you—
  someone who creates suffering by means of a law?
²¹ They gang against the life of the faithful person,
  they condemn the blood of the innocent person.
²² But Yahweh has been a haven for me,
  my God a crag that gives me refuge,
²³ and he has turned their wickedness upon them;
  he will put an end to them through their evildoing—
  Yahweh our God will put an end to them.

As I write, hundreds of people are encamped in a park near Wall Street, their base for protesting the fact that the 1 percent of the U.S. population, of whom Wall Street is a symbol, have a greater net worth than the entire bottom 90 percent, with many of the protesters being people without jobs and thus at the bottom of the 90 percent (but my wife likes to remind me that we in the West are the 10 percent to the two-thirds world's 90 percent). In cities in Israel, hundreds of its citizens are likewise encamped in tent cities in the name of a similar cause, with additional resentment at the cost of security spending and of concessions to special interest groups. In India, where increasing prosperity has also not benefited millions of ordinary people, a man called Anna Hazare recently undertook a twelve-day hunger strike until parliament agreed to some of his demands concerning an anticorruption measure to hold public officials accountable.

Psalm 94 speaks for the victims of such inequality and corruption. There is a sense in which they are by definition powerless and helpless. Demonstrations and hunger strikes are one way of denying powerlessness and helplessness. Prayer is another. Maybe the two are a good combination. The people the psalm complains about are eminent, important, powerful people, and they are **faithless** people. Their faithlessness expresses itself in the confident assertiveness of their talk; they always have a lot to say for themselves. It expresses itself in the way they treat ordinary people, and specifically in the way they ignore the needs of the vulnerable or even take advantage of their weakness. It expresses itself toward God by assuming that God does not take any notice of what happens. Perhaps they would not explicitly put it this way, but it is the implication of their action. It's hard for power and faithlessness not to go together. Either you get power by being faithless, or power tempts you into faithlessness.

The plaintive "How long?" near the psalm's beginning suggests the desperation that can characterize protest psalms, but the psalm's subsequent tone is more a gentle confidence. The middle section expresses that confidence toward the well-to-do people; they are stupid to make that assumption about **Yahweh's** lack of interest in what is going on in the world. Yahweh is one who disciplines and instructs, and it is hardly likely that he will then ignore the situation when people take no notice of his discipline and instruction. Heeding them is thus the way of blessing, even if it may sometimes look otherwise in the short term. The middle section closes with a brave declaration of confidence that corruption will not have its way for the long term. **Authority** will return to its proper basis, and upright people will be able to support the government rather than protesting it.

Once again, the plaintive "Who?" question that opens the final section is the kind of question that often marks desperation, but here it introduces a further statement of confidence. The beginning of the very last line speaks as if God has already put the well-to-do down, though the rest of that line implies that this process is by no means over. Maybe the question is also a way of recruiting the next generation into a **faithful** stance or into taking action if they can. Maybe the psalmist is sure someone will rise up and is watching the next generation to see who it might be. But its explicit point is that no, God does not sit by forever when 1 percent or 10 percent are doing well and the majority are impoverished. It is a scary psalm for anyone in the Western world to read, as well as for people in Wall Street.

PSALM 95

Will You Just Shut Up and Listen?

¹ Come, let's resound for Yahweh,
   let's shout for our crag who delivers us.
² Let's draw near his face with confession;
   we will shout for him with music.
³ Because Yahweh is the great God,
   the great king over all gods,
⁴ the one in whose hand are the far reaches of the earth,
   and to whom the mountain peaks belong,
⁵ the one to whom the sea belongs (he made it)
   and the dry land (his hands shaped it).

⁶ Come, let's bow down, let's bend low,
   let's bow the knee before Yahweh our maker.
⁷ Because he is our God
   and we are the people he pastures,
   the sheep in his hand.

   Today, if you listen to his voice,
⁸   do not stiffen your attitude as you did at Contention,
   as you did on the day at Testing in the wilderness,
⁹   when your ancestors tested me.
   They tried me, though they had seen my action;
¹⁰   for forty years I loathed that generation.
   I said, "They are a people who wander in attitude,
   because they have not acknowledged my ways,
¹¹ of whom I swore in my anger,
   'If they come to my place of rest. . . .'"

One of the most formative experiences of my life was being
a chorister in the choir at the cathedral in my home city in
England. I learned to sing and to read and write music, and
I wouldn't have become a music freak except for that experience. But more important, I got drawn into the actual worship of the services in which we sang, which doesn't happen
to every choirboy, and I wouldn't have become an Anglican
priest were it not for that experience. One of my memories is
the way every Sunday morning service began with the Venite,

which is the traditional title for Psalm 95. *Venite* is Latin for
the opening bidding "Come."

I'm not sure when it was that I realized that we sang only
the first two sections of the psalm and that this common practice involved a couple of first-rate ironies. The logic of using
the psalm at that stage of the service is that as well as inviting
people to join in praise, it challenges them to pay heed to what
God has to say through the Scripture readings that follow. In
using only the first two sections, however, we omitted the part
that issues this challenge, and we thereby omitted the part of
the psalm that marks it out as distinctive. Whereas the first two
sections speak in the regular manner of a psalm, from us to
God (or rather, in this case, from some people to other people
about God), in the last section God speaks back.

On their own, the first two sections form a textbook example of a praise psalm. They comprise an invitation to worship
followed by the reasons for the worship or the content of it,
then another invitation and more reasons. These opening two
sections both complement each other and form a significant
sequence. The psalm begins with an invitation to loud and
enthusiastic acclamation of God, more like the shouting and
singing at one of the soccer stadiums within three or four miles
of our cathedral than the elegant and graceful performance
of our choir. The basis for that acclamation is the greatness of
Yahweh as supreme God. The second section renews the invitation. It is another invitation to an act of outward and bodily
recognition of God, but the act now involves bodily prostration
more like that of Muslims in prayer than the dignified semi-
kneeling proper to Anglican worship. The basis for this bowing
down of the whole person is the awed recognition that Yahweh,
the supreme God over the entire world, has deigned to be our
God and to shepherd us.

The psalm ends perfectly well after those two sections, and I
like to fantasize that it existed perfectly well as a psalm of praise
until one day Yahweh got tired of all this shouting and prostration that could easily be unaccompanied by a commitment to
God outside of worship, so God gave some priest or prophet
the message in the last part. The message begins as if such a
person is speaking *about* God but then makes a transition to

78

speaking *as* God, which often happens in the words of prophets. The message refers back to incidents you can read about in passages such as Exodus 17. A couple of chapters previously, in Exodus 15, the Israelites have been praising God with great enthusiasm, like that of the first two sections of this psalm, but the enthusiasm and prostration soon evaporated.

As an alternative to my imaginative romance, it may be that all three sections were part of the psalm from the beginning and that it played a part in worship like the one it could play in Anglican worship when it was used as a whole. In the temple it would then have prepared people for listening to the reading of the **Torah**, as in the book of Exodus when God's giving his teaching at Sinai soon follows that story about what happened at Contention and Testing.

Another irony is that when the New Testament takes up the psalm, in Hebrews 3–4, it quotes the last part, not the first two parts. Like the Israelite congregation, the Christian congregation has to learn not to believe its own publicity if it is not to find itself the object of God's angry dismissal.

PSALM 96

Yes, Yahweh Has Begun to Reign

¹ Sing for Yahweh a new song,
     sing for Yahweh all the earth!
² Sing for Yahweh, worship his name,
     announce day after day his deliverance!
³ Tell of his honor among the nations,
     of his wonders among all the peoples!
⁴ Because Yahweh is great and much to be praised;
     he is to be held in awe above all gods.
⁵ Because all the nations' gods are nonentities,
     whereas Yahweh made the heavens.
⁶ Splendor and majesty are before him,
     strength and glory in his sanctuary.

⁷ Bestow on Yahweh, you families of the peoples,
     bestow on Yahweh honor and strength.
⁸ Bestow on Yahweh the honor due to his name,
     carry an offering and come into his courtyards.

⁹ Bow low to Yahweh in his holy splendor;
    tremble before him, all the earth.
¹⁰ Say among the nations, "Yahweh has begun to reign!"—
    yes, the world will stand firm, it will not collapse.
He will govern the peoples with uprightness;
¹¹   the heavens may celebrate and the earth rejoice.

The sea and its fullness may thunder,
¹²   the countryside and all that is in it exult.
Then all the trees in the forest may resound
¹³   before Yahweh, because he is coming.
Because he is coming to exercise authority over the earth;
    he will exercise authority over the world with faithfulness,
    over the peoples with truthfulness.

Today's news includes a report about forces in Yemen firing on people protesting the government and killing some of them. In Afghanistan, U.S. and Afghan soldiers have faced sharply increased attacks by insurgents from their base in Pakistan. Meanwhile in Kansas a bishop is being indicted for failing to report a priest who had taken pornographic pictures of children in his congregation. In Libya Muammar el-Qaddafi has been summarily killed by revolutionary forces finally taking the city that was his final refuge; he is only the last—or rather, probably, almost the last—of thousands of people to die in a conflict there. In Somalia, a wheelchair-bound woman has died after being abducted from Kenya.

It's hard to believe that **Yahweh** reigns or has begun to reign. Likewise, if Jesus' coming brought the reign of God near, it seems to have gone away. Yet Psalm 96 declares that Yahweh has indeed begun to reign, and it apparently speaks not only of the realm of creation and nature (like Psalm 93) but of the realm of politics and history. Its author and the people were well aware of realities in their own context that were equivalent to ones about which we learn from the media.

The psalm works in a similar way as Psalm 95 in beginning with an exhortation to worship and then giving the reasons for or the content of this worship, but it goes through that sequence not just once or twice but three times. But whereas

Psalm 95 said, "Let us worship," Psalm 96 gives an exhortation: "Sing . . . tell . . . bestow." The reason for the difference is that Psalm 95 speaks of Israel's worship while Psalm 96 speaks of the world's worship. In speaking of Israel's worship, the leader or the choir can speak to "us," people who are present. In speaking of the nations' worship, the people to whom the exhortation is addressed are not present. The call simply goes out into the ether. If anybody hears the call, it is again Israel that does so, overhearing the call and being reminded that its God is indeed the God of the nations, that he deserves to be acknowledged by the nations, and that he is destined to be acknowledged by them. On the other hand, when the psalm bids its hearers to tell of Yahweh's deeds among the nations, does it imply that this is one nation telling another? Or does it imply that Israel is to tell of God's deeds among the nations? When in due course more and more Gentiles became proselytes or "God-fearers," perhaps it is an indication that Jews were consciously or unconsciously fulfilling this commission to proclaim Yahweh's deeds among the nations.

Why should the nations sing Yahweh's praise, as the beginning of the psalm commissions them, and what is the evidence that Yahweh has begun to reign? The answer lies in Yahweh's **deliverance** and his wonders, terms that refer to events such as Yahweh's rescue of Israel from **Egypt** and his victory at the **Reed Sea**, and also his restoring the people from their **exile** in **Babylon**. Such events are the evidence that the gods the nations worship are nonentities whereas Yahweh reigns in glory in his sanctuary in the heavens.

Like the story in Exodus and the messages of the Prophets, the psalm assumes that these acts performed on Israel's behalf are significant not only for Israel but for the world. They show the pattern of God's involvement in the whole world, and they indicate the purpose God is pursuing for the whole world. So they are grounds for the nations to rejoice with Israel, even if the nations don't know it yet. There are reasons for the nations to join Israel in bringing offerings to Yahweh and bowing low before him. They can come right into Yahweh's palace, into his very courtyards, with those offerings.

They are also the evidence that Yahweh has indeed begun to reign. Oftentimes both Israel and the nations could not see the evidence of that reign, as it is tempting in the context of the chaos of world history in our own day to fear that the world is collapsing politically. The psalm urges us to see events such as the Israelites' deliverance from the Egyptians and from the Babylonians (we can add the death and resurrection of Jesus) as more reliable indicators of the direction the world is going than the grim events that they and we know in our own experience (or read about in the newspapers). They are the evidence that Yahweh is going to come to implement his **authority** in the whole world. Indeed, they are not only reason for Israel and for the nations to worship God but reason for the whole natural world to worship God, as it has the capacity to do.

PSALMS 97–98

The Real King of Kings

97:1 Yahweh has begun to reign, earth should celebrate,
  many foreign shores should rejoice!
2 Cloud and darkness are around him,
  faithfulness in exercising authority is the base of his
   throne.
3 Fire goes before him
  and has burnt his foes all around.
4 His lightning flashes have lit up the world;
  the earth has seen and convulsed.
5 Mountains like wax have melted at Yahweh's presence,
  at the presence of the Lord of all the earth.

6 The heavens have told of the way he acts rightly,
  all the peoples will see his honor.
7 They will be shamed, all those who serve an image,
  those who exult in nonentities;
  all the gods have bowed low to him.
8 Zion has listened and celebrated,
  the daughter-cities of Judah have rejoiced,
  for your authoritative decisions, Yahweh.
9 Because you, Yahweh, are the One on High over all the earth,
  you have ascended very high over all the gods.

¹⁰ You who are dedicated to Yahweh, repudiate evil;
    he guards the lives of people committed to him,
    he rescues them from the hand of the faithless.
¹¹ Light has been sown for the faithful person,
    joy for those who are upright in mind.
¹² Celebrate Yahweh, you who are faithful,
    confess his holy renown!

A composition.

^{98:1} Sing for Yahweh a new song,
    because he has performed wonders!
 His right hand has wrought deliverance for him,
    yes, his holy arm.
² Yahweh has caused his deliverance to be acknowledged,
    to the eyes of the nations he has revealed his faithfulness.
³ He has been mindful of his commitment and his truthfulness
    to the household of Israel.
 All the ends of the earth have seen
    the deliverance of our God.

⁴ Shout for Yahweh, all the earth,
    break out and resound and make music!
⁵ Make music for Yahweh with the guitar,
    with the guitar and the sound of music!
⁶ With trumpets and the sound of the horn,
    shout before the King, Yahweh!
⁷ The sea and what fills it should thunder,
    the world and the people who live in it,
⁸ rivers should clap hands,
    mountains should resound together,
⁹ before Yahweh, because he has come
    to exercise authority in the earth.
¹⁰ He exercises authority over the world with faithfulness,
    over the peoples with uprightness.

According to news reports, Muammar el-Qaddafi, who had ruled Libya for over forty years, once declared, "I am an international leader, the dean of the Arab rulers, the king of kings of Africa and the imam of Muslims, and my international status does not allow me to descend to a lower level." Two days ago the king of kings was dragged from a concrete sewer where he was hiding and shot. I don't know precisely how to associate God with the fall of Qaddafi, but I can see how people in Libya will be believing that God has at last delivered them from Qaddafi's rule and that God reigns a little more in Libya than was previously the case.

Psalms 97 and 98 are similar, so I deal with them together. If we can link them with a particular event in Israel's history, it would be one that was in some ways similar to the fall of Qaddafi's regime, the fall of **Babylon** in 539 that made it possible for **Judahites** in Babylon to return to Judah and rebuild the city. As Babylon was about to fall to the **Persians**, Isaiah 52 uses the same expression as these psalms when it declares, "Your God has begun to reign." It was a convulsion in world history that is portrayed in Psalm 97 as reflecting a kind of convulsion in the heavens, as **Yahweh** comes down to act in awe-inspiring fashion.

In a more overt way than the preceding psalms that also speak of Yahweh's reigning, these two psalms bring out the implications for Israel of the fact that Yahweh has asserted his **authority** as king. God's act in the world issued from his being mindful of his **commitment** and truthfulness to the household of Israel. It gives **Zion** and its daughter-cities (that is, the other cities in Judah) reason to rejoice. It is as if God has sown seeds that will issue in light (an image for **deliverance** and blessing) and joy. No wonder this event demands a "new song" and the sounding of all the instruments you can find.

One should not imagine the Judahite cities as simply empty ruins, but the fall of Babylon did mean that Yahweh had fulfilled his promises and put down their oppressive overlord. Yahweh has used his authority and acted in **faithfulness**— the exercise of authority in the right way that is basic to his reign. He has shown that the impressive images of gods that the Babylonians paraded are simply images—there was no real power to back up the outward impressiveness. As usual, the Old Testament does not deny that the other gods exist. It simply denies that they have anything like the power of Yahweh. There are many gods, but there is only one God. Judah had reason to rejoice all right.

As usual, also, these psalms that talk about Yahweh's reigning and acting on behalf of Israel go on to urge the world therefore to acknowledge Yahweh. It is reason for the world to rejoice. There are many peoples beyond Israel that benefited from Babylon's fall. Even foreign shores across the Mediterranean should rejoice, although they were not directly affected by that event. Yahweh's acting authoritatively in this way is a sign that their own history, too, will ultimately benefit from his beneficent reign. Even the natural world should use its vast capacity to thunder and clap and resound in acclamation of Yahweh.

Yet the psalms' references to Israel and Zion make it fitting that Zion in particular rejoices. Psalm 97 goes on to urge Zion's people to acknowledge Yahweh. It talks about them as people who are dedicated to Yahweh—the verb also means "love," but it suggests commitment, not just warm feelings. The implication of such dedication is that people repudiate evil—in turn this verb is one that also means "hate," but that word also suggests being against something and opposing it, not just having hostile feelings. In the context, the evil that people are expected to repudiate is the evil of recognizing other gods as if they were God. And the motivation for doing so is the faithfulness God shows to people who are committed to him.

Yes, light and joy have been sown for the faithful and upright. Yet actually they have been sown for the whole community. The fall of Babylon benefited everyone, whether or not they were faithful and upright. Anyone could enjoy the light and joy that God's assertion of his reign brought. It transpires that faithfulness and uprightness are as much a response to Yahweh's sowing light and joy as a condition of it. They are appropriate responses to God's gift of light and joy.

PSALMS 99–100

On Sacred Space, Sacred Acts, and Sacred Sound

99:1 Yahweh has begun to reign—peoples should tremble;
    the one who sits on the cherubs—the earth should shake.
2 In Zion Yahweh is great,
    and he is on high over all the peoples.

³ They should confess your name, great and awe-inspiring—
   he is holy.

⁴ With the might of a king you are dedicated to exercising
     authority,
   you are the one who established uprightness.
  You are the one who exercised authority
   with faithfulness in Jacob.
⁵ Lift Yahweh our God high
   and bow low to his footstool—he is holy.

⁶ Moses, and Aaron among his priests,
   and Samuel among the people who call his name,
  they were people calling to Yahweh,
   and he himself would answer them,
⁷   in the pillar of cloud he would speak to them.
  They kept his declarations, the law he gave them;
⁸   Yahweh our God, you answered them.
  You became a God who carried things for them,
   but one who exacted redress for their actions.
⁹ Lift Yahweh our God high
   and bow low to his holy mountain—
   because Yahweh our God is holy.

A composition. For the thank- offering.

¹⁰⁰:¹ Shout for Yahweh, all the earth,
²   serve Yahweh with joy,
   come before him with resounding.
³ Acknowledge that Yahweh is God
   he is the one who made us and we are his,
   his people and the sheep he pastures.

⁴ Come into his gates with thanksgiving,
   into his courtyards with praise,
   confess him, worship his name.
⁵ Because Yahweh is good,
   his commitment is forever,
   his truthfulness to generation after generation.

Yesterday I received what initially seemed a puzzling invitation to a weekly, early-morning prayer meeting, described as

"sacred space for a variety of prayer traditions." It seemed puzzling because I always thought of space as a place, but of course we can talk about space as a stretch of time, and it looks as if this sacred space is a sacred time. And I have now discovered that the idea of such a sacred space has become of some importance in the way people think about spirituality. I also suspected that part of the sacredness was that this time would be a time of quiet and reflectiveness that we need in our noisy and busy lives.

The idea of sacred space in the sense of place is important in Psalm 99, as it is in many psalms; indeed, it is implicit in most of them (the Old Testament also thinks in terms of sacred time, such as the Sabbath and the festivals). The way the Psalms think of sacred space is not identical with the modern way of using the idea, but it overlaps with it. In Israel, *the* sacred space, *the* holy place is Mount **Zion** and its temple. Mount Zion is **Yahweh's** holy mountain. Yahweh sits invisibly enthroned over the **cherubs** in the holiest room of the temple, and he has the **declaration chest** as his footstool there—so the footstool is holy, too.

But that is not the beginning of the story in Psalm 99. The psalm begins with the same motif that appeared in preceding ones, the fact that Yahweh has begun to reign. The reference to people trembling corresponds to the story of Yahweh's victory at the **Reed Sea** in Exodus 14–15, where Israel declared that Yahweh will reign forever and pictured other peoples trembling. That event meant that they should acknowledge that Yahweh's **name** is holy—naturally enough, because it sums up who Yahweh is (hence the warning in the Ten Commandments not to misuse Yahweh's name).

The kingship of Yahweh was then further expressed in his taking hold of the land of **Canaan** and giving it to Israel. This story comes to a climax with the eventual taking of Jerusalem and the building of the temple there, the place that became or that housed Yahweh's footstool. This kingship is expressed again in making it possible for the **Judahites** to return from **exile** and to rebuild the temple when it had been destroyed. A place becomes holy because it belongs to Yahweh because Yahweh has appropriated it and has taken it as a place to be.

Surprisingly, perhaps, you don't necessarily have to keep off of a place that is sacred. You could not go into the holiest room in the temple, which preserved the idea that Yahweh's holiness has the powerful and dangerous surge of an electrical current, but you could go into the temple itself on the holy mountain, which preserved the idea that Yahweh's supernatural nature did not make Yahweh inaccessible.

The sanctifying of a place requires at least God's cooperation. According to Genesis, the Sabbath became a sacred space or time because God said so. Mount Zion became a sacred space because David took an initiative and God accepted it. So we can take an initiative in saying, "This time or place is going to be a sacred space for us," but we have to do so humbly and inquiringly, hoping that God may acquiesce. Build it, and perhaps he will come.

The last part of Psalm 99 reprises the story, recalling the key roles of Moses, Aaron, and Samuel, but thereby tellingly omitting references to the kings themselves, the kind of people who take initiatives that may be dangerous or presumptuous. One significance of Moses, Aaron, and Samuel is that they prayed and did what Yahweh said. None of them was infallible, and they experienced two sides of Yahweh in that connection. Yahweh was capable of "carrying" their wrongdoing, accepting responsibility for handling its consequences rather than making them do so. Yahweh was also capable of exacting redress for their wrongdoing. You have to submit to Yahweh's **authoritative** decisions about whether a particular time is a moment for mercy or a moment for chastisement. Hence the way the psalm closes with the obvious but climactic declaration "Yahweh our God is holy."

Psalm 100 presupposes the notion of sacred space in the sense of a place that Yahweh has hallowed and made his home (it provides another textbook example of the way to go about praise, like several preceding psalms: bid people to praise Yahweh; say why; bid them again; say why again). So worship involves the extraordinary privilege of coming to Yahweh's home, entering his very gates into his very courtyards, like people being welcomed into a family's yard for a barbecue. Worshipers come bringing gifts, as you do when you come for a barbecue, which on this occasion is a thanksgiving affair. They come making a lot of noise, another characteristic of such an event. I suspect that the people who are organizing that sacred space for morning prayer, with which I started, see part of its sacredness as its quietness, and in Western culture we need such quietness. But the Bible much more often assumes that proper acclamation of God requires noise, like proper acclamation of a king or president or sports team. Worship involves sacred noise to accompany sacred acts at the sacred time in the sacred place.

PSALM 101

The Leadership Challenge

David's. A composition.

¹ I will sing of commitment and the exercise of authority,
    for you Yahweh I will make music.
² I will pay attention to the way that has integrity;
    when will you come to me?
  I will go about with integrity in my attitude
    within my household.
³ I will not set in front of my eyes
    anything worthless.
  I am against the action of deviant people;
    it will not stick to me.
⁴ A crooked mind will go away from me;
    I will not acknowledge evil.
⁵ The person who speaks against his neighbor in secret—
    I will put an end to him.
  The person who is [self-]important of eye and broad
      of mind—
    I will not tolerate.
⁶ My eyes will be on the person who is trustworthy in
      the country,
    to live with me.
  The person who is upright of way—
    he will serve me.
⁷ The person who practices deceit
    will not live within my household.

The person who speaks lies
   will not stand in front of my eyes.
⁸ Morning by morning I will put an end
   to all the people who are faithless in the country,
so as to cut off from Yahweh's city
   all who act wickedly.

The news yesterday reported that a recent poll indicates that people's distrust of government in the United States is at its highest level ever, and that people have a deep sense of economic anxiety and doubt about the future. The apparent air of surprise that accompanied the report was odd because these phenomena are of course related. They reflect the insight expressed in that phrase "It's the economy, stupid," which played a key role in Bill Clinton's 1992 presidential campaign. It reminds candidates that people are not so interested in foreign policy or in important moral issues. Their concern is their own security. You can hardly blame them.

Yet the psalm implies that if leaders give in to that aphorism they have missed their vocation. On reading the psalm's opening, one would initially assume that it heralds an act of praise concerning God's **commitment** and exercise of **authority**, but the bulk of the psalm suggests that it is something else. It further announces that it will describe the way that has integrity, which turns out to be the way of integrity to which the person who sings this psalm is committed. This way is not that of an ordinary person but that of a leader, so the significance of the psalm for ordinary people is that it both indicates how to pray for a leader and how to assess leaders or would-be leaders. To put it another way, "leadership ability" is above all a matter of character and moral commitment.

The appeal "When will you come to me?" perhaps indicates that the psalm issues from the leader's awareness of a need for God's intervention. The idea is likely not that he needs God to help him fulfill the moral vision for which he accepts responsibility, though that would be true, but that his description of his commitment is a vastly extended version of an element that appears in many prayer psalms: a declaration that one is committed to **Yahweh's** way and that there is thus no reason for

Yahweh to hesitate to act on the basis that the person praying is not morally or religiously deserving. So this single element that appears in many psalms dominates this psalm. On the basis of his affirming his moral commitment, the psalmist can appeal to Yahweh to come to him and protect him or deliver him from attack.

Most of his leadership commitment is expressed in negatives. Leadership involves taking tough action, stopping things that ought to be stopped. Some of the negative commitments are expressed quite generally—he is intolerant of wrongdoing and (moral) worthlessness within his "household," the equivalent of the White House staff, just as he also lives with integrity in that context himself. Rather than letting members of his staff do his dirty work for him, he surrounds himself with morally trustworthy people. The general point about wrongdoing and trustworthiness also suggests a link with the inner character of the leader and his staff; their position involves both an outward integrity and an inner integrity. Speaking untruth about other people makes the point more concrete, as does being a person who thinks he or she is very important, or being broad-minded about the moral commitment of other people. The psalmist closes with a claim that as well as being tough with himself and with his staff, he has been prepared to be tough with the people as a whole who he leads. It is in the morning that the king deals with cases that are brought before him and acts to defend the innocent and to put down the oppressor.

Many of the people involved in political leadership are in church on Sunday, and it is the pastor's job to rub their noses in the expectations implied by a psalm such as this one.

PSALM 102

I Have Hope for Zion, but Is There Hope for Me?

A plea. For a weak person when he is faint and pours out his murmuring before Yahweh.

[1] Yahweh, listen to my plea;
     may my cry for help come to you.

2 Do not hide your face from me
   on a day when there is trouble for me.
Bend your ear to me;
   on the day when I call, be quick, answer me.

3 Because my days are spent in smoke,
   my bones have burned as in a fireplace.
4 My heart has been stricken like grass, and has withered,
   because I have ignored eating my food.
5 Because of the sound of my groaning
   my bone sticks to my flesh.
6 I have come to resemble a tawny owl of the wilderness,
   I have become like a screech owl of the ruins.
7 I have been awake
   and I have become like a bird, alone on a roof.
8 All day long my enemies have reviled me;
   people I derided have sworn oaths by me.
9 Because I have eaten ashes
   and mixed my drink with tears,
10 in the face of your wrath and your fury,
   because you picked me up and threw me out.
11 My days are like an extended shadow,
   and I—I wither like grass.

12 But you, Yahweh—you will sit forever,
   your renown will continue for generation after generation.
13 You—you will arise, you will have compassion on Zion,
   because it is time to be gracious to it,
   because the appointed time has come.
14 Because your servants have favored its stones,
   and shown grace to its dirt.
15 Nations will be in awe of Yahweh's name,
   all earth's kings of your splendor.
16 Because Yahweh has built up Zion,
   has appeared in his splendor,
17 has turned to the plea of the naked person
   and not despised their plea.
18 May this be written down for the next generation,
   so that a people to be created may praise Yah,
19 because he has looked down from his holy height;
   from the heavens Yahweh has looked at the earth,

²⁰ to listen to the prisoner's cry,
     to release people doomed to death,
²¹ so that Yahweh's name may be proclaimed in Zion,
     his praise in Jerusalem,
²² when peoples gather together,
     yes, kingdoms, to serve Yahweh.

²³ He has humbled my strength on my way,
     he has cut my days.
²⁴ I will say, "My God, do not take me up
     in the midst of my days.
Your years continue
     generation after generation;
²⁵ before, you established the earth,
     and the heavens are the work of your hands.
²⁶ Whereas they may perish,
     you will stand.
All of them could wear out like a coat;
     like clothing you could pass them on.
²⁷ They would pass on, but you are the one,
     and your years will not come to an end.
²⁸ May your servants' children dwell,
     and their offspring endure, before you."

Every morning when we wake up, my wife prays our morning prayers, and almost invariably she thanks God for another wonderful day. An hour later, I sit at my desk thinking about that day's passage for The Old Testament for Everyone series. Today, the sun is shining, and I shall eat my breakfast outside in a little while. Tonight we will go to a bar to listen to Flat Top Tom and His Jump Cats, and I shall dance vigorously for the first time since I had surgery a little while ago (I have been needing to restrain myself for some weeks). There is great blessing on our personal life. Yet there is a contrast between that blessing and the state of the church, which is not "wonderful." Churches in the West are in decline, though this is not the case elsewhere. At the present rate our own congregation will have ceased to exist in a decade or so. Against that background I pray each day for God to have mercy on the church in my home country and in my adoptive country, and I am struck by the contrast between God's blessing of our personal life and God's abandonment of his church.

I am also struck by the difference between my experience, reflection, and prayer and those in Psalm 102, because the experience it presupposes and the reflection and prayer it expresses are almost the opposite of mine. On one side, the individual who prays this prayer does so out of a sense of being abandoned by God to the reviling of enemies. He has become the sort of person by whom people swear an oath, implying, "If I am lying, may I become like him!" He is alone, like an owl or an isolated bird. He withers like grass in the summer heat. His life resembles a person standing in the sun in the evening when the shadows lengthen, which signifies that darkness is about to fall.

In contrast, God's city is a place with a future. Admittedly, in the present it is a place that has been subjected to destruction, so that what its people have to love there are its stones and its dirt. But in the psalmist's imagination and anticipation it is a place built up, a place where God has appeared. He knows it will become like that again, because God is committed to it. Cities die, the way people do, but **Zion** will not do so, because its God does not die, and God's compassion for Zion does not die. Indeed, the psalm says boldly, "The appointed time has come," and it challenges God to disagree. The psalmist's faith is such that he can easily imagine the situation when the city's restoration has happened and he can speak of it as actual.

It is not the same with his personal suffering. The third section of the psalm comes back to that personal reality. There is little sign of anticipation and imagination here, only a renewed sense of the contrast between the shortness of our human life and the long duration of God's life. Or rather, there is a renewed sense of the way a human life can be cut short. While the body seems designed to last into a person's seventies or eighties, in a traditional society most people's lives are cut off "in the midst of their days." The cosmos is much more secure than my individual life, but one can also imagine it wearing out (imagining it is much more possible now, given realities such as global warming and possibilities such as some star crashing into us). The psalm's point is not that the cosmos *will* perish, only that one can imagine it perishing; one cannot imagine God's doing so. Rather touchingly, the psalm ends with the implicit plea "Okay, maybe you will not stop my life from being cut off. Given that your life will continue, please make it possible for the next generation to live before you" with your blessing. Such hopes are based on who God is, and on the way God is committed to the ongoing life of God's city, which is also the psalmist's city. I know a woman who has committed herself to praying every day for the next generation, the generation of her children and that of her grandchildren, whose grown-up life she will never see. It is quite a priority for prayer.

PSALM 103

How to Persuade Your Heart

David's.

1   Worship Yahweh, my heart;
      all my being, [worship] his holy name.
2   Worship Yahweh, my heart;
      do not ignore all his dealings.
3   He is the one who pardons all your waywardness,
      heals all your sicknesses,
4   restores your life from the pit,
      garlands you with commitment and compassion,
5   fills you in your finery with goodness,
      so that your youth renews like an eagle.

6   Yahweh performs faithful deeds,
      decisive acts for all the oppressed.
7   He would make his ways known to Moses,
      his deeds to the Israelites.
8   Yahweh is compassionate and gracious,
      long-tempered and big in commitment.
9   He does not contend forever,
      he does not hold onto it for a long time.
10 He has not acted toward us in accordance with our offenses;
      he has not dealt with us in accordance with our
          wayward acts.

¹¹ Because in accordance with the height of the heavens over
      the earth,
   his commitment has been strong over people who hold
      him in awe.
¹² In accordance with the distance of east from west
   he has distanced our rebellions from us.
¹³ In accordance with a father's compassion for his children,
   Yahweh has compassion for people who hold him in awe.
¹⁴ Because he knows our frame;
   he is mindful that we are dirt.
¹⁵ A mortal: his days are like grass;
   like a wild flower—that is how he blooms.
¹⁶ When the wind passes by it, it is no more;
   its place does not recognize it any more.
¹⁷ But Yahweh's commitment lasts from age to age
   for people who hold him in awe,
   and his faithfulness to their grandchildren,
¹⁸ to people who keep his covenant and are mindful of
      his orders,
   so that they perform them.

¹⁹ Yahweh established his throne in the heavens;
   his reign rules over everything.
²⁰ Worship Yahweh, his aides,
   mighty warriors performing his word,
   listening to the sound of his word.
²¹ Worship Yahweh, all his armies,
   his ministers doing his will.
²² Worship Yahweh, all his works,
   in all the places where he rules.
   Worship Yahweh, my heart.

Some years ago I went through one of those periods when God
didn't seem to be real. I don't mean I was going through some
intellectual questioning, though I have done that at other times,
but rather that I didn't *feel* that God was there. I would go to
the main seminary chapel service each week where I could see
many people were having an enthusiastic "experience of God,"
and I was just having an experience of coldness. When I said
as much to someone after the service one time, he commented
that maybe this experience was what God wanted for me at that

time. It seems a pretty insensitive response, now that I think about it, but maybe he was right. Anyway, eventually the sense of coldness went away.

I found Psalm 103 helpful in living with the experience. First, whereas worship may sometimes come naturally, it assumes that we may need to stir ourselves up to worship. Like some other psalms, it assumes we sometimes need to argue with ourselves. So "I" say to "my heart" and to "all my being" that they must worship God. The word for *heart* is usually translated "soul," but it refers to the whole person or the self rather than just a nonphysical part of me. So the psalm really does expect us to talk to ourselves.

But what do you say to your heart or self? It's not just that you tell yourself to feel things you don't feel or to sing loudly when it doesn't seem natural. It's rather that you remind yourself of the reasons for worship. You remind yourself of the way God acts toward us. In making the point more specific, the psalm points to two actions, pardon and healing, on which much of the following lines give more detail.

Instead of "pardon," translations often have "forgiveness," but the psalm uses a word that applies to a king's pardon rather than to the way one ordinary human being bears with the wrong of another ordinary human being. Later it spells out the implications. God isn't the kind of person who holds onto things, as if waiting for the strategic moment to come down on you like a ton of bricks. Rather he dismisses our rebellions (this word, too, suggests the relationship between a subject and a king) so that they go into **exile** as far as east is from west. Whether or not the psalmist knew it, that distance is infinity.

You could say that "pardons all your waywardness" is an exaggeration; if you don't apply for pardon, you probably don't get it. In the same way, "heals all your sicknesses" might seem an exaggeration; many sicknesses don't get healed (the period in my own life to which I referred was one in which my first wife was getting more and more affected by her multiple sclerosis, and God never healed her). But at least God *can* heal all sicknesses and is the origin of any healing that does come—no one else can heal. The psalm spells out the significance of healing as something much more spectacular than it might seem. I had the flu last week (apparently the result of having a flu shot, but the experts say that's impossible, so who knows?). I prayed for healing, and got it. But the kind of healing the psalm has in mind involves rescuing people when they were bound for the grave pit, and it involves putting a celebratory garland around their neck because there is something so spectacular to rejoice in and getting them to put on their finery. It's as if they are twenty years younger.

Talk of pardon and healing could make it sound as if God is interested only in people's individual personal needs. Actually God is also one who acts on behalf of the oppressed, as Israel's experience under Moses illustrates. How could a psalm of praise omit that fact? These and all God's actions are expressions of magnificent **commitment** and compassion, of grace and long-temperedness. The combination of terms indicates that the psalm is picking up God's own self-description in Exodus 34 and saying to God, "Yes, you are what you said you are." Given that "compassion" is the term for a woman's womb and that it suggests a woman's feelings for her children, it's noteworthy that the psalm assumes that compassion can also be a fatherly characteristic. And that fatherly compassion finds further expression in making allowances for the fact that we mortals are frail, made out of dirt, as we originally were according to the Genesis story. God knows how much we have to depend on him, and he is okay with that fact. All he asks is that we hold him in awe—that is, submit to him and live obediently before him like children.

It is not only human beings who appropriately honor **Yahweh** for being who he is. The whole supernatural world also appropriately does so. But the psalm ends by returning to "my heart," my soul, my self. It ends where it started, but it is a different place because of the road we have traveled.

PSALM 104

God of Light and God of Darkness

1 Worship Yahweh, my heart!—
     Yahweh my God, you became very great.

You put on honor and majesty,
2   wrapping on light like a coat,
stretching the heavens like a tent,
3   one fixing his lofts in the waters,
one making clouds his transport,
      one going about on the wings of the wind,
4 making his aides of winds,
      his ministers of flaming fire.
5 He founded the earth on its bases
      so that it would never collapse, ever.
6 You covered it with the deep like a garment
      so that the waters would stand above the mountains.
7 At your blast they would flee;
      at the sound of your thunder they would take flight.
8 They would go up mountains, they would go down valleys,
      to the place that you founded for them.
9 You set a boundary they were not to pass;
      they would not again cover the earth.

10 You are the one who sends out springs in washes
      so that they go between the mountains.
11 They water every wild animal;
      the donkeys break their thirst.
12 By them the birds of the heavens dwell;
      from among the branches they give voice.
13 The one who waters mountains from his lofts—
      from the fruit of your deeds the earth has its fill.
14 You are the one who grows grass for the cattle
      and plants for the service of human beings,
to bring forth bread from the earth
15   and wine that gladdens the heart of people,
to make the face shine with oil,
      and food that sustains the heart of human beings.
16 Yahweh's trees get their fill,
      the cedars of Lebanon that he planted,
17 where birds nest;
      the stork—the junipers are its home.
18 The high mountains belong to the ibex,
      the crags are a refuge for the rock badgers.
19 He made the moon for dates;
      the sun knows [the time for] its setting.

20 Bring darkness so that it becomes night:
   in it every creature of the forest moves about.
21 The lions roar for prey,
   yes, in seeking their food from God.
22 When the sun rises, they gather,
   and crouch in their lairs.
23 Human beings go out to their work
   and to their service until evening.

24 How the things you made multiplied, Yahweh;
   you made them all with discernment.
   The earth is full of your possessions;
25   that is the sea, great and wide in reach.
   There are moving things without number,
   living things small and great.
26 There ships go about,
   Leviathan that you formed to play in it.
27 All of them look to you
   to give their food at its time.
28 You give to them, they gather;
   you open your hand, they have their fill of good things.
29 You hide your face, they panic;
   you gather up their breath, they perish.
30 You send out your breath, they are created,
   and you renew the face of the ground.

31 May Yahweh's splendor be forever;
   may Yahweh rejoice in his deeds,
32 the one who looks on the earth and it trembles;
   he touches the mountains and they smoke.
33 I will sing for Yahweh while I live,
   I will make music for my God while I am still here.
34 May my murmuring be pleasing to him;
   I myself will rejoice in Yahweh.
35 May sinners come to an end from the earth;
   faithless people—may there be none of them anymore.
   Worship Yahweh, my heart;
   praise Yah.

When my older son got into his midteens, he declared that
he was no longer coming to church with his mother and me.

Fortunately this was not because he had decided that all church was stupid but that our demure Anglican church wasn't keen and lively enough; he intended to go to a more dynamic church with some of his friends. Obviously we were very glad that his rebellion against the parental stance on church was going to take this form and not mean simply giving up on church, and I used to go with him sometimes. On one of these occasions, the pastor preached on the verses from Psalm 104 that speak of bread, wine, and oil and talked about Jesus as the living bread, about the Holy Spirit who is poured out like wine, and about the anointing with power that God gives us.

I think it's fine to adapt verses from the Scriptures to make them say something different from what they literally say (as long as the "something else" is itself scriptural); after all, the New Testament does it. But it is also important to take note of what the verses actually say, and the inherent importance of Psalm 104 lies in what it says about God's relationship with our ordinary world and in the way it draws us into worship for that relationship.

The psalm starts with a vivid, poetic portrayal of the way God went about creation at the beginning, but it does not picture God as simply setting the world going and then letting it work on its own. The psalm's second section talks about the way that God is active in the world now. God makes the springs come out of the earth. God sits in the heavens with his watering can, watering the slopes where trees and crops grow. The psalm notes how the ecology of the world works. Plants, trees, animals, and human beings are all part of one whole, of which God takes ongoing care. The provision of oil, wine, and male cosmetics is part of this care. The movements of sun and moon form an aspect of that ecology. They signal to the creatures of the night when to go about their work, and they signal to human beings as creatures of the day when to go about theirs.

The richness of God's creative work is not confined to the plants and animals that lie close at hand for humanity. There is the sea with its ships and its exotic plenty, including (the psalm notes with a smile) a creature like Leviathan. In Psalm 74 Leviathan was a figure for immense power asserted against God, but it is a power that God had no problem defeating, so here it

101

becomes merely a joke figure, like the Loch Ness Monster. The creatures of the sea, like the creatures of the land, are ones that look to God for their food. We might suspect that they don't literally do so, but they are actually dependent on God every day. When God provides, they live on; when God withholds, they die. God is lord equally of life and death. Only God has life in himself to give. If God gives living breath, creatures live; if God withholds it, they die.

The psalm thus recognizes the dark side to creation—darkness as well as light, hunger as well as sufficiency, death as well as life, the quaking of the earth as well as the stability of the earth. Maybe there is a link between that resolute double recognition and the surprising note with which the psalm almost ends: a plea for the sinners and **faithless** to disappear from the earth. Human rebellion and waywardness spoil the world God created and keeps in being. The prayer also means that the people worshiping in the terms of this psalm cannot take the risk of being faithless sinners themselves.

PSALM 105

On Learning from Your Story

¹ Praise Yahweh, call in his name,
    make known his deeds among the peoples.
² Sing for him, make music for him,
    murmur about all his wonders.
³ Exult in his holy name;
    the heart of all who seek help from Yahweh should rejoice.
⁴ Have recourse to Yahweh and his might;
    seek help from his face continually.
⁵ Be mindful of his wonders, those which he has done,
    and of his portents, the decisions of his mouth,
⁶ you offspring of Abraham his servant,
    children of Jacob, his chosen ones.

⁷ He is Yahweh our God;
    his decisions are in all the earth.
⁸ He has been mindful forever of his covenant,
    the word he commanded to a thousand generations,

⁹ that which he sealed to Abraham
  and swore to Isaac.
¹⁰ He established it as a statute to Jacob,
  to Israel as a lasting covenant,
¹¹ saying, "I will give the country of Canaan to you,
  as a share of your very own."
¹² When they were few in number,
  little and aliens in it,
¹³ and they went about from nation to nation,
  from one kingdom to another people,
¹⁴ he did not allow anyone to oppress them,
  but reproved kings on account of them:
¹⁵ "Do not touch my anointed ones,
  do not do wrong to my prophets."

¹⁶ He summoned hunger onto the country;
  every staff of bread he broke.
¹⁷ He sent before them a man
  who was sold as a servant, Joseph.
¹⁸ They subjected his foot to the fetter;
  iron came onto his person.
¹⁹ Until the time his word came about,
  Yahweh's saying refined him.
²⁰ A king sent and freed him;
  a ruler of peoples [sent] and released him.
²¹ He made him lord of his household,
  ruler over all his property,
²² to constrain his officials according to his will
  and to teach discernment to his elders.

²³ Israel came to Egypt;
  Jacob stayed in the country of Ham.
²⁴ He made his people very fruitful,
  made them stronger than their foes.
²⁵ He made their attitude turn to be against his people,
  to scheme against his servants.
²⁶ He sent Moses his servant,
  Aaron whom he had chosen.
²⁷ They laid down among them words about his signs,
  his portents in the country of Ham.
²⁸ He sent darkness, and it became dark;
  they did not defy his word.

29 He turned their waters into blood
   and killed their fish.
30 Their country teemed with frogs,
   in their kings' rooms.
31 He spoke, and a swarm came,
   mosquitoes in all their territory.
32 He made their rain hail,
   flaming fire in their country.
33 He hit their vine and their fig tree,
   broke down the trees in their territory.
34 He spoke, and the locust came,
   the grasshopper without number.
35 It ate all the vegetation in their country,
   ate the fruit of their land.
36 He hit every firstborn in their country,
   the first of all their vigor.

37 So he brought them out with silver and gold;
   none among their clans collapsed.
38 Egypt celebrated when they left,
   because dread of them had fallen on them.
39 He spread a cloud for covering,
   and a fire to light the night.
40 They asked and he brought quail,
   and he would fill them with bread from the heavens.
41 He opened a crag and waters flowed,
   went in dry places as a stream.
42 Because he was mindful of his holy word
   with Abraham his servant,
43 he brought out his people with joy,
   his chosen ones with resounding.
44 He gave them the countries of the nations,
   and they entered into possession of the toil of the peoples,
45 so that they might keep his laws
   and observe his teachings.
   Praise Yah!

It's coming up to Thanksgiving/Advent Sunday, and I'm asking
the members of our church to think about the following four
questions:

1. "What are you particularly thankful for this year?"
2. "In your Christian faith, what are you finding nourishing or encouraging at the moment?"
3. "What questions about Christian faith do you have?"
4. "What might you covenant to do for the coming year?"

They will write down their answers in church anonymously; we will collect them and offer them to God; and I will read them and take up some of their themes in sermons over the next year.

It occurs to me that Psalm 105 offers pointers toward Israel's set of answers to these questions. You could say that it begins by raising the question "What have we got to be grateful for?" Its answer to the question doesn't relate to what God has done for a particular generation, for people alive in 900 or 700 or 500 BC, though in other contexts the Old Testament indicates that it does expect Israel to think about that question. Its answer reminds Israel to be grateful for the extraordinary sequence of events that lay at the foundation of every century in its life as a people. But by way of response to this sequence of events, gratitude isn't the only attitude to God that the psalm looks for. The story it will go on to tell is one that establishes how **Yahweh** is the one from whom Israel is to seek help, the one to whom it has recourse; that is another response. There are two other sorts of directions in which Israel was always tempted to look in this connection. It was inclined to look to different deities or to other nations as allies. The story that follows provides the basis for looking steadfastly to Yahweh.

The vast bulk of the psalm thus comprises a review of the story that appears in Genesis to Joshua, starting off with references to the **covenant** between God and Israel's ancestors. It uses the word *covenant* in the complementary sense from the one it will have for our congregation when it thinks about a covenant; it refers to God's covenant rather than ours. *Covenant* is a way of talking about commitment, a commitment that you make solemnly and that you know you can't get out of. The references to "sealing" it, "swearing" it, and establishing it as a "statute" underline the point. How risky of God to make a covenant to human beings, who can be expected to let God down!

God's covenant commitment to Abraham is the foundation of all that follows in the story that the psalm summarizes. From the beginning, in spelling out the implications of the covenant, the psalm's focus is on God's giving Israel a country of its own. That is the covenant gift. So it starts with the way God protected Israel's ancestors at the beginning of the story, when they were in the right country but it was controlled by other people. The psalm doesn't consider the question of how "fair" this was to the country's previous occupants, because that is not its agenda; the **Torah** answers that question by noting how the **Canaanites** were due for God's punishment.

Then the story has to undertake a strange and long diversion. God brought a famine on the country. The famine did not just happen. God caused it; the psalm does not ask why, as Western people would. Once again its angle on the story complements the angle in the Torah, which simply records that the famine happened, not that God deliberately caused it. The famine means that the ancestors have to leave the country to find food, but God has anticipated the crisis this raises for them and has sent Joseph ahead of them to **Egypt**, where he can see that they are looked after. Once more, the psalm complements Genesis, which holds back from saying that God's providence was involved in Joseph's being in Egypt, until Joseph interprets the story that way in the last chapter of the book. The psalm sees God's active involvement in the way the Egyptians turn against the Israelites, because this turning is the means by which God will work toward the fulfillment of that word to Abraham. In other words, the point about leaving Egypt isn't merely to find freedom from being serfs there; it's to gain access to the country God had promised. Thus God provided for them on their journey toward that country.

The opening of the psalm suggests two ways that the story told by this psalm is important—it is the basis for worshiping Yahweh and for relying on Yahweh. The end of the psalm adds a further point. If the psalm has a rationale for Yahweh's giving Israel the country that had belonged to the Canaanites, it is that Israel is to live there by Yahweh's laws and teaching. Perhaps it hints at the same rationale that Genesis 15 offers—the

Canaanites are thrown out of the country because of their waywardness; Israel is brought into the country so that it may live a different way. Although the psalm doesn't say that Israel is to make a covenant commitment to Yahweh that corresponds to Yahweh's covenant commitment to Israel, such is its implication. The relationship between God and Israel starts off as a covenant that God makes, but it continues as a covenant that Israel also makes. Obviously failure to keep that commitment means Israel risks being treated the same way as the Canaanites, which is what actually happened. So the psalm ends by giving Israel something further to think about.

PSALM 106:1–47
How Our Faithlessness Magnifies God's Faithfulness

1   Praise Yah!
    Confess Yahweh, because he is good,
        because his commitment is forever.
2   Who can utter Yahweh's mighty acts,
        get people to listen to all his praises?
3   The blessings of people who take care about decision making,
        of the person who does what is faithful at all times!

4   Be mindful of me, Yahweh, when you favor your people,
        attend to me when you deliver them,
5   so that I may see the good things that come to your chosen,
        rejoice in the joy of your nation,
        exult with your own.

6   We have offended along with our ancestors,
        we have been wayward, we have been faithless.
7   Our ancestors in Egypt did not discern your wonders,
        they were not mindful of the magnitude of your acts of
            commitment.
8   But he delivered them for the sake of his name,
        so that his might would be acknowledged.
9   He blasted the Reed Sea and it dried up,
        and he enabled them to go through the deeps like
            a wilderness.

107

¹⁰ He delivered them from the hand of their opponent,
     restored them from the hand of the enemy.
¹¹ Water covered their adversaries;
     not one of them was left.
¹² They trusted in his words,
     and sang his praise.

¹³ They quickly ignored his deeds;
     they did not wait for his plan.
¹⁴ They felt a deep desire in the wilderness,
     and tested God in the wasteland.
¹⁵ He gave them what they asked,
     but sent a wasting within their spirits.
¹⁶ They were jealous of Moses in the camp,
     of Aaron, Yahweh's holy one.
¹⁷ The earth opened and swallowed Dathan,
     closed over Abiram's group.
¹⁸ Fire blazed among their group,
     a flame that burned the faithless.
¹⁹ They made a bullock at Horeb,
     bowed down to an image.
²⁰ They exchanged their splendor
     for the representation of a bull that eats grass.
²¹ They ignored their deliverer,
     the one who had done great things in Egypt,
²² wonders in the country of Ham,
     awe-inspiring deeds at the Reed Sea.
²³ He said he would wipe them out,
     except that Moses, his chosen,
stood in the breach before him,
     to turn his wrath from destroying.

²⁴ They rejected the beautiful country
     and did not trust in his word.
²⁵ They muttered in their tents
     and did not listen to Yahweh's voice.
²⁶ So he raised his hand [to swear] to them,
     to make them fall in the wilderness,
²⁷ and to make their offspring fall among the nations,
     to scatter them among the countries.
²⁸ They joined the Master of Peor
     and ate sacrifices offered for the dead.

²⁹ They provoked by their deeds,
and an epidemic broke out among them.
³⁰ But Phinehas stood and intervened,
and the epidemic stopped.
³¹ It counted for him as a rightful deed,
generation after generation forever.
³² But they angered at Strife Waters;
it was displeasing to Moses because of them.
³³ Because they rebelled against his spirit,
he was rash with his tongue.

³⁴ They did not destroy the peoples,
as Yahweh had said to them.
³⁵ They mixed with the nations,
and learned what they did.
³⁶ They served their images;
they became a snare for them.
³⁷ They sacrificed their sons
and their daughters to demons.
³⁸ They shed innocent blood,
the blood of their sons and daughters,
whom they sacrificed to the images of Canaan;
the land became polluted through the bloodshed.
³⁹ They became taboo through their deeds;
they were immoral in their deeds.

⁴⁰ Yahweh's anger burnt against his people,
he loathed his own.
⁴¹ He gave them into the hand of the nations;
their opponents ruled over them.
⁴² Their enemies oppressed them,
and they bowed down under their hand.
⁴³ Many times he would rescue them, but those people—
they were rebellious in their planning.
They sank low because of their waywardness,
⁴⁴   and he saw the trouble that came to them.
When he heard their resounding,
⁴⁵   he was mindful of his covenant to them.
He relented in accordance with the magnitude of his acts
of commitment
⁴⁶   and made them the objects of compassion
before their captors.

⁴⁷ Deliver us, Yahweh our God,
     gather us from the nations,
   to confess your holy name
     and glory in your praise.

From six thousand miles' distance I have been astonished to follow the London equivalent to Occupy Wall Street, which has involved protesters camping out at St. Paul's Cathedral, where I was ordained, near the London counterpart of Wall Street. I was not surprised to discover that the cathedral is going to court to get the protesters removed, though I was glad to know that some of the cathedral staff have resigned in their own protest, in the conviction that the cathedral should self-evidently be on the side of the protesters. I share that conviction and take the cathedral's action as sadly typical of the church's capacity to shoot itself in the foot on such occasions.

I am slightly comforted to be reminded by Psalm 106 that it has always been so. From the beginning, the story of the people of God is the story of our missing the point, of our failing God. Of course the story of the church can be told in other ways; it can be told as a story that keeps illustrating the commitment of people to God in sharing the gospel with the world and showing it the love of God. Psalm 105 has told the story of Israel as the story of God's protection and **faithfulness**. But Psalm 106 goes over much of the same story (though it starts later and finishes later) in order to bring out a different message. While it does talk about God's blessing the people and **delivering** them, it concentrates on their unresponsiveness. If Psalm 105 corresponds broadly to the arc and dominant message of Genesis to Joshua (where Israel's unresponsiveness is set in the framework of God's acts of grace), Psalm 106 corresponds more to the arc and dominant message of Exodus to Judges (which ends with Israel's unfaithfulness). If Psalm 105 is thus more a salvation story, Psalm 106 is more a disobedience story.

The people's unresponsiveness to God goes back to their time in **Egypt**, when Moses and Aaron had a hard time convincing the people that God was acting on their behalf. God delivered them anyway, and they recognized this fact, but they then soon forgot, and the story of their journey toward the promised land is one of testing God, being jealous of Moses, making images, failing to trust in the nature of the country that God was taking them to, and joining in the worship of the **Masters**. The story continued in **Canaan**. They failed to destroy the peoples who were there already and instead followed the kind of practices for which these people had incurred God's wrath, such as sacrificing their children. Yet **Yahweh** still could not avoid being mindful of his **covenant** to them. Here is a note that Psalms 105 and 106 have in common. It is this covenant on God's part that is the basis of the people's life, whether or not they are responsive to God.

It is for this reason that the psalm can begin the way it does. Its opening is otherwise astonishing in light of where the psalm eventually goes, as the direction the psalm takes is astonishing in light of the way it opens. A long account of the failure of the people of God can be the dominant theme of this psalm that begins in praise, because the account of failure and **faithlessness** actually magnifies God's faithfulness and mercy. The opening and closing of the psalm point to some other implications. One emerges from the fact that God does chastise his people even if he does not cast them off. The corollary is that blessing rests on the people who give themselves to acting faithfully in the way they make **authoritative** decisions. At the most selfish level, people are unwise to infer from God's **commitment** that therefore they might as well do what they like. Israel's story shows it is not the way of blessing.

Another implication is that chutzpah makes it possible to pray for mercy and deliverance when you are in a mess that you deserved. God has been unwise enough to show that he has a hard time resisting being merciful, so the close of the psalm takes advantage of that fact. You can add the motivation that it will lead to God's being recognized and praised. Yet another implication is that this entire pattern applies both to the people as a whole and to the individual. The point is expressed in the fact that blessing comes to the faithful yet the individual benefits from God's inability to turn away from being faithful to the people as a whole.

111

PSALM 106:48

Another Amen

⁴⁸ Yahweh, the God of Israel, be worshiped,
    from age to lasting age!
All the people is to say, "Amen."
    Praise Yah!

Whereas the amen at the end of Book Three of the Psalter stands in contrast to Psalm 89 to which it is appended, this amen at the end of Book Four follows nicely on Psalm 106, though perhaps it issues a challenge in that it involves recognizing that our story as the people of God is indeed a story of rebellion and waywardness.

PSALM 107

Let the Redeemed of the Lord Say So

¹ Confess Yahweh, because he is good,
    because his commitment is forever.
² The people restored by Yahweh are to say it,
    those whom he restored from the hand of the foe,
³ and gathered from the countries,
    from the north and from the west.

⁴ They wandered in the wilderness, in the wasteland;
    they did not find the way to a settled city.
⁵ Hungry, thirsty too,
    their spirit within them fainted.
⁶ But they cried out to Yahweh in their trouble,
    and he rescued them from their pressures.
⁷ He directed them by a straight way,
    to get to a settled city.
⁸ They are to confess to Yahweh his commitment,
    his wonders for human beings,
⁹ because he has sated the person who is scurrying about,
    and filled the hungry person with good things.

¹⁰ People living in darkness and deathly gloom,
    prisoners of affliction and iron,

¹¹ because they had defied the words of God,
 despised the plan of the One on High:
¹² he subdued their heart with trouble;
 they collapsed without a helper.
¹³ But they cried out to Yahweh in their trouble
 and he delivered them from their pressures.
¹⁴ He brought them out of darkness and deathly gloom,
 and broke their bonds.
¹⁵ They are to confess to Yahweh his commitment,
 his wonders for human beings.
¹⁶ because he has broken up bronze doors,
 shattered iron bars.

¹⁷ Stupid people, because of their rebellious way
 and their acts of waywardness, suffered affliction.
¹⁸ Their spirit loathed all food;
 they reached the gates of death.
¹⁹ But they cried out to Yahweh in their trouble,
 and he delivered them from their pressures.
²⁰ He sent his word and healed them;
 he released them from their deep pit.
²¹ They are to confess to Yahweh his commitment,
 his wonders for human beings.
²² They are to offer thanksgiving sacrifices,
 and tell of his deeds with resounding.

²³ People who go down to the sea in ships,
 doing work in great waters,
²⁴ these people—they saw Yahweh's deeds,
 and his wonders in the deep.
²⁵ He spoke and raised a storm wind,
 and it lifted its waves.
²⁶ They went up to the heavens, they went down to the depths;
 their spirit melted away in their trouble.
²⁷ They reeled and staggered like a drunk,
 and all their insight swallowed itself up.
²⁸ But they cried out to Yahweh in their trouble,
 and he delivered them from their pressures.
²⁹ He made the storm into stillness;
 their waves went quiet.
³⁰ They rejoiced when they became silent,
 and he led them to the haven they longed for.

³¹ They are to confess to Yahweh his commitment,
    his wonders for human beings.
³² They are to exalt him in the congregation of the people,
    and praise him in the session of the elders.

³³ He turns rivers into wilderness,
    springs of water into thirsty land,
³⁴ fruitful land into salt marsh,
    because of the evil of the people who live in it.
³⁵ He turns wilderness into a pool of water,
    dry land into springs of water.
³⁶ He has settled hungry people there;
    they have established a settled city.
³⁷ They have sowed fields and planted vineyards,
    and they have produced fruit, a harvest.
³⁸ He has blessed them and they have increased greatly,
    and he does not let their cattle decrease.

³⁹ But they have decreased and become low
    through oppression, trouble, and sorrow.
⁴⁰ He pours shame on leaders,
    and makes them wander in wastes where there is no path.
⁴¹ But he secures the needy person from affliction
    and makes their families like flocks.
⁴² The upright will see and rejoice;
    all wickedness has stopped its mouth.
⁴³ Who is the person of insight who will note these things?—
    they will consider Yahweh's acts of commitment.

As a teenager, I used to go to camps run by the National Young Life Campaign, now known as Young Life (but I think unrelated to Young Life in the United States, though with aims that are not so different). We would go off to the beach or climb mountains during the day and have services in the evening. It was at one of those camps either in England or in Wales that I had the sense of God's calling me to the ministry. I think it was at the same camp that Raymond Castro, one of the leaders, used to organize "Say so" times during those evening meetings, times when he got people to volunteer to talk about what God had done for them or what God was saying to them. He knew that giving your testimony in that way had a powerful effect on other young people, more powerful than adults talking about what God had done for them or was saying to them, and that it also had a powerful effect on the individual who did the sharing.

It was on the basis of the opening of this psalm that they were called "Say so" times. In the King James Version, verse 2 of Psalm 107 reads, "Let the redeemed of the LORD say so." While the psalm wants to get Israel as a community to testify to what God has done for it, otherwise its presupposition is the same as the one Raymond Castro used. The opening three lines suggest that the testimony urged by the psalm relates to the return of people from **exile** and what this event meant to them. The following sections celebrate their restoration from four types of experience rather than from four places. For some people the experience meant being lost, hungry, and thirsty. For some it meant captivity and darkness. For some it meant sickness or injury and the likelihood that they would die. For some it meant a hazardous journey across the ocean to start a new life on some other Mediterranean shore.

There were aspects of this experience that the people all had in common. First, they couldn't complain; it was their own fault, the result of the kind of waywardness that is described in 1 and 2 Kings and in the Prophets. But second, they **cried out** to **Yahweh** in the midst of their trouble. Third, Yahweh responded and **delivered** them from whatever was their experience of trouble—typically, Yahweh was not held back by their sinfulness from rescuing them. In each case, the rescue deals with the particular trouble they were in—Yahweh enables them to find the way to where there is food to eat, or breaks open the prison doors, or heals them and pulls them back from the gates of death, or stills the waves that threaten their sea crossing. All these people, then, have been redeemed or restored by Yahweh, and they ought to say so—because that testimony honors Yahweh, builds up the people themselves, and encourages other people.

The last major section of the psalm implies a stress on that last consideration. The fact that people were free to return to **Judah** as decades went by did not solve their problems in the way you might have expected. You can read the story in the books of Prophets such as Haggai and Zechariah and in the books of

Ezra and Nehemiah. It's therefore important that people draw the right conclusions from the psalm's four vignettes. Those acts whereby Yahweh rescued people were not one-time-only events, because getting into trouble isn't a one-time event. They showed the kind of God Yahweh is and the way Yahweh characteristically acts. But decrease, oppression, trouble, and sorrow have reasserted themselves in the people's experience. And therefore they need to listen to the testimony that a previous generation could give. The redeemed of the Lord are to say so for the sake of their grandchildren and great-grandchildren.

So people of insight will meditate on their story in order to have possibilities opened up in their imaginations and in order to pray the way their grandparents did.

PSALM 108

What to Do When God's Promises Fail

A song. A composition. David's.

1. My mind is set, God,
   I will sing and make music; yes, my soul [is set].
2. Wake up, harp and guitar;
   I will wake the dawn.
3. I will confess you among the peoples, Yahweh,
   I will make music for you among the nations.
4. Because your commitment is great, over the heavens,
   your truthfulness up to the skies.
5. Be high over the heavens, God,
   over all the earth your honor.
6. So that the people you love may be rescued,
   deliver me by your right hand and answer me.

7. God has spoken by his holiness:
   "I will exult as I allocate Shechem
   and measure out Sukkot Valley.
8. Gilead will be mine, Manasseh will be mine.
   Ephraim will be my helmet, Judah my scepter.
9. Moab will be my wash basin, over Edom I will throw
   my shoe,
   over Philistia I will shout out.

¹⁰ Who will conduct me to the fortress city,
    who will lead me to Edom?
¹¹ Have you not rejected us, God?—
    you do not go out with our armies.
¹² Grant to us help against the foe,
    as human deliverance is empty.
¹³ By God we will act with force;
    he will trample our foes.

I was talking the other day with a friend who has been an associate pastor in a flourishing Pentecostal church for a year. He did not have a Pentecostal background, but this fact had not seemed to matter, because nothing very Pentecostal remained in this Pentecostal church. It had become indistinguishable from other lively churches outside mainstream denominations. My friend said he had experienced no one prophesying or speaking in tongues or being miraculously healed in his year in the church. That account cohered with impressions I have had from other people and from occasional visits to Pentecostal churches in the United States (the situation is different in the two-thirds world). I am sad about this fact, though I am not necessarily faulting the churches. Prophecy, speaking in tongues, and healing are God's gifts, not something we can generate. Yet this aspect of the way things are in the church in the West does raise some questions. God once promised to pour out his Spirit on his people (see Joel 2). He isn't doing so.

A different concrete topic is the focus of Psalm 108 (which reworks material that also appears in Psalms 57 and 60), but there is a similarity in an underlying issue. What do you do when God doesn't fulfill his promises? The middle section of the psalm recalls undertakings God made way back at the beginning of Israel's life. It was a really solemn undertaking— God spoke by his holiness, putting his own nature as God on the line.

The promises concern his taking the country of **Canaan**. They presuppose the situation when **Yahweh** and Israel were not yet in the promised land. They are poised to enter it, located to the south or southeast of the country, near the end of the journey from **Egypt**. Yahweh intends to allocate the area west

117

of the Jordan, which is symbolized by Shechem, modern-day Nablus, the biggest city at the beginning of Israel's history when Jerusalem was not very important. Yahweh intends similarly to measure out and thus allocate the Sukkot Valley, east of the Jordan, which stands for that area in general. Talking then about Gilead and Manasseh suggests reference to the Israelite clans that settled east of the Jordan, while **Ephraim** and **Judah** are the two most prominent clans west of the Jordan. The Israelite clans will be the beneficiaries of Yahweh's allocating the land; while the land will always belong to Yahweh, they become Yahweh's tenants. But in the first instance, they are Yahweh's agents in taking the country. It is as if Ephraim is the helmet worn by warrior Yahweh and Judah is the baton this general waves at his troops.

And it is going to be impossible for anyone to get in Yahweh's way. Moab, Edom, or **Philistia** might try, but they will fail. Edom is the area that Yahweh and Israel will reach first, so Yahweh asks who is going to take the lead as they draw near to Edom. You can read the story about Edom and Moab in Numbers 20–21. The Philistines won't feature in the story for a while as they arrive on the border of Canaan at about the same time as the Israelites but on the opposite side, coming from across the Mediterranean. In line with that fact, you can't read an account of this promise in the Old Testament story in the **Torah**; this account of the promise sums up the implications of Yahweh's promises as they could be expressed in a later age.

The problem is that the reality of Israel's subsequent experience often contrasted with what was explicit or implicit in the promises. So what do you do then? The psalm has two answers, expressed on either side of the recollection of the promises. As you might expect, the recollection leads into protest, prayer, and the expression of a conviction that God will fulfill the promises. More surprising is the way the psalm begins, with an extended expression of praise for God's **commitment** and truthfulness or reliability, though this praise also ends with a prayer. Maybe there is an irony there; the praise will in due course imply that the (alleged) reality of God's commitment and reliability is why God must respond to the prayer.

I intend to pray more for God to fulfill the promises expressed in Joel and to praise God for his commitment and reliability.

PSALM 109

How to Deal with Being Swindled

The leader's. David's. A composition.

¹ God, my praise, do not be silent,
²   because it is a faithless mouth and a deceitful mouth
    that people have opened against me;
        they have spoken with me by means of a lying tongue.
³ With aggressive words they have surrounded me
    and made war on me without reason.
⁴ In return for my friendliness they accuse me;
    so I [am making] a plea.
⁵ They have brought upon me evil in return for good,
    aggression in return for my friendliness.
⁶ "Appoint a faithless person over him,
    an accuser who will stand at his right hand.
⁷ When he is up for a decision, may he come out as faithless,
    his plea will lead to condemnation.
⁸ May his days be few;
    may another person take his property.
⁹ May his children become orphans,
    his wife a widow.
¹⁰ May his children wander about, beg and solicit,
    from their ruins.
¹¹ May the creditor strike at all that he has,
    may strangers plunder his earnings.
¹² May he have no one showing commitment,
    may there be no one being gracious to his orphans.
¹³ May his succession be for cutting off,
    in the next generation may their name be blotted out.
¹⁴ May the waywardness of his ancestors stay in mind
        for Yahweh,
    may his mother's offenses not be blotted out.
¹⁵ May they be before Yahweh always;
    may he cut off their memory from their land.

¹⁶ Because of the fact that he was not mindful to keep
　　　　commitment,
　　　but pursued the person who was lowly and needy,
　　　and the person crushed in spirit, to kill him.
¹⁷ He liked cursing, and it came about for him;
　　　he did not wish [to utter] blessing, and it was far
　　　　from him.
¹⁸ He put on cursing like a coat,
　　　it came into his insides like water,
　　　into his bones like oil.
¹⁹ May it be for him like clothing that he wraps on,
　　　and as a belt that he always puts around."

²⁰ May this be the wages of my accusers from Yahweh,
　　　the people who speak evil against me.
²¹ So you, Yahweh, my Lord,
　　　deal with me for the sake of your name;
　　　because your commitment is good, rescue me.
²² Because I am lowly and needy,
　　　and my spirit hurts within me.
²³ Like a shadow as it lengthens, I am gone;
　　　I am shaken off like a locust.
²⁴ My knees have collapsed from hunger;
　　　my body has wasted, away from fatness.
²⁵ I—I have become an object of reviling to them;
　　　when they see me, they shake their head.

²⁶ Help me, Yahweh my God,
　　　deliver me in accordance with your commitment,
²⁷ so that people may acknowledge that this is your hand,
　　　that you, Yahweh, you have done it.
²⁸ Those people may curse, but you—may you bless;
　　　they will have arisen and been shamed, but your servant
　　　　will rejoice.
²⁹ May my accusers put on disgrace,
　　　may they wrap around their shame like a coat.
³⁰ I will confess Yahweh greatly with my mouth,
　　　in the midst of many people I will praise him,
³¹ because he stands at the right hand of the needy person
　　　to deliver him from the people who make decisions
　　　　about him.

This weekend we plan to go to a new movie about some of the victims of the financial meltdown in the first decade of this century. They are the staff of a high-end condo block who discover that the occupant of the penthouse has been engaged in a billion-dollar fraud that (among other things) has robbed them of their pension fund. They decide to get their redress by robbing the financial mogul. "At least for a little while it will make you laugh instead of cry about the current state of affairs, which is more than you can say about a lot of things," one reviewer comments. In real life, in the aftermath of that meltdown, the media have reported how the victims of such a swindler threatened to kill his wife and children.

The kind of person for whom this psalm speaks is someone who indeed wants to get back at people who have swindled him. I take the long middle section (vv. 6–19) as their words about him, about the person who prays this psalm. He is quoting the swindlers' words. They plan to get him found guilty for acts he has not committed, so that the result will be his personal ruin or death, the forfeiture of his land and property, and the community's turning its back on him. Most chillingly, they bring God into the way they speak. Their words provide a great example of what it means to take **Yahweh's name** in vain, to attach Yahweh's name to something that is devoid of reality and truth. For that matter, they take his parents' names in vain, speaking as though they were great sinners and deserve their memory to be cut off the same way as they say the psalmist does. Ironically, they accuse him of the offenses they are themselves guilty of—a failure of **commitment**, a heartlessness, a love of cursing rather than blessing, which they hope may rebound on him.

How do you deal with an experience of being treated falsely? We might think there are two alternative ways. Either you go in for the action of the victims of that fictional or real-life swindler; you take action to get your own back. Or you suck it up and turn the other cheek. Along with other parts of the Scriptures, Psalm 109 thinks that you pray. You do suck it up, but you also batter on God's chest about it. You are right to be enraged, and you are entitled to express your rage rather than pretending it does not exist, but you express it to God. In the psalm, at least, part of the reason that the victim needs God to

121

take action against the plotters is the need to be **delivered** from their plots; he needs them to be put down. But the psalm's rage goes beyond that need to the more general need to see redress on wrongdoing.

New Testament passages such as Matthew 23 reaffirm the psalm's stance in this respect; retribution must come to people who do such wrong to others. The New Testament's quoting from Psalm 109 in connection with Judas in Acts 1 suggests it doesn't think it was odd for God to have this psalm in his book. If we ourselves are not people who need to pray it, we are called to put ourselves into the position of people who need to do so. This identification is particularly chilling if we imagine people in other parts of the world praying it about us who live in the Western world. Indeed, the importance of psalms to us often emerges when we realize we play a different role in them from the one we assume. We are the people psalms complain about, not the people who have a right to complain. It may be one reason that psalms make us feel uncomfortable.

PSALM 110

A Question of Power

David's. A psalm.

¹ Yahweh's word to my lord:
   "Sit at my right
   until I make your enemies your footstool."

² Yahweh will send your strong scepter out from Zion;
   rule in the midst of your enemies.
³ Your people are willing offerings
   on the day you deploy your forces.
   In holy splendor from the womb of dawn
   the dew of your youth is yours.
⁴ Yahweh has sworn, and will not relent:
   "You are a priest forever after the manner of Melchizedek."

⁵ The Lord is at your right;
   he has crushed kings on the day of his anger.

⁶ He exercises authority among the nations,
    filling [the scene] with bodies;
  he has crushed heads over the earth,
    far and wide.
⁷ From the stream by the way he drinks;
    therefore he can raise his head.

My wife keeps going on about power. I don't take it personally. Actually, it works in my favor, because her fixation lies with the way contemporary Western thinking is preoccupied by questions about who has power and about how power features in the relationships of men and women, parents and children, pastors and congregations, and professors and students. She thinks that our understanding and appreciation of these relationships is being spoiled by the focus on power and by an obsession with obtaining it, with the powerless gaining power, or with empowering people. The dynamics parallel those that apply in connection with the significance of sacred places such as the temple. Their importance is perverted by the way they become symbols of power, so that in the present day the key question about the Temple Mount in Jerusalem is who controls it. Yet such considerations confirm the principle that human willfulness makes it dangerous to concentrate power and important to diffuse it.

That principle makes Psalm 110 worrying. In Israel, religious power was diffused among priests, kings, and prophets. Kings could not take over the role of priests and might be struck down if they did so, as happened to King Uzziah (2 Chronicles 26). Prophets could confront priests or kings. Here in Psalm 110 it is presumably a prophet who speaks, a prophet exercising the kind of power possessed by Nathan or Gad in David's court (see e.g., 2 Samuel 7), and he declares that **Yahweh** appoints the king as also priest. That means David is put into a position like that of Melchizedek. Genesis 14 tells of Melchizedek, who was king of Salem, which Psalm 76 has confirmed is the same as Jerusalem. In keeping with common practice in traditional societies, he was priest as well as king in Salem. It meant his position was not so different from that of Abraham, who in effect held both sorts of power in the clan in Genesis. But when

123

Israel became a nation, you could say that in effect power was diffused between Moses, who was rather like a king; Aaron, who was priest; and Miriam, who was a prophet. In Judges there are no kings, and we don't read much about priests or prophets. Once there are kings and a temple in Jerusalem, the story is a bit ambiguous about how much power the kings had in the temple. Alongside the story about Uzziah's being struck down, there are stories about kings offering sacrifice without getting into trouble—but maybe it means that they provided the sacrifice and a priest actually made the sacrifice.

In Psalm 110, Yahweh's opening and closing words are promises that the king will be able to lead his people successfully, that they will willingly serve in his army, and that he will defeat his enemies. Such promises might seem to give him too much encouragement to make wars that are merely designed to bolster Israel's power in the world, though several considerations reduce that worry. One is that Israel was never in the position of a great power like the United States or Britain. It was usually a little power under pressure from the great powers or from neighbors that were at least as powerful. Another consideration is the point made in the psalm's closing verses, that Israel and its king were designed to be Yahweh's means of exercising **authority** in the world. If they did try to use their power to build themselves an empire, they would risk being treated the same way as the other powers that Yahweh acted against.

Perhaps Yahweh's solemn declaration that the king is also priest acts as constraint. If the king is also a priest, it could mean that he is in a position to claim religious sanction for wars that are actually undertaken for purely political reasons. But it could also mean that decisions about war can never be taken on a purely political basis. The king is not merely the commander-in-chief. He has to face God over the wars he undertakes, and he has to do so quite publicly and officially. Further, he is a priest after the manner of Melchizedek, who appears in the Old Testament not as someone who makes war but as someone who blesses.

The New Testament uses Psalm 110 to help it understand the significance of Jesus, but the psalm itself gives no indication that it is about the Messiah, and as is often the case the New

Testament is giving the psalm different significance in applying it to Jesus.

PSALM 111
Yahweh's Covenant and Our Covenant

¹ Praise Yah!
  I will confess Yahweh with my whole mind
    in the counsel of the upright, the assembly.
² Yahweh's doings are great,
    looked into for all their delights.
³ His action is majestic and glorious,
    his faithfulness stands forever.
⁴ He gained renown for his wonders;
    Yahweh is gracious and compassionate.
⁵ He has given meat to people who are in awe of him;
    he is mindful of his covenant forever.
⁶ He told his people of the might of his doings
    in giving them the possession of the nations.
⁷ The doings of his hands are true and decisive;
    all his decrees are truthful,
⁸ established forever and ever,
    done in truth and uprightness.
⁹ He sent redemption to his people,
    he commanded his covenant forever.
  His name is holy and to be held in awe;
¹⁰   awe for Yahweh is the essence of insight.
  Good sense belongs to all who do them;
    his praise stands forever.

I noted in connection with Psalm 105 that this Thanksgiving/ Advent we are suggesting to the people in our church that they think about what they have to thank God for over the past year and what they might make a covenant about for the coming year. It hadn't occurred to me that their covenant commitments could be a response to their reflection on the past year, but the point is obvious when you think about it. Today we gave the congregation the four questions I listed in the comment on Psalm 105 so that they could think about them before we do so in the context of our worship next Sunday, and on the way home my wife asked me whether I was going to think about them ahead of time myself. Whether I do so or whether I rely on what occurs to me next Sunday (which fits with my usual approach to life), I shall now be linking together the way I may covenant and the way God has blessed me over the year.

Psalm 111 points in the same direction in that it begins by making a commitment to confessing **Yahweh** and ends with a reference to "doing" the requirements of his **covenant.** The first part of the psalm refers to the covenant commitment Yahweh made to Israel; near the end it talks about Yahweh's *commanding* a covenant, suggesting the covenant commitment Yahweh looks for from the people. Similarly, the psalm three times refers to Yahweh's "doings" on behalf of the people; then at the end it refers to what people need to "do" in response to Yahweh's "doings." God's covenant commitment and God's doing have to come first, but our covenant commitment and our doing have to follow. In our congregation's thanksgiving and covenanting we will be thinking about the specific and personal blessings that God has given us and about the specific and personal response we make. The psalm is thinking about the foundational blessings God has given the people and the foundational response they make.

You could say that it sums up the nature of the people's relationship with God, and it is therefore fitting that it is an alphabetical psalm—that is, after the opening "Praise **Yah**," each of the half-lines begins with a different letter of the Hebrew alphabet. There are thus eleven lines for the twenty-two letters in the alphabet, and the psalm is able to cover the nature of worship and of a relationship with God from *A* to *Z*.

The questions about thanksgiving and covenanting are the first and last of the questions we will be considering. The psalm also offers insight on our middle two questions. Question two asks about what aspects of Christian faith are especially important and helpful to people; the *A* to *Z* might help in considering that question. Question three asks about concerns people might have about Christian faith, and it is noteworthy that this psalm that begins with reason for praise ends by talking about insight. It assumes that what God has done and said contains

126

the answers to our questions. It also assumes that insight is a matter of an attitude we take to God and to what God says and of the way we live out that attitude.

PSALM 112

The Prosperity Gospel Redefined

1   Praise Yah!
   The blessings of the person who lives in awe of Yahweh,
      who delights much in his commands!
2   His offspring will become a mighty man in the country;
      the generation of the upright will be blessed.
3   Wealth and riches are in his house,
      and his faithfulness stands forever.
4   He rises in the darkness as light for the upright,
      gracious, compassionate, and faithful.
5   Good is the person who is gracious
      and lends as he fulfills his concerns with decisiveness.
6   Because he will not collapse, ever;
         the faithful person will become an object of renown
            forever.
7   He is not afraid of bad news;
         his mind stands firm, reliant on Yahweh.
8   His mind is held firm so that he is not afraid,
      until he looks on his foes.
9   He spreads abroad as he gives to the needy;
         his faithfulness stands forever.
   His horn will stand high in honor;
10   the faithless person will see and fret.
   He will grind his teeth and waste away;
      the desire of faithless people will perish.

My wife used to work for one of the most successful and wealthy people in the United States (this did not mean she brought a wonderful dowry into our marriage). Her job was to help him do something with his money, and the projects she was involved in were worthwhile, impressive, interesting, and often educational. One entailed the remodeling of a mansion in a posh neighborhood in Europe, where she recently dreamed all our combined extended family was moving to live, and another entailed the restoration of a number of World War II military aircraft. Often the projects were of direct benefit to ordinary or needy people, and her boss had pledged to give away most of his money in his lifetime.

The Bible has no ideal of everyone having the same wealth. It hints at the awareness that some people are better off than others, which might be because they are better or more hard-working farmers, or just luckier. It assumes that there is a correlation between the **faithfulness** of a farmer's life and the success of his farm, though it also recognizes that things do not always work out that way. It does not assume that your skill, hard work, and faithfulness simply entitle your family to enjoy the fruits of being better off than other families and ignore the less well-off.

Psalm 112 is another *A–Z* psalm, like Psalm 111. Maybe it implicitly offers a rounded spirituality of wealth and a rounded attitude to life. Using a certain structure, however, also enables psalmists, like all poets, to think things they would not otherwise have thought. The psalm starts as if it is simply giving faithful farmers an excuse to congratulate themselves on the prosperity that issues from their faithfulness, but it then trips them up when it redefines the blessings that come from faithfulness. It thus affirms the prosperity gospel but then deconstructs it. The blessing it affirms does not lie in a farmer's simply doing very well for himself and his family. It lies in the fact that he can get up when it is dark in order to bring light to people who are upright, gracious, compassionate, and faithful. That declaration in itself implies a recognition that not every upright, gracious, compassionate, and faithful person gets on okay in life. And the declaration maybe has a double meaning. Light and darkness are common symbols for blessing and calamity. So the psalm might be saying that the wealthy farmer is in a position to get up when it is literally dark in order to be a blessing to other people. Or it might mean that he is in a position to rise up when things are dark for the family of another upright person that is having a hard time and bring that person light. Or it might mean both.

Either way, as a person with some wealth he is able to be gracious and to lend to another family that is having a hard time in order to tide them over until the next harvest. He thus takes **decisive** action with his family's assets in order to benefit another family that is in need. As usual, the Old Testament assumes that when you have surplus assets, you don't lend them in order to make more money; you lend them in order to be compassionate to needy people in a way that doesn't just make them the beneficiaries of a handout. But as you live this generous and faithful life and stay reliant on God, the psalm promises that your assets will increase. Not only so; you will be honored in the community and will do better than people who focus on their own needs, who ridicule you, and who then find that their self-centered concern with building up their own portfolio gets them nowhere.

PSALMS 113–114

On Being Open to the Unexpected

113:1 Praise, Yahweh's servants,
   praise Yahweh's name!
² May Yahweh's name be worshiped,
   now and forever!
³ From the rising of the sun to its setting,
   the name of Yahweh be praised!
⁴ Yahweh is on high above all nations,
   his honor is above the heavens!
⁵ Who is like Yahweh our God,
   the one who is on high in order to sit [enthroned],
⁶ who gets down low in order to look,
   in relation to the heavens and the earth,
⁷ who lifts up the poor person from the dirt,
   raises the needy person from the trash heap,
⁸ to enable them to sit with the leaders,
   with the leaders of the people,
⁹ who enables the childless woman to sit in the household,
   a joyful mother of children?
   Praise Yah!

114:1 When Israel went out from Egypt,
   Jacob's household from a jabbering people.

129

² Judah became its sanctuary,
    Israel its realm.
³ When the sea saw, it fled;
    the Jordan—it turned back.
⁴ The mountains—they jumped like rams,
    the hills like lambs.

⁵ What was it with you, sea, that you fled,
    Jordan, that you turned back,
⁶ mountains, that you jumped like rams,
    hills, like lambs?

⁷ Tremble before the Lord, earth,
    before Jacob's God,
⁸ who turned the crag into a pool of water,
    basalt into a spring of water.

In commenting on Psalm 108, I spoke of a friend's Pentecostal church that seemed to have no more expectation of God's acting than evangelical or mainline churches do. But yesterday I sat in the ophthalmologist's waiting room reading a book recommended to me by my boss (so obviously I had to read it), a book by James Smith with the provocative title *Thinking in Tongues* (Grand Rapids: Wm. B. Eerdmans Publishing Co., 2010). One chapter begins with the testimony a woman gave in a service to the way she and her husband had been trying for a baby for eight years and had become frustrated and hopeless and angry with God. But the previous month the women in her Bible study group had laid hands on her and prayed for her. She was too tired to believe that the stories of women such as Hannah could become her story, and she didn't think much about the event afterwards. But she was now pregnant.

Yahweh is one who enables the childless woman to sit in the household as the joyful mother of children, the psalm says. Of course, of course, of course, **Yahweh** doesn't always do so. Many childless women remain childless, and many other prayers don't get answers. The psalmist had not failed to notice that fact. But it didn't make him decline to recognize that Yahweh did sometimes answer prayers, and it didn't make him give into the temptation to infer that a childless woman's unexpected pregnancy was just one of those odd things, explicable on the basis of some hormonal event, and that it was nothing to do with God. It can be more comfortable to assume you know how life works and how God works, and that God does not do miracles of that kind today even if he did them in Bible times. It's more unsettling to acknowledge that you don't know how life works or how God works, and that we don't have the criteria for deciding why some prayers get answers and others don't. Psalm 113 encourages us to live unsettled lives and implies that we may then see miracles that we would not otherwise see. James Smith expresses it in terms of being open to God's surprises, of expecting the unexpected. It isn't your openness that makes the unexpected happen; your openness is not even a condition of the unexpected happening (the woman in that story had given up hoping, though maybe it's significant that her friends hadn't). It's God who decides when to act; and if we don't expect the unexpected, we may not recognize it when it happens.

For an Israelite family, great sadness attaches to a woman's not being able to have children, because having children is a key way she plays a part in the future of the people and in the future of her family. Equivalent sadness attaches to a man's not being able to make the family farm work. Maybe he's a poor farmer; maybe he's unlucky; maybe he's lazy; maybe he's the victim of loan sharks or enemy invasion; but one way or another he ends up in the dirt, on the trash heap. As is the case in our world, sometimes that might be a metaphor, and sometimes it might be a literal reality. And many failed farmers no doubt never got their farms back. But sometimes God made it possible for them to gain a new start and rejoin the village elders in their position of honor as the community's leaders. Once again the psalm invited people not to see that event as mere chance or the result of human initiative but as the surprising gift of God.

Such experiences on the part of a husband or a wife are reflections of the fact that God is both one who sits on high enthroned and one who looks down at what is happening on earth and gets involved there. In this connection, this psalm was not so much a prayer to expect the man on the trash heap to pray (your job was to pray for him and help him off the trash heap) or to expect the childless woman to pray (your job was to pray for her and see whether she is getting enough nourishment). It was one for people in general to use as an expression of praise and prayer, partly so that they know how to respond when they are childless or on the trash heap.

Psalm 114 offers a parallel encouragement to Psalm 113, but one oriented to the community rather than the individual. In later centuries, these two psalms were used together at the beginning of the Passover meal. As people gathered for this family meal, they might find it significant that Psalm 113 invites people to celebrate the way that God is involved in the life of families while Psalm 114 would be appropriate specifically to Passover. It begins by recalling the exodus, God's **deliverance** of people at the **Reed Sea**, and God's taking them across the Jordan into their new country, and it pictures nature pulsating at what it sees God doing for Israel—a different sound from the jabbering of the **Egyptians** in their alien tongue.

In a later context where people were not really free but were under the rule of a superpower, there would be some poignancy about that recollection. You couldn't blame them for thinking that they had still not experienced the kind of restoration of the community that the Prophets promised would come about. It's then telling that the psalm ends with that reference to a pool of water and a spring, because Isaiah 41 promised such provision for the poor and needy (which takes us back to Psalm 113) as a way of describing that coming restoration and the bringing of people back from **exile**. So the psalm says, "You know how God provided for the people on the way from Egypt to the promised land? Well that's not just something God did once, way back at the beginning. It's something God did again in bringing people back from exile. It's the kind of thing God does in delivering and restoring his people. So it's the kind of thing you can look forward to again."

PSALM 115

Trust or Control

¹ Not to us, Yahweh, not to us, but to your name give honor,
   for your commitment, for your truthfulness.

² Why should the nations say,
  "Where is their God, then?"
³ when our God is in the heavens;
  everything that he wishes he has done.
⁴ Their images are silver and gold,
  the making of human hands.
⁵ They have a mouth but they do not speak,
  they have eyes but they do not see,
⁶ they have ears but they do not hear,
  they have a nose but they do not smell,
⁷ [they have] their hands but they do not feel,
  [they have] their feet but they do not walk about;
  they do not make a sound with their throat.
⁸ Their makers become like them,
  everyone who trusts in them.

⁹ Israel, trust in Yahweh!—
  he is their help and their shield.
¹⁰ Household of Aaron, trust in Yahweh!—
  he is their help and their shield.
¹¹ People who are in awe of Yahweh, trust in Yahweh!—
  he is their help and their shield.
¹² In that Yahweh has been mindful of us, he will bless us;
  he will bless the household of Israel.
  He will bless the household of Aaron,
¹³   he will bless the people who are in awe of Yahweh,
  small along with great.
¹⁴ May Yahweh add to you,
  to you and to your children.
¹⁵ May you be blessed by Yahweh,
  maker of the heavens and the earth.

¹⁶ The heavens are heavens belonging to Yahweh,
  but the earth he gave to human beings.
¹⁷ Whereas the dead do not praise Yah,
  nor any who go down to silence,
¹⁸ we—we will worship Yah,
  now and forever.
  Praise Yah!

Today I received a much-forwarded e-mail with a moving story about a woman showing a caring attitude to a homeless guy and his mentally challenged friend who showed up in a fast-food restaurant. The e-mail promised that if in turn I forward the e-mail to my friends, I can make a wish, and it will come true. If I send it to five people, my wish will come true in three months; if I send it to ten people, it will come true in five weeks; and so on. The people who send and forward the e-mail want to be in control of their lives and their destinies, and they think they know how to get that control.

The people the psalm describes seek to fulfill the same desire by making images of gods for themselves. An image is something you can see and control, and the gods the images represent are beings you can control. Offer the right offerings to them, and you will get the right result. This theology is not so different from one Christians sometimes hold, a vending-machine theology: insert the right coin, and your candy bar will come out. Similarly, although the psalm speaks of the image makers as belonging to other nations, Israelites often went in for making images, so that one point (maybe the main point) of the psalm is to speak to them.

The image makers could naturally ask, "Where is your God, then?" Elsewhere the Psalms refer to that question in contexts where people are mocking someone because God is failing to act on the person's behalf, but here the question has different significance. People are mocking because you couldn't see the God the Israelites believed in (or were supposed to believe in). The psalm turns that apparent weakness into a strength: "You know why you can't see our God? That's because he's in the heavens, stupid!" Of course the mockers also believed that their gods were in the heavens; they didn't think they were contained in their images (at least, in theory they didn't believe so). But they hadn't drawn the obvious inference that the idea of making images of such gods therefore doesn't make sense. At least it doesn't make sense if you believe that these gods can do things. The very nature of an image makes the point. Images have all the right body parts to suggest a capacity to be active. But none of their body parts work. A result of trusting in these entities that cannot do anything means you cannot do anything, either—a sad result, because it is the exact opposite to one aim of making them, which is to be in control of your life and your destiny.

134

Yahweh has a mouth, eyes, ears, nose, hands, feet, and vocal chords that work. One shouldn't be literalistic in understanding that point, but neither should we dismiss it as mere metaphor. It is as people with mouth, eyes, ears, hands, feet, and vocal chords that we are made in God's image; and it is because God has these that Jesus could have all these as a being who embodies God. Being in the heavens and thus in a position of power and having the capacity to do things mean that Yahweh is the real God who can act in the world. He can be a help and a shield and one who blesses you and makes it possible for you to have children. In a sense it is more difficult to trust your future to a God whom you can't see, but it is actually more sensible. You won't have such a feeling of control, but you will actually be safer.

The reference to the dead comes as a surprise, but maybe the point is that another way in which people try to control their destinies is by consulting dead people, especially family members, maybe by asking them to mediate with God on their behalf. The psalm thus closes off another avenue that's an alternative to relying directly on Yahweh. Dead people are no more use to you than images. Dead people are dead. They can't worship Yahweh (they will be able to do so on resurrection day, of course, but that's another story). You can. Once again the psalm pushes people into direct dealings with the real God.

PSALM 116

Reason to Believe

1   I give myself, because Yahweh listens to
    my voice, my prayers for grace.
2   because he has bent his ear to me,
    and through my days I will call.

3   Death's ropes encompassed me,
    Sheol's restraints found me.
4   When I find constraint and sorrow,
    I call out in Yahweh's name:
    "Oh now, Yahweh, save my life!"
5   Yahweh is gracious and faithful;
    our God is compassionate.

135

⁶ Yahweh watches over simple people;
    I sank low, and he delivered me.
⁷ Turn, my spirit, to your rest,
    because Yahweh—he has dealt with you.
⁸ Because you pulled out my life from death,
    my eye from tears, my foot from being pushed down,
⁹ I can walk about before Yahweh
    in the land of the living.
¹⁰ I trust, because I could say,
    "I—I have become very weak."
¹¹ I—I said in my trepidation,
    "Every human being deceives."

¹² What shall I return to Yahweh
    for all his dealings with me?
¹³ I will lift the deliverance cup
    and call out in Yahweh's name.
¹⁴ I will fulfill my promises to Yahweh,
    yes, right before his people.
¹⁵ Valuable in Yahweh's eyes
    is the death of people who are committed to him.
¹⁶ Oh now, Yahweh, because I am your servant,
    I am your servant, the son of your maid;
    you loosed my bonds.
¹⁷ I will offer a thanksgiving sacrifice to you,
    I will call out in Yahweh's name.
¹⁸ I will fulfill my promises to Yahweh,
    yes, right before his people,
¹⁹ in the courtyards of Yahweh's house,
    in the middle of Jerusalem.
    Praise Yah!

Last night I had dinner with a young man who is a faithful church worshiper. He has been so for most of his life, but he isn't sure whether the worship in which he takes part is real in the sense of corresponding to the truth. As he put it, he isn't sure whether the Christian story is true. He was brought up as a Christian, and he really wants it to be true, and he is willing to give his life to serving God. But he is not certain whether God is really there to be served, and he doesn't know how to move from this uncertainty to a greater certainty, either way. I didn't have much idea about how to help him move except (in response to his questions) to tell him how and why I live on the basis of its being true.

Psalm 116 points toward one answer to those questions, though there is a sense in which it doesn't help my friend very much. It doesn't give him a procedure to follow, such as those used to solve math or science problems, nor does it evoke a sign similar to those that he thinks other people have received. What often convinces people that the Christian or the Israelite story is true is the way that God reaches out to them personally, but Psalm 116 assumes that if that happens to you, your job is to talk about it to other people. And though hearing about how God has reached out to you may not be as good as God's reaching out to them in person, it's at least something.

So Psalm 116 is an example of a psalm that is at the same time a thanksgiving and a testimony. Toward the end it speaks specifically of thanksgiving and of the thanksgiving offering that people might bring to God when they are aware of having had their prayers answered. This psalm also presupposes that in the midst of the experience that drives people to call on God (such as severe illness or other people's hostility), they might say to God, "And I will look forward to bringing you an offering to express my thanksgiving." The psalm then rejoices in their being able to enter the very courtyard of God's house to make that offering. And people's experience of **deliverance** is enhanced by articulating their gratitude and expressing it in something concrete, such as an offering. It is also enhanced by their joining in the festive meal accompanying this kind of sacrifice: a thanksgiving sacrifice would involve family members and friends sharing in eating the animal that was sacrificed as part of the worship, all in God's presence.

The experience of deliverance is further enhanced by the fact that the thanksgiving is also a testimony—that is, while the last part of the psalm addresses God, most of it addresses other worshipers, people such as those family members and friends who would accompany an individual to the temple to make the offering and share in the rejoicing. So there is another aspect to the individual fulfilling his promises. He does so by "calling out in **Yahweh's name**" as he utters his thanksgiving and proclaims

137

how great Yahweh is. And other people's trust in God is built up by hearing his testimony. We might worry whether a testimony about God's acting in our lives makes other people saddened over a lack of God's action in their lives. A friend of mine commented that he might sometimes want to give thanks for what God has done, but he is hesitant because he doesn't want other people to feel bad. Would it be insensitive to thank God for healing when other people haven't experienced God's healing in response to their prayers? My answer is that through the years when we prayed for my first wife's healing and God never granted it, such testimonies were a blessing rather than another hurt. My trust was built up by their testimony.

The psalm begins in a slightly abrupt way. The word for "giving oneself" is also the word for "love," but when we speak of loving God we often mean having warm feelings for God whereas we noted in connection with Psalm 98 that "love" in the Bible means action. "If you love me, you will keep my commandments," Jesus says in John 14. Here, too, "loving" means giving oneself to God. It is another way of saying to God, "I am your servant." That is why God is bound to me and has accepted an obligation to reach out to me; it is also why I am bound to God and why I both give myself and trust—the verb "trust" is also used in an abrupt way in the psalm. The object of my giving and my trust is God, but both times the psalm leaves out the object and concentrates on the attitude.

I am praying that God will reach out to my friend or that other people will tell him how God has acted in their lives, and that such testimony will pull him toward a conviction that the Israelites' story and the Christian story correspond to reality.

PSALM 117

How to Say a Lot in a Few Words

¹ Praise Yahweh, you nations,
   extol him all you peoples.
² Because his commitment to us has been powerful;
   Yahweh's truthfulness is forever.
   Praise Yah.

If you want to know how to praise God, here is the answer.
Summon people to do so, and then give the reasons.

PSALM 118

This Is the Day That the Lord Has Made

¹ Confess Yahweh, because he is good,
    because his commitment is forever.
² Israel is indeed to say,
    "His commitment is forever."
³ Aaron's household is indeed to say,
    "His commitment is forever."
⁴ The people who are in awe of Yahweh are indeed to say,
    "His commitment is forever."

⁵ Out of constraint I called Yah;
    Yah answered me with roominess.
⁶ Because Yahweh is mine, I will not fear;
    what can human beings do to me?
⁷ Yahweh is mine as my helper,
    and I shall look on the people who are against me.
⁸ It is better to rely on Yahweh
    than to trust in human beings.
⁹ It is better to rely on Yahweh
    than to trust in leaders.
¹⁰ All nations surrounded me;
    in Yahweh's name I can indeed wither them.
¹¹ They surrounded me, yes, surrounded me;
    in Yahweh's name I can indeed wither them.
¹² They surrounded me like bees;
    they have been extinguished like a fire of thorns—
    in Yahweh's name I can indeed wither them.
¹³ You pushed me hard, so as to fall,
    but Yahweh helped me.
¹⁴ Yah was my strength and protection,
    and he became my deliverance.
¹⁵ The noise of resounding and deliverance was in the tents
        of the faithful:
    Yahweh's right hand acts with force,
¹⁶ Yahweh's right hand lifts up high,
    Yahweh's right hand acts with force.

¹⁷ I shall not die, but live,
    and tell of Yah's deeds.
¹⁸ Yahweh severely disciplined me,
    but did not give me over to death.

¹⁹ Open the faithful gates to me;
    when I come through them, I shall confess Yahweh.
²⁰ This is Yahweh's gate;
    faithful people come through it.
²¹ I will confess you, because you answered me
    and became deliverance for me.
²² "The stone that the builders spurned
    has become the head cornerstone."
²³ This came about from Yahweh;
    it has been wonderful in our eyes.
²⁴ This is the day that Yahweh has made;
    we will celebrate and rejoice in it.
²⁵ Oh now, Yahweh, will you deliver us?—
    Oh now, Yahweh, enable us to succeed.

²⁶ Blessed be the one who comes in Yahweh's name;
    we are blessing you from Yahweh's house.
²⁷ Yahweh is God; he has shone light to us—
    tie the festal offering with cords to the horns of the altar.
²⁸ You are my God and I will confess you—
    my God and I will exalt you.
²⁹ Confess Yahweh, because he is good,
    because his commitment is forever.

I joined the faculty of my seminary in England at the time
when it moved to a new campus in a different city, so the beginning of my first year was a big moment for the seminary, not
just for me. As I walked onto the campus on that first morning,
I remember singing "This Is the Day That the Lord Has Made."
As it happens, we are going to sing it as our opening hymn in
church tomorrow, but the organist is concerned that it is too
short. He's probably right that there will hardly be time for the
procession to get from the back of our little church and reach
our places before the song is over, so I told him we will sing it
twice. Or three times. The more interesting question is what

we mean when we sing this song. Is Sunday the day that God made? Or does the song apply to every day? Or what?

In origin, in its context in Psalm 118, the song's title refers to a day when **Yahweh** has acted in a spectacular way to **deliver** his people from a crisis. Quite likely the better translation is "This is the day when Yahweh acted," but I don't want to spoil the song. Like Psalm 116, it is a thanksgiving and testimony psalm. It involves the whole congregation, but it particularly involves the voice of an "I," someone such as the king, a leader such as Nehemiah in a period when Israel didn't have kings, or a worship leader. Initially this leader urges the congregation as a whole to join in praise, then urges the priests in particular, and then the people who are in awe of Yahweh (in later centuries that phrase denoted non-Israelites who had committed themselves to Yahweh, and perhaps that reference applies here).

Then the leader speaks and recalls some crisis—the words are quite general, perhaps because as usual the psalm was designed to be used on any occasion when the people came to give thanks for a deliverance. It combines past recollection with affirmations about the ongoing significance of what has happened. Because I have experienced God's acting to deliver me, this experience has built up my trust in him. One implication is that I can approach the next crisis with less fear. Another is that I have proved that relying on Yahweh works better than relying on human resources—that is, relying on making alliances with other peoples and their leaders. Part way through, the leader addresses an opponent as if he is present—maybe he is literally there, paraded before the people, but maybe he is just there in the leader's imagination as he recalls the crisis. It was an experience of severe discipline, one that put huge pressure on him in order to get him to learn those lessons about whom to trust and how to have confidence.

As you get to the last section of the psalm, it becomes more explicit that the psalm involves some alternating between the leader's speaking and the people's speaking. We might imagine the leader actually standing at the gates of the city or the gates of the temple. They are "**faithful** gates" because they lead into what was supposed to be a faithful place and therefore a place where faithful people could come. The leader and the people bring a thank offering to give concrete expression to their thanksgiving for what God has done. So this festival offering is to be bound by ropes and taken to the **altar** for sacrifice. The plea for God now to deliver and grant success reflects the awareness that a particular act of deliverance is never the last one you will need and is often only a stage in God's granting you real safety and security. The earlier declarations about trusting and not fearing are not just pious theory; they need to be implemented in new contexts.

When Jesus comes to Jerusalem on a colt and people shout "Hosanna" in Mark 11, they are using the Hebrew expression for "Will you deliver us?" It's no coincidence, because they go on to take up the words "Blessed be the one who comes in Yahweh's **name**." Then in Mark 12 Jesus takes up the line about the stone, which looks like a proverb that is illustrated by the way the city's attackers had discounted the people and their leader, but he has triumphed against all odds. In different ways the people and Jesus see the psalm as illuminating what Jesus is about.

PSALM 119:1–24

God's Laws as the Way to Blessing

¹ The blessings of people of integrity in their way of life,
  who walk by Yahweh's teaching!
² The blessings of people who observe his declarations,
  who inquire of him with their whole mind!
³ Yes, they have done no wrong;
  they have walked in his ways.
⁴ You have commanded your orders
  to be well kept.
⁵ Oh that my ways may be firm
  in keeping your laws!
⁶ Then I shall not be ashamed
  when I look at all your commands.
⁷ I will confess you with uprightness of mind
  as I learn of your faithful decisions.

⁸ I will keep your laws;
do not totally abandon me.

⁹ How can a youth keep his way pure?—
by guarding it in accordance with your word.
¹⁰ I have inquired of you with my whole mind;
do not let me stray from your commands.
¹¹ I have treasured your words in my mind
so that I may not offend you.
¹² You are to be worshiped, Yahweh;
teach me your laws.
¹³ With my lips I have proclaimed
all the decisions of your mouth.
¹⁴ In the way of your declarations I have rejoiced
as over all wealth.
¹⁵ I shall murmur about your orders
and look on your paths.
¹⁶ In your laws I will take pleasure;
I will not ignore your words.

¹⁷ Deal with your servant while I live,
and I will keep your word.
¹⁸ Open my eyes so that I may look on
wonders from your teaching.
¹⁹ I am a sojourner on the earth;
do not hide your commands from me.
²⁰ My spirit has failed with longing
for your decisions all the time.
²¹ You have blasted the willful;
cursed are the people who stray from your commands.
²² Take away from me taunt and shame,
because I have observed your declarations.
²³ Although officials have sat, have spoken against me,
your servant murmurs about your laws.
²⁴ Yes, your declarations are my pleasure,
my advisers.

After church today, a friend asked me a question that had arisen out of a conversation he'd had with a coworker. My friend was surprised that the coworker was willing to work seven days a week—what about the commandment concerning a Sabbath day's rest? The coworker's reply was that all such Old Testament laws had been abolished by Jesus. At first I was bemused, because the coworker is a Jehovah's Witness, and one hears that Witnesses have some pretty strict rules (such as refusing blood transfusions), but I guess these are rules for Gentiles and Christians. The coworker was right that observing Sabbaths had not been required of Gentiles and had ceased to be an obligation for Jews who came to believe in Jesus (as Paul notes in Colossians 2). Yet we assume that the other commandments still have something to teach us, and it seems likely that this is the case with the Sabbath commandment, something about time for God and time for rest. The rules in the Old Testament were not merely random taboos or prohibitions designed to keep you from enjoying your life. They were given to help you live a truly human life.

Psalm 119 is full of enthusiasm for these rules. Its author was so passionate about them that it ended up as another alphabetic psalm—it waxes lyrical over God's word from *A* to *Z*. And this does not mean merely beginning one line with each letter of the alphabet. The psalm comprises twenty-two sections, each with eight verses, and each of the eight verses begins with the same letter—so verses 1 to 8 all begin with the equivalent of *A*; verses 9–16 all begin with the equivalent of *B*; and so on. One of the results of adopting that pattern is that there isn't much sequencing in the content of the lines—what they have in common is the letter they begin with ("Okay, what else does the letter *B* make me think of?"). Which in turn means we can meditate on each line independent of its context. I won't attempt to comment on every line—you can make any line an object of that meditation.

First, the psalm teaches, adhering to God's rules is the way of blessing. Things go well in your life. You can hold your head high. You can expect God to be with you and not finally abandon you. Conversely, a curse rests on people who turn away from God's commands. The third section indicates that the psalmist does not go around with eyes shut to the realities of life. Notwithstanding the declaration in the first section that adhering to God's rules means being able to hold your head high and not be ashamed, the third section articulates the feeling of someone who is being shamed. People who ought to know better have spoken against the psalmist, but that hasn't made the psalmist abandon a commitment to sticking by those rules. Sometimes you have to live in light of the way you believe things will work out in the long run. If these important people show that their words ought not to be heeded, so much the worse for these people who ought to be good counselors. Their behavior will reinforce the psalmist's conviction that it is God's declarations that are the best counselors.

So God's laws are a pleasure. These opening sections use that word twice; it is a word that elsewhere describes the delight and happiness that a child brings to its mother. They are a joy. You realize that even if you understand them reasonably well, there is always more to learn from them. You give your whole energy to getting your mind around them and then to living by them. The psalm can speak of people who have done no wrong in relation to these laws, which shows that they are not setting an impossibly high standard. The Ten Commandments illustrate the point. It's not so complicated to worship **Yahweh** alone and not worship other gods, to avoid making images, to keep the Sabbath, to avoid adultery, and so on. It's not so esoteric, though it may be difficult in that other people are worshiping other gods and making images and working 24/7 and having affairs. The question is whether we want to do so. The psalm encourages us to keep reminding ourselves that being desirous of living by God's rules is worthwhile. It's not the only key to being able to make that commitment, but it's one such key.

PSALM 119:25–48

Standing on the Promises

25 My spirit is stuck in the dirt:
    bring me to life in accordance with your word.
26 I proclaimed my ways and you answered me;
    teach me your laws.
27 Help me understand the way of your orders,
    so that I may murmur about your wonders.
28 My spirit has wept itself away through sorrow;
    lift me up in accordance with your word.

²⁹ Remove the way of falsehood from me;
  grace me with your teaching.
³⁰ I have chosen the way of truthfulness;
  I have set out your decisions [before me].
³¹ I have stuck to your declarations;
  Yahweh, do not shame me.
³² I run the way of your commands,
  because you broaden my mind.

³³ Teach me the way of your laws, Yahweh,
  so that I may observe it to the utmost.
³⁴ Help me understand, so that I may observe your teaching,
  and keep it with all my mind.
³⁵ Direct me in the path of your commands,
  because I delight in it.
³⁶ Bend my mind to your declarations
  and not to profit.
³⁷ Help my eyes pass from seeing emptiness;
  bring me to life by your way.
³⁸ Establish for your servant what you have said,
  that which was for the people who are in awe of you.
³⁹ Make my reviling, which I dread, pass,
  because your decisions are good.
⁴⁰ Now: I long for your orders;
  in your faithfulness bring me to life.

⁴¹ So may your commitment come to me, Yahweh,
  your deliverance in accordance with what you have said.
⁴² And I shall answer the person who reviles me with a word,
  because I have trusted in your word.
⁴³ So do not snatch right away from my mouth your truthful
    word,
  because I have waited for your decisions.
⁴⁴ And I will keep your teaching always,
  forever and ever.
⁴⁵ So I will walk about in roominess,
  because I have inquired of your orders.
⁴⁶ And I will speak of your declarations before kings,
  and not be shamed.
⁴⁷ So I will take pleasure in your commands,
  to which I give myself.

146

⁴⁸ And I will lift my hands to your commands, to which I give
   myself,
   and I will murmur about your laws.

Yesterday I got our congregation to write out their thanksgivings, uncertainties, and commitments for the coming year, in
line with the plan I mentioned in connection with Psalm 105.
Just before doing so, I realized that there was another question
it would have been good to include (but it seemed too late to
add it): What might they want to pray for during the next year?
It would be exciting to check back on the answers to that question in a year's time. Today I realize that there is yet another
question that might lie behind that one: What promises has
God given us that might form the basis for our prayers?

Psalm 119 stimulated that thought, for one of its notable features is the way it interweaves talk about God's commands and
God's promises. It assumes that you can't really expect to claim
God's promises unless you are living in light of God's commands. On the other hand, it assumes that if you are indeed
living in light of God's commands, you can expect to claim
God's promises. It doesn't imply a vending-machine theology of the kind that Psalm 115 questions; like many psalms,
it presupposes and frequently refers to the fact that life often
doesn't work out that way. There is a positive side to this fact:
when we ignore God's commands, often God just rolls his eyes
and keeps his promises to us anyway. But the psalm doesn't get
overwhelmed by the converse experience, the occasions when
the principle's limited applicability operates in our disfavor,
and bad things happen to good people. The psalm still assumes
that it is worthwhile to live on the basis that a link between
commands and promises generally holds.

Although the psalm keeps talking about God's promises, you
won't find the word "promise" in the psalm. Hebrew doesn't
have a word for promises that God makes—it has a word for
human promises, but that word implies a vow, and the psalm
doesn't use it to refer to God's promises. God's promise is just
his "word." God says it, and that means God will do it. So this
part of the psalm starts with the fact that I have fallen into the

dirt and am stuck there. Maybe the idea is that I am as good as dead, because dirt is where human beings come from and where they return to. So I pray, God, bring me (back) to life, "in accordance with your word," your promise that you do grant life to people who live in accordance with your word of command. Or again, "my spirit has wept itself away through sorrow." Literally it has melted away, but maybe the way it has done so is by weeping. So I pray to be lifted out of my sorrow "in accordance with your word," your promise not to leave people in that position.

I could be tempted to look elsewhere for the solution of my problems, for some other means of being lifted out of my sorrow, so I pray that God will make such temptations pass away, because in my heart of hearts I know that such other resources are empty. The empty thing would be other deities for an Israelite—the Christian reader can fill in the blank. So here I pray, God, give me life by your way—through my walking in **Yahweh's** way. I ask God thereby to establish and confirm and thus fulfill and vindicate what he has said in promising to be that kind of God; he *is* that kind of God for people who are in awe of him and thus obey his word of command. It is the way God's **commitment** will become a reality, as God acts to **deliver** me "in accordance with what [God has] said" in making promises. I can ignore other people's words (the kind of words that revile me by saying that God is not with people like me) because I trust in God's words. And if God keeps his word, it means I shall have a chance to testify to its truth; so asking God not to snatch away his true word out of my mouth is another way of asking him to fulfill his promises by making the **authoritative** decision I need, to deliver me from my predicament.

PSALM 119:49–72

Teach Me

⁴⁹ Be mindful of your word to your servant,
       upon which you have made me hope.
⁵⁰ This is my comfort in my lowliness,
       that what you have said has brought me to life.

51 Though the willful have mocked me greatly,
    I have not diverted from your teaching.
52 I have been mindful of your decisions from of old, Yahweh,
    and found comfort.
53 Rage has gripped me because of the faithless people,
    people who abandon your teaching.
54 Your laws have been my protection
    in the house where I stay.
55 I have been mindful by night of your name, Yahweh,
    and I have kept your teaching.
56 This is how it has been for me,
    because I have observed your orders.

57 Yahweh being my share,
    I have said I would keep your words.
58 I have courted you with all my heart;
    be gracious to me in accordance with what you have said.
59 I have thought about my ways
    and turned my feet to your declarations.
60 I have hurried and not delayed
    to keep your commands.
61 Though the ropes of the faithless were around me,
    I have not ignored your teaching.
62 In the middle of the night I get up to confess you
    for your faithful decisions.
63 I am a friend to all the people who are in awe of you
    and to the people who keep your orders.
64 The earth is full of your commitment, Yahweh;
    teach me your laws.

65 You have done good things with your servant, Yahweh,
    in accordance with your word.
66 Teach me goodness of discernment and acknowledgment,
    because I have trusted in your commands.
67 Before I became low I was going astray,
    but now I have kept what you said.
68 You are good and you do good;
    teach me your laws.
69 The willful have smeared falsehood over me,
    whereas I observe your orders with my whole mind.
70 Their mind is thick like fat,
    whereas I have delighted in your teaching.

71 It was good for me that I was brought low,
    so that I might learn your laws.
72 The teaching that comes from your mouth is better for me
    than thousands of pieces of gold and silver.

I'm grading student papers, and one effect that has on me
(alongside making me want to commit suicide) is to make
me puzzle over what it is that enables people to learn. There
are people who have read the Scriptures with fresh eyes, seen
things they had not seen before, and seen things I had not seen
(maybe through making links with things they had seen before
or experiences they have had)—which is the way they get an
A. There are other people who continue to write what their
Sunday school teachers told them the Bible says rather than
reading for themselves what the Bible says. There are people for
whom discovering what the Bible says is an exciting adventure;
there are others who simply want confirmation of what they
already think.

The speaker in Psalm 119 keeps asking to be taught by God.
I guess it is some comfort to me to know that God also puz-
zles over how to enable people to learn and how to get them
to think in new ways. The nature of learning is that you cannot impose it on people, even if you are God. But at least you
are getting somewhere if people want to learn. If you are the
learner rather than the teacher, that introduces you to another
paradox. You want to learn, but you know you may not be "getting it." So one of the poignant notes that recurs in Psalm 119 is
the plea "Teach me," which comes two or three times in these
three sections.

When the psalmist entreats, "Teach me your laws," I assume
the entreaty does not merely mean "apprise me of the content
of your laws." Israelites knew very well that they were supposed
to worship Yahweh alone, to forswear the making of images,
to be careful about what they attached Yahweh's **name** to, to
keep the Sabbath, and so on. They did not need to be taught
these commands. If they had a question about which animals
they could eat and which they could not eat, not having memo-
rized the lists in the **Torah**, they could go and ask a priest. They
did not need Yahweh to teach them in this sense. The problem

150

about teaching and learning is about whether they have internalized those commands about worshiping Yahweh alone, forswearing images, and so on. Yahweh's commands go against the grain. It is more natural to worship several gods and thus be able to hedge your bets, to make an image that will help you to worship, to attach God's names to your favorite projects, or to work 24/7 so as to be sure that your family has enough to eat.

It is at least something that the psalmist wants to learn. That desire is a necessary though not a sufficient condition for learning. But we can know we want to learn yet be held back by forces inside us of which we are hardly aware. How does God answer that prayer to teach us?

One of the psalm's unwelcome answers is that being knocked over can help us. It refers three times to lowliness, becoming low, being brought low—each time the expressions are variants on the same word. The psalmist knows what it is like to be put down. "When you've got nothing, you've got nothing left to lose," says a song by Dave Morrison, one of my favorite songwriters. Or "Freedom's just another word for nothing left to lose," as Janis Joplin sang. The psalm knows that being brought low can push you to more trust and openness to what God needs to teach you. A more welcome aid is awareness of the positive facts that push me toward obedience. The psalm speaks of Yahweh's being my "share," using the word that describes an Israelite family's allocation of land. Maybe it's significant that your share is not exactly your property. Legally speaking, you can't sell it, but neither can anyone take it off you. In that sense your possession of it is secure. Our having a relationship with God with the same security is a motivation to obedience (rather than encouraging us to take it for granted). Another awareness that is almost an inversion of that first one is that I can see the evidence of God's **commitment** to us throughout the world, not just on my plot of land; that awareness, too, pushes me toward obeying this gracious God. Yet another is the goodness God shows to me personally and the way God keeps his promises.

We are dependent on God to teach us, but it doesn't mean that we don't need to take hold of the keys to learning that are available to us.

PSALM 119:73–96

On Raising the Ceiling of Our Hope

73 Your hands made me, established me;
     help me understand so that I may learn your commands.
74 People who are in awe of you will see and celebrate,
     because I have waited for your word.
75 I have acknowledged, Yahweh, that your decisions are faithful,
     and in truthfulness you have brought me low.
76 Do grant that your commitment becomes my comfort,
     in accordance with what you said to your servant.
77 May your compassion come to me so that I may live,
     because your teaching is my delight.
78 May the willful be shamed, because they have put me in
          the wrong by means of falsehood,
     whereas I murmur about your orders.
79 May the people who are in awe of you return to me,
     the people who acknowledge your declarations.
80 May my mind be of integrity in your laws
     so that I may not be shamed.

81 My spirit is spent [with looking] for your deliverance;
     for your word I have waited.
82 My eyes are spent [with looking] for what you have said,
     in saying "When will you comfort me?"
83 When I have become like a water skin in smoke,
     I have not ignored your laws.
84 How many are your servant's days—
     when will you make a decision about my persecutors?
85 The willful have dug pits for me,
     which is not in accordance with your teaching.
86 All your commands are truthful;
     when people persecute me with falsehood, help me.
87 They have almost consumed me in the country,
     but I have not abandoned your orders.
88 In accordance with your commitment bring me to life,
     so that I may keep the declarations of your mouth.

89 Your word endures forever, Yahweh,
     standing in the heavens.
90 Your truthfulness lasts generation after generation;
     you established the earth and it has stood firm.

⁹¹ As for your decisions, they have stood firm today,
   because everything is your servants.
⁹² Were not your teaching my delight,
   I would then have perished in my lowliness.
⁹³ Never will I ignore your orders,
   because by means of them you have brought me to life.
⁹⁴ I am yours, deliver me,
   because I have inquired of your orders.
⁹⁵ Whereas faithless people have hoped to make me perish,
   I show understanding of your declarations.
⁹⁶ As for every end, I have seen the limit,
   but your command is very broad.

For the first time for some months, I talked yesterday to a friend who lost his job in construction a couple of years ago, not long after he had moved with his wife and baby to another town where they could afford to buy a house and where the job situation looked good. But then the bottom dropped out of the construction business. I had been meaning to call him for a while but kept failing to get around to it. He and his wife had a plan for establishing a business to tide them over until construction picked up, but it seemed to me an implausible plan, and one reason I had failed to call was that I was afraid what the news would be. It transpired that they are still waiting for construction to pick up (though their business is helping to tide them over). As I was thinking about them, I went to seminary chapel, and we began with a meditation that talked about raising the ceiling of our hope. It's very easy for hope to have a ceiling, a limit beyond which we will not hope.

The middle of the above three sections of Psalm 119 works with that fact. Waiting can be really hard. It can eat you up. It's as if you are deprived of physical food and your body starts to consume itself. Here the wait is not for physical food but for the fulfillment of God's promises. It's as if the strain of waiting and looking has made your eyes so tired that they can no longer stay open. Once again the wait is for a response to the question of when God will bring comfort. "When?" the psalm twice asks. "How many days are going to pass with me being harassed by people?" And as usual, asking, "When?" is not actually a request for information (any more than when the kids ask,

"Are we there yet?" at a point when a car journey is only half over). If God replies, "In about four years," the questioner would not respond by saying, "Oh, thanks, that's okay, then." Asking, "When?" is an indirect way of pleading, "Let it be now." This fact links with something about the nature of "comfort." In the Old Testament, comfort is sometimes a matter of words (as in English) but sometimes a matter of action—God comforts us by doing something. The second is the kind of comfort the psalmist is thinking of. The same applies to the reference to comfort in the first section above and also to the reference there to God's compassion. God's compassion is not just God saying, "There, there." It's God doing something about our predicament.

Another way of expressing the need for God to act is suggested by the image of a water skin in the smoke. To be truthful, we don't know what the image refers to, though the traditional guess is that a water skin would shrivel and blacken in the smoky atmosphere of an Israelite family's courtyard. But it's easy to see that it suggests a nasty experience. So, the psalmist says, my spirit is consumed, my eyes are consumed—in fact I myself am almost consumed.

Against the background of the requirement that one live waiting for God's word to be fulfilled, in the third section there are noteworthy declarations of faith in God's word. The section suggests two reasons why it is possible to maintain that faith. One is that I have proved the trustworthiness of God's word before. I have experienced it giving me life in the sense that my obedience to God's word to me has meant that God has kept his word for me. The other is suggested by the last line. Though it's also obscurely expressed, its point is along the lines of "I have seen the limitations or the limits of everything, such as the kind of priorities and actions the persecutors believe in, but I know that God's commands open up broader vistas for my life than those priorities, beliefs, and actions." People often think that God's commandments narrow down our thinking and our lives. The psalmist knows that they broaden them.

Thus (to go back to the beginning of these three sections) the psalmist knows that the wait will be worthwhile and that other people will recognize this fact. Indeed, even the obligation to wait can do something constructive to us.

PSALM 119:97–120

I Can Be Wiser Than My Professor

⁹⁷ How I give myself to your teaching—
    all day it is my murmur.
⁹⁸ Your commands make me more discerning than my enemies,
    because they are mine forever.
⁹⁹ I have gained more insight than all my teachers,
    because your declarations are my murmur.
¹⁰⁰ I show more understanding than the elders,
    because I have observed your orders.
¹⁰¹ I have kept back my foot from every evil way,
    so that I might keep your word.
¹⁰² I have not turned from your decisions,
    because you have instructed me.
¹⁰³ How smooth the things you say have been to my taste,
    more than honey to my mouth.
¹⁰⁴ Through your orders I show understanding;
    therefore I oppose every false path.

¹⁰⁵ Your word is a lamp to my foot,
    a light to my pathway.
¹⁰⁶ I swore and confirmed
    that I would keep your faithful decisions.
¹⁰⁷ I am low, very low, Yahweh;
    bring me to life in accordance with your word.
¹⁰⁸ Will you favor the free offerings of my mouth, Yahweh,
    and teach me your decisions.
¹⁰⁹ My life is in my palm continually,
    but I have not ignored your teaching.
¹¹⁰ Faithless people have set a trap for me,
    but I have not strayed from your orders.
¹¹¹ I have made your declarations my own forever,
    because they are the joy of my heart.
¹¹² I have inclined my mind to do your laws
    forever, to the utmost.

¹¹³ I oppose divided people,
    and give myself to your teaching.
¹¹⁴ Since you have been my shelter and shield,
    I have waited for your word.

¹¹⁵ Get away from me, you wrongdoers,
      so that I may observe my God's commands.
¹¹⁶ Hold me up in accordance with what you said, so that
            I may live;
      do not let me be ashamed of my expectation.
¹¹⁷ Sustain me so that I may find deliverance,
      and have regard to your laws continually.
¹¹⁸ You have thrown out everyone who wanders from your laws,
      because their deceptiveness is false.
¹¹⁹ You have finished off all the faithless people in the country
            like dross;
      therefore I give myself to your declarations.
¹²⁰ My flesh shivers in reverence for you;
      I am in awe of your decisions.

After my class on the Prophets last night, we invited the students back to our home for scones and tea, and during the conversation one of them asked what I enjoyed most about teaching. My response was that I love sending people away to read part of the Old Testament and having them come back with their eyes wide open (it can be in a good way or a disturbed way!). Afterward I wished I had drawn her attention to a feature of that evening's class, when I had some people read a dialogue between the Prophets Nahum and Jonah that had been written by a previous student in the class. One reward of teaching is profiting from the insights and creativity of your students. Their questions are part of that dynamic because they often make you think through issues that you would not otherwise have considered. There had been examples of that process in the class last night, too.

At points, at least, studying the Scriptures makes students wiser than their teachers or their elders, let alone their enemies. In the United States, my students are inclined to think of their professors as people who have the answers, as if I have access to a secret appendix to the Old Testament that contains the resolutions to questions raised by the main text. It is an aspect of their trust in experts, which is more common in U.S. culture than in British culture and which glorifies the amateur (an attitude that also has its weaknesses). In the United States, therefore, part of my job is to get students to see that we are all in the same position before the Bible. The commentators can sometimes help us, but it is not our job to read the Bible through someone else's eyes (including the eyes of the author of The Old Testament for Everyone series).

It is the Bible that is the source of wisdom (not the only source, of course, but the one we are concerned with at the moment). So it's worth my giving my whole day to studying it. For different reasons, it would be easy to think that the people with wisdom in the world are teachers, elders, and enemies, but the wisdom in God's teaching puts all these people into the shade. So studying the Bible is like eating something sweet; it slides down our throats like honey. It's like a flashlight that makes it possible to walk a path that would otherwise be dark and dangerous, where we would not be able to see snakes or other pitfalls (when my life is in my palm, as the psalm puts it—that is, in a position that means anyone can take it). It's something that brings us joy, though paradoxically it is also something that makes us shiver. We know that the stakes are high when we study this teaching. It's a life-and-death matter.

The word for "teaching" is *torah*, and it wouldn't be surprising if the psalm has especially in mind *the* **Torah**, Genesis to Deuteronomy, which in its capacity as *the* Teaching both tells Israel the story of God's early relationship with the people and lays down God's consequent expectations. The study of God's teaching commended by the psalm involves "murmuring." The psalm uses the word a number of times in this connection. When Jews study the Torah, traditionally they murmur it out loud; they take it on their lips not only in order to declaim it to someone else but to encourage it to be part of their own selves, of their very bodies.

PSALM 119:121–44

The Faithful Master

[121] I have made faithful decisions;
    do not leave me to oppressors.
[122] Make a pledge to your servant for good things;
    the willful must not oppress me.

¹²³ My eyes are spent [with looking] for your deliverance,
for what you said about your faithfulness.
¹²⁴ Act with your servant in accordance with your commitment,
and teach me your laws.
¹²⁵ As I am your servant, help me understand,
so that I may acknowledge your declarations.
¹²⁶ It is a time for Yahweh to act;
people have violated your teaching.
¹²⁷ Therefore I give myself to your commands,
more than to gold and silver.
¹²⁸ Therefore I have treated as upright every order concerning
everything;
I have opposed every way of falsehood.

¹²⁹ Your declarations are wonders;
therefore my spirit has observed them.
¹³⁰ The opening up of your words gives light,
helping the simple to understand.
¹³¹ I opened wide my mouth and panted,
because I longed for your commands.
¹³² Turn your face to me and be gracious to me,
in accordance with your decision for people who give
themselves to your name.
¹³³ Establish my feet by what you say,
so that no wickedness may master me.
¹³⁴ Redeem me from human oppression,
so that I may keep your orders.
¹³⁵ Shine your face on your servant,
and teach me your laws.
¹³⁶ My eyes have run down streams of water,
because people have not kept your teaching.

¹³⁷ You are faithful, Yahweh,
and upright in your decisions.
¹³⁸ You have commanded the faithfulness of your declarations,
and the truthfulness, exceedingly.
¹³⁹ My passion has devoured me,
because my foes have ignored your words.
¹⁴⁰ What you say has been much proven,
and your servant gives himself to it.
¹⁴¹ Although I am small and despised,
I have not ignored your orders.

¹⁴² Your faithfulness is a faithfulness that lasts forever,
   and your teaching is truth.
¹⁴³ Although trouble and distress have found me,
   your commands are my delight.
¹⁴⁴ The faithfulness of your declarations lasts forever;
   help me understand so that I may live.

One of my former colleagues used to delight to talk about
her first appointment with her boss. His opening words to
her were "How can I serve you?" "What can I do for you?"
"How can I help you do your job?" In a way the questions
seem smarmy (the *Oxford English Dictionary*'s definition of
smarmy: "ingratiating and wheedling in a way that is per-
ceived as insincere or excessive"). But I know the boss in
question, and I know he meant it. From time to time he had to
make or recommend **authoritative** decisions that were tough
for staff, faculty, and students (in hard times it might issue in
people losing their jobs), but I knew that he was seeking to
serve when he did so. The boss, the master, had a servant's
heart, and the employees, the servants, could know the nature
of his heart and know that they could appeal to it.

The psalm makes that assumption about the heart of God.
The relationship of God to us is that of master to servant, and
one might think that this model for a relationship puts us firmly
in our place. This assumption is encouraged by the fact that the
word for servant is often translated "slave." But the Old Testament describes the relationship of master to servant in much
warmer terms than is implied by that understanding, and the
Old Testament shows virtually no knowledge of slavery in our
sense of one person owning another person for life and being
free to do as one likes with that person. The mutually trusting relationship of Abraham and his servant, whom Abraham
commissions to go find a wife for Isaac (Genesis 24), is a more
telling indicator of the Old Testament's ideal of master-servant
relationships. You could almost say that the master is also a
servant.

It is in light of this understanding that this section of Psalm
119 appeals five times to the servant status of the suppliant.
Its implication is that the servant indeed has obligations to the

master, but that the master also has obligations to the servant. First, it means that when the servant is in trouble, the master is bound to take the servant's side and put energy into offering protection and rescue where necessary. With some boldness the psalm urges the master to make a pledge to the servant; the giving of pledges usually works the other way around. The servant goes on (second) to urge the master to act in light of his **commitment**. It is another bold image. You make a pledge to someone when you are indebted to him or her and must offer some guarantee that you will fulfill your obligations. The implication is that the master has taken on obligations that he can't get out of.

At the same time, the relationship implies that the servant has obligations to the master, though even here the servant can put some responsibility onto the master. So third, says the servant, "You have to tell me what my obligations are. I am willing to fulfill them, but you have to lay them down and help me understand them." Abraham's servant indeed relates to Abraham in that way in connection with the matchmaking commission. There is further straightness in the way the servant continues. He reminds me of myself when I was still a rookie professor and became irate at what I saw as the administration's dilatoriness in dealing with an issue. I stormed into my boss's office to tell him that it was time he got a grip and got his act together and sorted the issue out. It's amazing I didn't get fired. In effect this servant acts the same way I did. You can almost see him standing before his master and shouting, "**Yahweh**, it is a time for you to act! People have violated your teaching, and you are doing nothing about it."

There's a contrast with his fourth appeal to being a servant— "Shine your face on me." When a suppliant comes before a king or a master, if the king or master frowns, the suppliant is in trouble. But if the master smiles, then it means the suppliant's plea will be granted. Whether it happens will depend in part on what kind of servant he or she has been. Finally, in these verses the servant declares that he has given himself to what his master says, which has been much proven. He has had chance in the past to find out whether the master's words are wise, reliable, and effective—that opportunity might relate both to his commands and to his promises. He has proved them to be so. So he gives himself to them. The verb is often translated "love," but once again the verb denotes not mere warmth of feeling. It doesn't really matter whether we feel warm and fuzzy about God's words. The question is whether we base our lives on them in trust and obedience.

It's telling that these sections of the psalm that keep coming back to the master-servant relationship also keep coming back to the idea of **faithfulness**; they begin with reference to the servant's faithfulness but talk much more about the master's faithfulness.

PSALM 119:145-76

The Appeal of the Lost Sheep

145 I have called with all my heart; answer me, Yahweh,
　　so that I may observe your laws.
146 I have called you—deliver me,
　　so that I may keep your declarations.
147 I have anticipated the twilight and cried for help,
　　as I waited for your word.
148 My eyes have anticipated the watches,
　　to murmur about what you have said.
149 Listen to my voice in accordance with your commitment;
　　　Yahweh, bring me to life in accordance with your decision.
150 People who pursue schemes are near;
　　they are far from your teaching.
151 You are near, Yahweh,
　　and all your commands are true.
152 Of old I have acknowledged from your declarations
　　that you founded them forever.

153 See my lowness, rescue me,
　　because I have not ignored your teaching.
154 Contend for my cause and restore me;
　　in light of what you have said, bring me to life.
155 Deliverance is far from the faithless,
　　because they have not inquired of your laws.
156 Your compassion is great, Yahweh;
　　bring me to life in accordance with your decisions.

161

¹⁵⁷ Although my pursuers and foes are many,
    I have not diverted from your declarations.
¹⁵⁸ I have seen betrayers and loathed them,
    people who did not keep what you said.
¹⁵⁹ See that I have given myself to your orders;
    Yahweh, bring me to life in accordance with your
        commitment.
¹⁶⁰ Truthfulness is the first principle of your word,
    and every faithful decision of yours stands forever.

¹⁶¹ Officials have pursued me without reason,
    but my heart has stood in awe of your word.
¹⁶² I rejoice over what you have said,
    like someone who finds much plunder.
¹⁶³ Whereas I oppose and abhor falsehood,
    I give myself to your teaching.
¹⁶⁴ I have praised you seven times a day
    for your faithful decisions.
¹⁶⁵ There is much well-being for people who give themselves
       to your teaching,
    and there isn't anything that can make them fall.
¹⁶⁶ I have looked for your deliverance, Yahweh,
    and done the things you command.
¹⁶⁷ I have kept your declarations with my whole being,
    and I give myself totally to them.
¹⁶⁸ I have kept your orders and your declarations,
    because all my ways are before you.

¹⁶⁹ May my resounding come near your face, Yahweh;
    in accordance with your word, help me understand.
¹⁷⁰ May my prayer for grace come before your face;
    in accordance with what you have said, rescue me.
¹⁷¹ May my lips pour forth praise,
    because you teach me your laws.
¹⁷² May my tongue sing of what you have said,
    because all your commands are faithful.
¹⁷³ May your hand come to my help,
    because I have chosen your orders.
¹⁷⁴ I have longed for your deliverance, Yahweh,
    and your teaching is my delight.
¹⁷⁵ May my spirit live,
    so that I may praise you.

¹⁷⁶ I have wandered like a lost sheep: search for your servant,
    because I have not ignored your commands.

A Bedouin herdsman tells of how he was tending a flock of
goats in the Judean wilderness near the Dead Sea. Before sleep-
ing, the herdsmen would count their flocks, but for some reason this herdsman failed to do the count for two days. On the
third morning he did so and found that a goat was missing.
So he told the other herdsmen that he wanted to leave the rest
of his flock with them and go and search for the lost goat. He
describes how he had to climb hills and go down into valleys
and thus roam far away from his flock and the other herdsmen.
Eventually he came across a cave with its entrance open at the
top, like a cistern. He thought maybe the goat had fallen into
the cave, so he threw a stone into the cave to see if it startled the
goat. What it did was hit a pot. The herdsman heard the sound
of the pot breaking, and it was the beginning of the discovery
of the Dead Sea Scrolls.

This gargantuan psalm ends with the plea of such a lost
sheep. The story implies that the goat of which it speaks was
lost through the neglect of the herdsman more than through
its own willfulness, and the psalm implies that we can get lost
even when we have not willfully wandered. The psalm's long
closing line goes on to affirm, "I have not ignored your commands." The psalm presupposes careful study of the **Torah**, of
what **Yahweh** has said. On one hand, that means study of Yahweh's laws, declarations, commands, and orders. On the other
hand, it means study of Yahweh's word of promise and Yahweh's
authoritative decision about what is to happen, which are
expressions of Yahweh's **commitment** and **faithfulness**. The
psalm implicitly recognizes that we always need to beware of
merely following our natural human instincts or conforming to
the attitudes that are taken in our culture. So we always need to
pay attention to such study. That need applies both to the moral
shaping of our lives and to the shaping of our expectations and
hopes. Such attentiveness to the Torah is not mere theoretical
study that results in acquaintance with what the Scriptures say.
It is study that issues in observing the expectations of Scripture, keeping them, loving them in the sense of giving oneself

to them, standing in awe of them in the sense of obeying them. It also issues in calling, crying for help, pleading for grace, and looking for God to act—that is, in prayer that presses God to act in consistency with the commitments that God has made, to act like the shepherd who gives his all to find one lost sheep whether or not the sheep is responsible for its wanderings.

So study of the Torah is set in the context of a life of prayer as prayer is set in the context of a life of study. The point is expressed most vividly in the talk about anticipating the twilight and the watches. Twilight is the moment of transition from day to night, and thus it is one of the times when sacrifices were offered each day in the temple and when prayers were prayed and praise offered. The allusion to the watches looks like a complementary reference to the moment of transition from night to day, the other time when the daily sacrifices were offered. It is another natural time to pray, even if you are not in Jerusalem and thus not in a position to go to the temple to pray at those moments. The psalm thus speaks of not being able to wait for the "official" moment for prayer. The two anticipations relate both to prayer and to murmuring, or reading the Torah out loud. The hyperbole involved in the use of that verb "anticipate" is complemented by the talk of praising God seven times a day, five times more each day than those two occasions that were literally part of the community's rule of life.

Part of the genius of Psalm 119 is its unified nature. Maybe its being an alphabetical psalm helps; it covers life with God from A to Z. These last four sections thus comprise eight lines beginning with each of the last four letters of the Hebrew alphabet, which are q, r, s, and t (if you are curious about the letters that come later in the English alphabet, then the answer is that u doesn't feature because the Hebrew alphabet includes only consonants; v, w, y, and z come earlier in the alphabet; and who needs x if you have k and s?). It expresses more systematically than any other the consistent assumption that runs through the Psalms: that the people of God both must and can commit themselves to doing what God says. It does not encourage any idea that we can offer excuses for failing to live a life that is consistent with the Torah.

PSALMS 120–121

Peaceableness and Peacefulness

A song of the ascents.

120:1 To Yahweh in my trouble
    I called and he answered.
  2 Yahweh, save my life from lying lips,
    from a deceitful tongue.

  3 What will it give you, what will it add to you,
    deceitful tongue?
  4 The arrows of a warrior, sharpened,
    with coals of broom shrubs.
  5 Oh for me, that I have stayed with Meshek,
    dwelt with the tents of Kedar.
  6 A long time I have been dwelling
    with one who opposes peace.
  7 I am for peace,
    but when I speak,
    they are for war.

A song for the ascents

121:1 I lift my eyes to the mountains:
    from where does my help come?
  2 My help comes from Yahweh,
    maker of the heavens and the earth.
  3 He does not give your foot to faltering;
    your guard does not doze.
  4 There, he does not doze and he does not sleep,
    Israel's guard.
  5 Yahweh is your guard,
    Yahweh is your shade, at your right hand.
  6 By day the sun will not hit you,
    or the moon by night.
  7 Yahweh guards you from everything evil;
    he guards your life.
  8 Yahweh guards your leaving and your coming,
    from now and forever.

After a journey that took twenty-four hours, some friends of mine arrived yesterday in the capital of one of the toughest and poorest countries in Africa, which they visit from time to time seeking to help refugees there make their voices heard in the West. Their work is not exactly admired by the government that turned these people into refugees, who are in recurrent danger as are people who aid them. We who support the people who go on these trips live with some anxiety through the weeks they spend in Africa, and we breathe a sigh of relief after they complete a mission, are transported back to the capital, and board a plane back to the country's gateway in Europe.

For the duration of this trip, at least, I shall say these two **songs of the ascents** on their behalf. They go to a context where they are for **peace**, but the people whom they seek to stand with are the victims of people who oppose peace and are for war, even while claiming the opposite. The government claims that the refugees are rebels and are for war and that the government is for peace, and they use this claim as an excuse for violent military action. It is a context where one cannot take for granted the trustworthiness of the words and intentions of the refugees' home government. Being for peace and living in peace does not rule out the idea that one is enraged at the deceit and aggression of such people.

The first psalm follows a common pattern in which one begins by recalling the way God has answered prayer in the past. That recollection gives one renewed confidence to pray for God to act in that way again. On this basis, the psalm declares that the deceptiveness will not achieve what it aims to achieve; rather, it will rebound on the deceivers. The psalm speaks for someone who has no alternative at the moment but to live far away from home. Meshek is in Turkey; Kedar, in Arabia; so these are metaphorical expressions to suggest living in some place that is a long way away from Jerusalem.

Whereas frustration and rage are more dominant than tranquility in Psalm 120, the balance in Psalm 121 is the reverse. Mountains surround Jerusalem, and Psalm 125 indicates how they provide a metaphor for the way God surrounds the city. So looking at the mountains is not a cause of worry, as if the enemy may ride over their brow any moment (the enemy would just as likely come up from the plains). It is instead a reason for encouragement, not because the mountains were in themselves a protection but because of what they symbolize. Looking at them provides the answer to the question of where help will come from, the answer that is made explicit in the declaration that help comes from **Yahweh**. He is, after all, the creator and thus the one who is quite capable of protecting you.

At this point, too, Psalm 121 complements Psalm 120. One basis for trust is the way that Yahweh has answered prayer in the past; another basis is who Yahweh is. He's got the whole world in his hands; therefore he's got you and me sister, you and me brother, in his hands. He is not the kind of guard who drops off to sleep in the middle of the night when everything seems quiet but actually an enemy is advancing on the city or the camp. He is alert 24/7, day and night (the reference to the moon is a kind of poetic balance for the reference to the sun, not an indication that people thought the moon was dangerous in the way that the midday sun is dangerous). He watches over you as you leave the city to go out to battle or into the fields, or to return from somewhere like Meshek or Kedar after your pilgrimage, or to go into **exile**, and he watches over you as you come back after the battle, the day's work, or your exile, or as you make your pilgrimage again next year, and through all the time in between.

PSALMS 122–123

Praying for Jerusalem, Praying for Grace

A song of the ascents. David's.

122:1 I was glad when people said to me,
    "We'll go to Yahweh's house."
2 Our feet have been standing
    in your gates, Jerusalem,

3 Jerusalem, which is built as a city
    that is joined together to itself,
4 where the clans went up,
    Yah's clans,
  (a declaration for Israel),
    to confess Yahweh's name,

167

⁵ because thrones for making decisions sat there,
    thrones for David's household.
⁶ Ask for the well-being of Jerusalem;
    may people who dedicate themselves to it be secure.
⁷ May there be well-being in your rampart,
    security in your citadels.
⁸ For the sake of my kinfolk and my friends
    I will indeed speak of well-being for you.
⁹ For the sake of the house of Yahweh our God
    I will seek good things for you.

A song of the ascents.

¹²³:¹ To you I lift up my eyes,
    you who sit in the heavens.
² Now: like the eyes of servants
    toward the hand of their masters,
  like the eyes of a servant girl
    toward the hand of her mistress,
  so are our eyes toward Yahweh our God,
    until he is gracious to us.

³ Be gracious to us, Yahweh, be gracious,
    because we have become very full of shame.
⁴ Our spirit has become very full for itself
    of mockery in relation to complacent people,
    of shame in relation to important people.

When people would ask me what I expected to miss about leaving England to move to the United States, I would say that one of the main things was proximity to Israel. From London I could get there in four hours or so, and I used to enjoy taking groups of students and watching the Bible come alive before their eyes. Yet in another sense I didn't mind such visits becoming less practical. Though the situation in Jerusalem had always been troubled and troubling, it became more and more so. It was not the city of peace that its name suggested. Further, like Western countries, Israel as a whole was becoming a place that knew great prosperity, but the prosperity was more and more unequally distributed.

Psalm 122 urges us to pray for the *shalom* of Jerusalem. For Israelites, the city's importance as the central place of worship and of the administration of justice made it a place for which it was natural to pray, whether or not they personally lived there. The word *shalom* has two main connotations: Praying for *shalom* implies praying for peace, as the parallel talk about security implies. It also implies praying for broader **well-being**, as the parallel talk about good things implies. People pray for Jerusalem in this way both for the sake of kinfolk and friends, because the capital city matters to those in far-off villages, and for the sake of Yahweh's house. The most important thing about Jerusalem was that the temple was there. Yahweh lived there.

Like Psalm 84, the psalm speaks for people who have had the chance to go to Jerusalem for a festival, for Passover in spring, Pentecost in early summer, or **Sukkot** in fall, and who have now gone home to resume their ordinary lives. Maybe it presupposes that they could not go to Jerusalem for all three festivals every year, even though the **Torah** speaks in terms of their doing so. They would have to think about the practicalities of life on the farm. But this year they had made a group commitment to going, and they have had that experience of actually standing in the gates of Jerusalem, the city that is so impressively and securely built. They have joined people from all Israel's clans in worship of **Yahweh**. The thrones for the Davidic king and other people involved in **authoritative** decision making in the capital might relate to the city's political importance, or they might relate more immediately to the royal administration's being the people's supreme court. If your village's elders cannot sort out a matter of conflict in the village, then it becomes the royal administration's job to do so, and you might take these matters to Jerusalem when you made pilgrimage there.

God has not lately been answering prayers for the peace of Jerusalem. Maybe we should pray some more, and pray in the manner of Psalm 123. The way Christians argue with Jews and with Muslims over Jerusalem and the way these different groups of believers fight one another is good reason for unbelievers to mock us and for us to feel shame. What we can do is come shamelessly before God like servant boys and servant

169

girls. Servants don't have any power or prestige, but they have a master or a mistress, and this person has power and prestige and can intervene on the servant's behalf. As failures in our relationship with Jerusalem as in other aspects of our lives, all we can do is appeal to God for grace, as the psalm does three times.

PSALMS 124–125

Mountains around Jerusalem, Yahweh around His People

A song of the ascents. David's.

124:1 Were it not Yahweh who was ours,
     Israel is indeed to say,
  2 were it not Yahweh who was ours
     when people arose against us,
  3 then they would have swallowed us alive
     in their angry burning against us,
  4 then the waters—they would have carried us off,
     the torrent—it would have passed right over us,
  5 then it would have passed right over us,
     the seething waters.
  6 Yahweh be worshiped,
     who did not give us as prey to their teeth.
  7 Our life is like a bird that has escaped from the hunters' trap.
     The trap—it broke; and we—we escaped.
  8 Our help is the very name of Yahweh,
     maker of heavens and earth.

A song of the ascents.

125:1 The people who trust in Yahweh are like Mount Zion,
     which will not fall down—it will abide forever.
  2 Jerusalem—mountains are around it;
     Yahweh—he is around his people, now and forever.
  3 Because the faithless baton will not rest
     over the allocation of the faithful,
   so that the faithful do not put
     their hands to wrongdoing.
  4 Do good, Yahweh, to the people who are good,
     yes, to the upright in mind.

⁵ But the people who bend their crooked ways—
  may Yahweh make them go [away], the people who act
    wickedly;
  well-being [be] on Israel!

Last weekend we overheard a conversation on the San Fran-
cisco subway in which the father of two small children who was
on his way to the airport with some people from different parts
of the country was recounting a story. They live in Illinois, and
the children had been impressed by the tall buildings when the
family visited Chicago. Then they went on vacation in Yosem-
ite National Park, and the children were overwhelmed by El
Capitan, the breathtaking granite rock formation. One of the
children commented, "Gee, God is a more impressive builder
than human beings, isn't he?"

When translations have the Psalms likening God to a mountain, the Hebrew word usually denotes something more like a
crag. Psalms 94 and 95, for instance, describe God as the crag
who provides us with refuge and who **delivers** us. Psalm 121
speaks of looking to the mountains in a more general sense,
as a symbol of God's strength and protection. Psalm 125 also
starts from the fact that from Jerusalem you look around at
higher mountains such as the Mount of Olives. The image
would be stronger the further you go back in Old Testament
times, because David's Jerusalem is the lowest part of the city
as the city eventually developed (though it is immediately surrounded by steep slopes that give it protection from attackers):
"Jerusalem—mountains are around it," like a mother's arms
around a baby. So that expression provides people with an
encouraging image: "**Yahweh**—he is around his people," too.

Mountains are also a symbol for stability and permanence.
When an earthquake happens, it makes the ground shift,
but it does so nowhere near as spectacularly or dangerously
as it makes humanly constructed skyscrapers collapse. On
the whole, you can assume that the mountains around Jerusalem are going to be there forever, and you can make the
same assumption about Jerusalem. The psalm also incorporates another riff on this imagery. Mount **Zion** has a distinctive strength and invulnerability that derives from its being

not merely a mountain like others but the peak to which Yahweh has made a commitment. So Yahweh is strong and stands firm, and Mount Zion is strong and stands firm, and people who trust in Yahweh are strong and stand firm. Given our psychologically influenced way of thinking, we are inclined to infer that this firmness lies in an inner strength that people gain through their trust in Yahweh, and there is truth in that assumption, but it is not the psalm's point. People's security lies not in an inner strength but in the way their trust in Yahweh means Yahweh watches over them and protects them. Yahweh does not merely give them inner strength, but in a situation when they are objectively and externally vulnerable, he protects them from falling under the authority of some foreign power that wields its baton over the land that God has given them. It is as well that Yahweh will thus protect them, because such an event might put pressure on them to share the **faithless** ways of their conquerors—to worship their gods or follow their ways in other respects.

The convictions expressed in the first part of the psalm do not make it unnecessary to pray for God's protection. Rather, they make such prayer possible. The kind of testimony expressed in Psalm 124 also makes it possible. The security of which Psalm 125 speaks does not rule out crises and threats. There were indeed occasions when Jerusalem came under attack and when it all but fell. In Isaiah's day, the **Assyrian** king Sennacherib speaks of having shut up King Hezekiah in Jerusalem, his own capital, "like a bird in a cage." But the cage was shut from the inside as well as the outside, and the city did not fall (of course it did so when Yahweh decided to withdraw his protection as an act of punishment). Yahweh was indeed its protection. The city is still there now.

PSALMS 126–127

Weeping and Insomnia

A song of the ascents.

126:1 When Yahweh renewed Zion's fortunes,
    we became like people dreaming.

² Then our mouth filled with laughter,
   our tongue with resounding.
 Then they said among the nations,
   "Yahweh has shown greatness in acting with them."
³ Yahweh has shown greatness in acting with us;
   we became people celebrating.

⁴ Renew our fortunes, Yahweh,
   like channels in the Negev.
⁵ May people who sow in tears
   reap with resounding.
⁶ The person who goes, but goes weeping,
   carrying a seed bag—
 as he comes, may he come with resounding,
   carrying his sheaves.

A song of the ascents. Solomon's.

127:1 If Yahweh does not build the house,
   in vain the builders have labored on it.
 If Yahweh does not guard the city,
   in vain the guard has been wakeful.
² It is in vain for you, being people early to rise,
   people late to sit down,
 people who eat bread of toil—
   yes, he gives sleep to his beloved.
³ Now: sons are your own possession from Yahweh;
   the fruit of the womb is a reward.
⁴ Like arrows in a warrior's hand—
   so are the sons of youth.
⁵ The blessings of the man who has
   filled his quiver with them!
 Of them he will not be ashamed
   when they speak with opponents in the gate.

Like anybody else, when I am worried, anxious, or preoccupied, I can't sleep. Sometimes I don't even know what it is that is preoccupying me. While I found sleep problematic for a while after my first wife died, in general I have this difficulty much less than I did when I was younger. In particular I remember being unable to sleep when I was first ordained and involved in parish

173

ministry, I guess because I was anxious about that involvement. I must have told my rector, because I recall his quoting Psalm 127 to me: "He gives sleep to his beloved." I guess he meant it as a promise for me to lay hold of, but it came across as a reminder that made me feel more guilty. Not only was I unable to sleep; I was at fault for not claiming God's promises.

The psalm's own point about sleep is slightly different, though in the end it does carry the implication my rector saw in it. Its comment about sleep relates, indeed, to an issue that lies behind some of our problem with insomnia. I read somewhere that the insomnia champions of the world are the United States, Germany, and the United Kingdom, and the first two of these are the biggest economies of the world and of Europe. One reason that they are so successful is that their people work so hard. The message of the psalm is thus "Whoa! Hold back! What do you think you are doing, and why?" You can put much energy into seeking to achieve and to safeguard, but it may get you nowhere in the long run, or even in the short run. The psalm does not imply that people should not build houses or guard their cities from attack. It reminds us that we do not have as much control of our destinies and our futures as we would like to think. The paradoxical implication is "Relax. God loves you. And anyway, it's God's building activity that counts."

I have a friend who complains that his father spends so much time working to safeguard the family's future that he has no time for the family itself. It would be nice if the second part of Psalm 127 made that link, but it makes a different point. It doesn't implicitly devalue daughters but makes a comment on an aspect of the particular value of sons. When you are growing older and you don't have the strength you once had, it helps if you have a bunch of hefty young men to go with you when there is some conflict that needs resolving and you might otherwise be a pushover (or when there is a field that needs plowing and the oxen are hard to handle).

It wouldn't be surprising if insomnia also underlies Psalm 126. Each autumn and winter you might well feel some anxiety as you went out of the village to plow your fields and sow your seed. You might weep as you did so. You could never know whether there would be enough rain at the right times during the coming months to generate a crop. The psalm begins by encouraging people to remind themselves about the way they have previously had the chance to let weeping give way to noisy rejoicing. It was something that made other people notice and acknowledge how great their God is. In a situation where the community once more needs restoring, the psalm reminds itself and reminds God of that event. Maybe sowing in tears and reaping with joy is a metaphor for another, broader kind of restoration of the community, like the one that took place after the **exile**. It would be like the time when summer came and the farmers were able to come back from the fields to the village carrying their sheaves of grain. But the annual experience of being able to do so would be indescribably joyful as people knew there could be food to eat for the next year. The psalm is often used on Thanksgiving, and it makes one think of the tears the original English settlers in the colonies must have shed during their first year when they had virtually nothing to eat, and of the joy they must have felt when they saw their first harvest.

PSALMS 128–129

Blessings and Atrocities

A song of the ascents.

128:1 The blessings of anyone who is in awe of Yahweh,
    who walks in his ways!
2 Because you will eat the fruit of your hands;
    your blessings and good things will be yours:
3 your wife like a fruitful vine in the inner rooms of
      your house,
    your children like the slips of olive trees around
      your table.
4 So: surely thus will someone be blessed,
    a man who is in awe of Yahweh.
5 May Yahweh bless you from Zion;
    you can look at all the good things of Jerusalem,
  all the days of your life,
6   look at your grandchildren.
  Well-being [be] on Israel!

175

A song of the ascents.

^{129:1} People have attacked me much since my youth,
    Israel is indeed to say,
 ² people have attacked me much,
    though not prevailed over me.
 ³ Over my back plowmen have plowed;
    they made long furrows.
 ⁴ Yahweh is faithful;
    he cut through the ropes of the faithless people.
 ⁵ May they be shamed and may they turn away back,
    all the people who are against Zion.
 ⁶ May they become like the grass on roofs
    that withers before someone has plucked it,
 ⁷ with which a reaper has not filled his hand,
    or a gatherer his arm,
 ⁸ and passersby have not said,
    "Yahweh's blessing on you—
    we bless you in Yahweh's name."

On the satirical Web site *The Onion*, one of last week's headlines proclaimed, "Lack of Media Interest Makes Genocide Cover-Up Unnecessary." The "story" explained that an African warlord had declared that global disinterest in the wholesale slaughter of one of the ethnic groups in his country had made him regret the effort he put into covering up the atrocities—burying the corpses in secret mass graves, burning villages to destroy evidence, and so on. He had expected media scrutiny or a U.N. fact-finding mission. "Next time, I'll leave them lying where they fall with the machetes still in their heads." *The Onion* specializes in bad taste, but its report makes one say, "Ouch." Genocide in Sudan raises little interest in the West.

It's as if a militia is laying people on the ground and running a plow over them, making the kind of furrows that a plow makes in the soil. Psalm 129 uses this image to describe Israel's experience. The people tells its national story as if it is an individual being treated in this barbaric way, and it sees this abuse as one that has characterized its entire history, its entire lifetime. It began with the Amalekites' unprovoked attack when the Israelites were a tired, thirsty, hungry crowd of serfs who had just escaped from **Egypt** (Exodus 17). It was an attack they survived only because of a miracle, and when one considers the Jewish people's subsequent experience over the centuries, the millennia that the psalm does not know about, it is indeed miraculous that the nations "have not prevailed" over them.

Western people are inclined to look down on a prayer like the one the psalm goes on to express, but prayer is the only recourse of a defenseless people without machine guns or drones at its disposal. The psalm assumes it is okay for the defenseless victims of would-be ethnic cleansing to look to God not only for protection but for the putting down of the perpetrators of atrocities. Implicitly *The Onion* is taking the same view when it satirizes the West's tolerance of war crimes.

The juxtaposition of Psalms 128 and 129 neatly juxtaposes sets of convictions and experiences that stand in tension yet are both part of the experience of the people of God. Israel does not let the experience described in Psalm 129 make it stop holding onto the promises expressed in Psalm 128. Indeed, the hope that oppressors can be put down is hardly possible without the conviction that blessings come to people who live in awe of **Yahweh**. Israel does not deny the reality of its experience of abuse, but neither does it let that experience make it stop believing that God is one who blesses. Maybe it is significant that Psalm 128 talks of family life whereas Psalm 129 speaks of national life. The war crimes of Psalm 129 certainly affect the family, and the promises of Psalm 128 are made to the nation. Yet the possibility of closing the gate on the outside world and rejoicing in the life of the family is often a resource in the Western world, and perhaps that was so for the head of an Israelite household of whom Psalm 128 directly speaks. You fulfill your responsibilities in leading the family and playing your part in the leadership of the village, doing so in a fashion that works by Yahweh's ways, not those of the **Canaanites** across the valley, and you enjoy the fruits in the life of your family. The reference to blessing/good things coming from **Zion**/Jerusalem suggests that the psalm belongs in the context of a festival such as Passover, Pentecost, or **Sukkot** when people rejoiced in Yahweh's deeds on the people's behalf and prayed for such blessings to recur. It would be the celebration of the festival with its reminders of Yahweh's deeds that encouraged people to believe that the vision in Psalm 128 counted for more than the atrocities described in Psalm 129.

PSALMS 130–131

Wishing and Hoping

A song of the ascents.

130:1 From the depths I have called you, Yahweh:
²   Lord, listen to my voice.
  May your ears become attentive
    to the sound of my prayers for grace.
³ If you keep wayward acts, Yah—
    my Lord, who can stand?
⁴ Because with you there is pardon,
    so that you may be held in awe.
⁵ I have been expectant for Yahweh, my spirit has been
      expectant,
    and for his word I have waited.
⁶ My spirit [has waited] for my Lord
    more than guards for the morning, guards for the morning.
⁷ Israel, wait for Yahweh,
    because with Yahweh there is commitment.
  With him the redemption will be great,
⁸   when he redeems Israel from all its wayward acts.

A song of the ascents. David's.

131:1 Yahweh, my mind has not been lofty,
    my eyes have not looked high.
  I have not gone about with great ideas
    or wonders beyond me.
² If I have not conformed
    and quieted my spirit. . . .
  Like someone nursed with its mother,
    so my spirit is nursed with me.
³ Israel, wait for Yahweh,
    now and forevermore.

It's the beginning of Advent, when we start thinking about the first coming of Jesus but also about his second coming. The sermon on Sunday related to why the second coming matters and the reason for believing it will happen. It matters because Jesus still has a job to finish; the basis for believing that it will happen is that he really has begun it. Thinking about the need for Jesus to finish the job he has begun, I recalled a conversation I had last week over Thanksgiving dinner with a nurse who had come straight to the dinner from a day's work at the E.R. "What sort of thing takes people to the E.R. at Thanksgiving?" I asked. "Well, there was the teenager who got shot over dinner. And then of course there is the usual attempted suicide that happens on a holiday." Yes, there is a job for Jesus to finish. Fortunately, the fact that Jesus brings harmony to many families and gives many people a reason to carry on living is the kind of thing that provides the evidence that he has begun the work that he will indeed finish.

Psalms 130 and 131 use the verbs "expect" and "wait" five times, and near the end both issue exhortations to "wait for **Yahweh**." Translations use the word "hope," which is fine, though it is capable of being misunderstood. We can talk about having hope or being hopeful without implying anything about the object of our hope. "Hope" suggests an attitude. But the words *expect* and *wait* need an object—we expect something or wait for someone. So Christians are not merely people who are hopeful. They are people who are expecting Christ to come and waiting for Christ to come. The psalms thus talk about being expectant for Yahweh or for Yahweh's word and about waiting for Yahweh.

The word *wait* can also have a misleading implication. Waiting may suggest an attitude of patience, of calm mellowness. In the Old Testament, waiting is impatient. It implies urgency. Yet Psalm 131 also implies that there is a patient side to such waiting. All being well, a baby nursing on its mother is content and settled; it knows it has nothing to worry about. Israelites can be in a similar position. They don't have to have big ideas about their importance. They don't have to feel that they are responsible for their destiny or for the world's destiny. It isn't their job to convert the world; that is God's job. They can relax.

Yet at the same time they can and must wait expectantly for God to do his job.

The combination of quiet relaxation and urgent expectancy is more demanding, more important, and trickier when you pray "from the depths." The psalms regularly pray from the depths, but Psalm 130 nuances the nature of these depths. "The depths" suggests a place where you are overwhelmed by suffering and oppression—not merely emotionally but physically and materially (Psalm 69 twice uses the word in connection with being overwhelmed by enemies). As Stevie Smith put it in a poem about someone who metaphorically got too far out into deep water in life, you are not waving but drowning. Psalm 130 presupposes such depths. Its distinctiveness lies in the way it associates that experience with our waywardness. Often the fact that you are drowning is not your fault; in this psalm it *is* your fault. In some circumstances you can't say to God, "You must rescue me—I don't deserve this experience." All you can do is appeal to God's grace and mercy, to God's capacity for pardon.

And then once more you have to wait. Like Psalm 103, Psalm 130 uses the word "pardon" rather than the word "forgive." Whereas *forgiveness* is a word that belongs in the context of relationships between friends and family, *pardon* is a word that belongs to relationships with people in power. Someone seeking pardon is a person who has committed a crime and comes before a king or a president hoping to find mercy. You cannot be sure you will find it. The king or president has to balance the importance of mercy with the importance of preserving standards and doing so in a way that draws attention to their importance. So you wait hopefully but take nothing for granted. Will the word of pardon issue from the king's mouth? You wait with more urgency than a city's guards watching for the dawn and thus for the assurance that the city is not in danger of some secret attack and/or for the moment when they can go home and sleep. Or you wait with more anticipation than the temple staff watching for the dawn and thus for the moment when morning prayers are to be made and sacrifices are to be offered.

A neat aspect of the analogy is that there is no doubt that the dawn will come, hard though it sometimes is to believe. In one sense you cannot take for granted that Yahweh will grant you pardon. But the analogy with a king or president is incomplete. You know that Yahweh is big in **commitment** and big in redemption. You know that you ought to pay for your wayward acts but that actually Yahweh will do so. Yahweh will pay the price of your not being stuck in the depths forever.

PSALM 132

If You Build It, He Will Come

A song of the ascents.

¹ Yahweh, be mindful for David
     of all his being weighed down,
² in that he swore to Yahweh,
     promised to Jacob's Strong One,
³ "If I come into my tent, my house,
     if I climb into my bed, my couch,
⁴ if I give sleep to my eyes,
     slumber to my eyelids,
⁵ before I find the place belonging to Yahweh,
     the dwelling belonging to Jacob's Strong One. . . ."
⁶ So: we heard of it at Ephrata,
     we found it in the Forest region.
⁷ Let's come to his dwelling,
     let's bow low to his footstool.
⁸ Rise, Yahweh, to your residence,
     you and your mighty chest.
⁹ Your priests put on faithfulness,
     the people who are committed to you resound.
¹⁰ For the sake of David your servant,
     do not turn away the face of your anointed one.

¹¹ Yahweh swore to David in truthfulness;
     he will not turn from it.
   "One from the fruit of your body
     I will put on your throne.

¹² If your sons keep my covenant,
    my declarations that I will teach them,
  for all time their sons,
    also will sit on your throne."
¹³ Because Yahweh chose Zion,
    which he wanted as a seat for himself.
¹⁴ "For all time this is my residence,
    where I will sit, because I wanted it.
¹⁵ Its supplies I will greatly bless;
    its needy people I will fill with bread.
¹⁶ Its priests I will clothe with deliverance,
    its committed people will resound loudly.
¹⁷ There I will make David's horn flourish;
    I set up a flame for my anointed one.
¹⁸ Its enemies I will clothe in shame,
    but on him his crown will sparkle."

In an hour's time, I am off to our diocesan convention, where clergy and laypeople will make decisions about policies and initiatives for the coming year. We will begin by asking for God's guidance and wisdom in connection with our discussions and decisions, but we won't then expect a number of divine interventions to tell us what to decide. I guess that theologically we assume or hope or trust that God's wisdom operates through our exercising our human wisdom. There are indications within the Scriptures of another way of looking at this process. God relates to us like a parent to (adult) children, telling us to go and make our decisions and then going along with those decisions. You could say it's a frightening aspect of God's way of running the world that God leaves decisions to us in that way.

Psalm 132 points to a spectacular example. It offers another take on the story of the origin of the Jerusalem temple, told in 2 Samuel 6–7. There it is David's idea to bring the **declaration chest** to Jerusalem and build a temple in the city. God is not very keen on the idea of a temple. "I like being able to move around, not being fixed in one place," God says, "and anyway this initiative of yours reverses the proper relationship between me and you. I'm the one who is going to build a house, a house

for you" (in the sense of a household, a line of succession).
"That building needs to come first."

There is no indication in the story in 2 Samuel that **Yahweh**
had chosen **Zion** (as the psalm says). The whole enterprise was
David's idea, and it is easy to see the pragmatic political thinking that underlies it. The new nation needs a center, and pref-
erably one located in a place that is both secure and neutral, a
place with which none of the clans is specifically associated.
Because Jerusalem is still occupied by the Jebusites, locating
the temple in David's capital reinforces its position as a center for the Israelite clans. You could hardly blame Yahweh for
reacting negatively to being used to prop up David's administration. Yet Yahweh does more than acquiesce grudgingly in
David's action. Yahweh puts a retrospective seal of approval on
Zion as a dwelling place. His stance parallels his attitude to the
idea of having kings, which was also Israel's idea rather than
his, and also an idea that clashed with Yahweh's own thinking,
yet an idea that he then embraced with enthusiasm—as the
psalm also assumes.

The first half of the psalm incorporates a kind of reenactment of the events that led to the building of the temple. It
indeed starts from David's initiative and thus points to that
interrelation between human initiative and divine desire. It
begins with the way David had imposed a burden on himself
and made a solemn promise, which concerned locating the
declaration chest. First Samuel 4–6 relates how the Israelites
had taken the chest into battle, only for it to be captured by
the **Philistines**. The Philistines found it too hot to handle, and
it eventually ended up in Forest Town, way down the mountains from Jerusalem, just inside **Judahite** territory. There it
stayed for decades. Apparently in David's day no one in Israel's
leadership now knows where it is, but David sets about finding
out and succeeds, and he determines to go there to bow down
before this symbol of Yahweh's presence in Israel. From there
David invites Yahweh to come up to Jerusalem, where he has
determined to provide a dwelling worthy of Yahweh. So the
priests and the people as a whole (the people **committed** to
Yahweh) join in **faithfulness** and celebration in bringing the

183

chest up to Jerusalem. Following on the reenactment of this act on David's part, and in light of it, the psalm pleads with God to pay heed to the prayers of the current anointed king.

The first half of the psalm thus speaks from the congregation to God, in the usual manner of a psalm. But sometimes psalms turn into a conversation in which God responds, and Psalm 132 is an example. In the second half God speaks—or rather, the reenactment continues in the second half, as the psalm also recalls God's commitment to David back at the time of his becoming king and his initiating the building of the temple. God made a promise that there would always be a descendant of David on the throne. The reaffirmation links with the prayer for God to heed the prayers of his anointed because that phrase denotes the current Davidic king. It thus offers reassurance that the prayer will be answered. From Zion God will bless the people as a whole. The psalm further points to another aspect of the two-sided relationship between God and David. The promise about David's successors presupposes that they will be faithful to their side of the **covenant**. Maybe God in his grace will be merciful when they are faithless, but they cannot assume that God will keep his side of the covenant when they fail in theirs. And after 587 no Davidic kings sat on David's throne in Jerusalem.

PSALMS 133-134

How to End the Day

A song of the ascents. David's.

^{133:1} Now: how good and how lovely
    is kinfolk living as one,
 ² like good oil on the head,
    going down onto the beard,
  Aaron's beard,
    which goes down upon the collar of his clothes,
 ³ like the dew of Hermon,
    which goes down upon the mountains of Zion.
  Because there Yahweh commanded blessing,
    life for evermore.

A song of the ascents.

134:1 Now: worship Yahweh, all you servants of Yahweh,
    you who stand in Yahweh's house each night.
² Raise your hands to the sanctuary
    and worship Yahweh.
³ May Yahweh bless you yourself from Zion—
    the one who is the maker of the heavens and the earth.

When my wife and I got married fifty-one weeks ago, we discovered the *Episcopal Prayer Book*'s "Daily Devotions for Individuals and Families," four one-page sets of psalms, Scripture readings, and prayers that you can use when you wake up, at lunch, at dinner, and before going to sleep. They are a version of the "liturgy of the hours" that goes back to the early Christian centuries and has appeared in various forms in different Christian confessions. We have found this version a great way of framing our lives—we can almost invariably begin and end the day with them, and we use the midday and early evening forms when we are at home for lunch and dinner and thus reset our minds on God during the day.

Psalm 134 begins the form of prayers "for the close of the day." I imagine that in origin it will have belonged to the close of the day in the sense of sunset, when the evening sacrifices were offered and prayers were prayed in the temple, and when the day is in a sense over. The body of Israel as a whole did not stand in **Yahweh's** house each evening, so maybe the servants of Yahweh here are the priests and Levites whose job was to offer those sacrifices and prayers on behalf of the people as a whole. But one can imagine that Israelites in general, living all over the country, could remind themselves as the sun set that this moment was the occasion for those sacrifices and prayers, and in spirit they could join in. There is a parallel in the way the parson's ringing the church bell could remind workers in the fields that he was about to say prayers in the church and could invite them to join him in spirit.

Whereas the opening lines address the servants of God as a group, the last line addresses an individual; maybe it's the response of the ministers to their leader. The word for *worship* is traditionally translated "bless," though the idea of "blessing God" is a bit odd, and "worship" more likely conveys the idea. The word in question is similar to the word for "knees," so maybe it suggests going down on your knees before God. But the psalm's double use of words that at least look the same (*worship* and *bless*) points to the reciprocal nature of the relationship between worship and blessing. We worship; God blesses. God blesses; we worship.

Psalm 133 ends on a similar note with its reference to blessing. It wouldn't be surprising if there was a link between blessing and the unity or harmony of the extended family, the theme with which the psalm begins. Such harmony is a great blessing. The link between these **songs of the ascents** and the annual pilgrimage festivals to Jerusalem undertaken by families might make people rejoice in the togetherness of such occasions. It might also make them aware of the need to preserve that harmony. In the West we know that occasions such as Thanksgiving and Christmas are times when families come under great strain, and it wouldn't be surprising if the same was true of Israel's pilgrimage festivals—as the story of Joseph and Mary's Passover pilgrimage suggests (Luke 2), like the story of Elkanah, Hannah, and Peninnah (1 Samuel 1).

But in the Old Testament "blessing" is concrete and down to earth; it suggests the fruitfulness of human beings and animals and the flourishing of the crops, and it is easy to see that the absence of unity and harmony would imperil the work of the family and thus threaten its having enough to eat. For practical reasons as well as because of their inherent value, then, unity and harmony are something to wax poetic about, in the way that the psalm does. Such harmony makes the face shine as makeup does, and the reference to abundant anointing also speaks of God's appointment of the priests and of the festivity attached to their ministry. The "dew" of Hermon is presumably a metaphor. An inland mountain such as Hermon would hardly be known for its dew, but it is known for its snow, which seeps through to feed the rivers that flow from it even during the dry summer. The metaphorical dew of Hermon thus plays a key role in providing water for Israel and in being a means of God's blessing the land.

PSALM 135

Holy Wind

¹ Praise Yah!
  Praise Yahweh's name;
      praise, servants of Yahweh,
² you who stand in Yahweh's house,
      in the courtyards of the house of our God.
³ Praise Yah, because Yahweh is good;
      make music for his name, because it is lovely.
⁴ Because Yah chose Jacob for himself,
      Israel as his special possession.
⁵ Because I myself acknowledge that Yahweh is great;
      our Lord [is great] above all gods.
⁶ Anything that Yahweh has wished, he has done
      in the heavens and on the earth,
  in the seas and all the depths,
⁷   making clouds rise from the end of the earth.
  He has made flashes of lightning for the rain,
      bringing out wind from his storehouses,
⁸ the one who hit the firstborn of Egypt,
      human beings and cattle.
⁹ He sent signs and portents in the midst of Egypt
      against Pharaoh and against all his servants,
¹⁰ the one who hit many nations
      and slew powerful kings,
¹¹ Sihon, the king of the Amorites,
      Og the king of Bashan,
  and all the kingdoms of Canaan,
¹²   and gave their country as a possession,
      a possession for Israel his people.

¹³ Yahweh, your name is forever;
      Yahweh, your fame is through generation after generation.
¹⁴ Because Yahweh governs his people
      and gets relief in connection with his servants.
¹⁵ The nations' images are silver and gold,
      the work of human hands.
¹⁶ They have a mouth but they do not speak,
      they have eyes but they do not see.
¹⁷ They have ears but they do not listen;
      no, there is no breath in their mouths.

¹⁸   Their makers will become like them,
        anyone who relies on them.
¹⁹   Household of Israel, worship Yahweh;
        household of Aaron, worship Yahweh.
²⁰   Household of Levi, worship Yahweh;
        you who are in awe of Yahweh, worship Yahweh.
²¹   Yahweh be worshiped from Zion,
        the one who dwells in Jerusalem.
     Praise Yah!

Two nights ago, we had a huge windstorm in our city, with gusts up to ninety-seven miles per hour. The wind felled hundreds of trees, including century-old oaks and tall palms. Hundreds of thousands of people lost power, and many still lack power. Schools and restaurants were closed. Trees falling on buildings led to the evacuating of an apartment block and the abandoning of at least forty buildings that will simply need to be demolished. Elsewhere, trucks were blown over on freeways. I don't know how long it will take to clear up the debris from the streets.

It is what happens (Psalm 135 makes one say) when God brings winds out of his storehouses. Coincidentally, today is the second Sunday in Advent, John the Baptizer's Sunday, when we recall his declaration that Jesus will baptize with the Holy Spirit and fire—with holy wind and fire, you could easily translate it. The windstorm has provided a frightening illustration of what it could be like to be blown over by the Holy Wind. The psalm, too, assumes that such an experience would be scary.

Whereas we were fortunate that the windstorm was not accompanied by rain or fire, the psalm notes that lightning and rain are natural accompaniments of wind as the clouds arise on the far horizon and come to fill the sky. It goes on to note some further terrifying aspects of God's activity in the world, associated with the Israelites' escape from oppressors in **Egypt** and from attackers on the edge of **Canaan**, and with their arrival in Canaan itself. The Bible does not imply that massacres and natural disasters generally emerge from God's deliberate purpose; usually they are "just one of those things." After the windstorm we wondered whether the collapse of a big tree on our property onto a car on the street would make us financially liable for the damage, or is it "an act of God"? Maybe the storm is another result of global warming, my wife comments. If so, maybe it thus counts both as something for which we are corporately responsible and as something that signifies God's judgment upon us.

To a small, powerless people such as the Israelites, this power of God embodied in natural and political events was not frightening but reassuring. It was easy for them to feel overwhelmed by the power of the mighty nations around them and to be impressed by the power of the gods these peoples worshiped. The psalm reminds them of the power that the real God has shown in their history and of the significance that God has given to this insignificant people by choosing them to be his special possession. It reminds them of the powerlessness of the images that represented those other gods. Such images look impressive and have the physical features of living, speaking, active, sentient, responsive beings, but these features do not work. Whereas Israelites might be tempted to think that these gods are powerful, their images give you a picture of their actual impotence. In contrast, **Yahweh** governs his people and leads them in the way he has in mind for them. Yahweh gets relief in connection with them—that is, he sees them being oppressed by people such as the Egyptians or the Amorites, and he hates what he sees. He is thus motivated to terminate their affliction in order to express the concern he feels. In contrast, people who rely on the gods represented by the images, or on the images themselves, end up as helpless, feeble, and vulnerable as the images they had made.

PSALM 136

His Commitment Is Forever

1. Confess Yahweh, because he is good
   (because his commitment is forever).
2. Confess the God of gods
   (because his commitment is forever).
3. Confess the Lord of lords
   (because his commitment is forever),

189

⁴ the one who did great wonders alone
  (because his commitment is forever),
⁵ who made the heavens with discernment
  (because his commitment is forever),
⁶ who spread the earth over the water
  (because his commitment is forever),
⁷ who made the great lights
  (because his commitment is forever),
⁸ the sun to rule over the day
  (because his commitment is forever),
⁹ the moon and the stars to rule over the night
  (because his commitment is forever),
¹⁰ who hit Egypt in their firstborn
  (because his commitment is forever),
¹¹ and brought Israel out from their midst
  (because his commitment is forever),
¹² with a strong hand and an extended arm
  (because his commitment is forever),
¹³ who divided the Reed Sea into two
  (because his commitment is forever),
¹⁴ who let Israel pass through the midst of it
  (because his commitment is forever),
¹⁵ but shook Pharaoh and his force into the Reed Sea
  (because his commitment is forever),
¹⁶ who took his people through the wilderness
  (because his commitment is forever),
¹⁷ who hit great kings
  (because his commitment is forever),
¹⁸ who slew powerful kings
  (because his commitment is forever),
¹⁹ Sihon, king of the Amorites
  (because his commitment is forever),
²⁰ Og, king of Bashan
  (because his commitment is forever),
²¹ and gave their country as a possession
  (because his commitment is forever),
²² a possession for Israel his servant
  (because his commitment is forever),
²³ who was mindful of us in our lowliness
  (because his commitment is forever),

²⁴ and tore us away from our foes
    (because his commitment is forever),
²⁵ who gave food to all flesh
    (because his commitment is forever).
²⁶ Confess the God of the heavens
    (because his commitment is forever).

A former student of mine served as an armed forces chaplain in Iraq for two years after graduating from seminary. One week he called me from there. He had felt compelled to preach on the idea of God's steadfast love. He remembered my explaining one evening the Hebrew word that represents it, the word *hesed*. He added that as I talked about this idea, I was at the same time giving Ann, my disabled wife, her formula down her feeding tube, and what struck him was that we weren't just *talking* about steadfast love or covenant love; it was something that was being acted out. (I apologize that this is a story about me, though I think of it more as a story about Ann and about something God did through her illness, and I ask you to think about it that way.) He told this story in his sermon. A few days later one of the soldiers who heard the sermon was killed in a mortar attack, and the chaplain had to pray with him as he died. He was glad that the last sermon the soldier had heard concerned God's steadfast love. The following Sunday the set psalm in our worship at church was Psalm 51, and in my sermon in connection with the psalm's opening appeal to God's steadfast love, I told this story. A woman came to talk to me in tears afterward because since childhood she had been given a deep conviction that God was full of wrath. She couldn't internalize the idea that God was characterized by grace, steadfast love, and compassion.

It's that word for steadfast love that recurs in the second part of every line of Psalm 136. I think the word **commitment** best represents the idea in English. There might be more than one reason that the word keeps recurring like that. One is that it's a kind of refrain—maybe the temple choir sings the first half of each line, and the people as a whole respond with the second half. But another is that the effect of the repetition might be to encourage the process whereby people internalize the fact that commitment is one of God's most basic characteristics. In the foundational description of **Yahweh's** character that Yahweh gives Israel at Sinai in Exodus 34, along with words such as *compassion* and *grace* and *steadfastness*, it's the only word that comes more than once.

The declarations about God that accompany this testimony to God's commitment compare with the ones in Psalm 135. You could say that they are summed up by the first two lines. On one hand, God is good. That goodness finds expression in the way that God does not sit there unconcerned when the Israelites are oppressed by the **Egyptians,** or are wandering through the wilderness, or are attacked by powerful kings such as Sihon and Og. God is mindful of the Israelites in their lowliness. They are an unimpressive, powerless people, and God takes account of that fact. But that mindfulness would be worth nothing if God were incapable of doing something about their situation. So the other key truth about God is that he is God of gods, Lord of lords, the creator who has a strong arm to extend against oppressors and attackers. As the psalm puts it vividly, he can tear Israel away from its foes like a thief snatching a purse from its owner or like a wind tearing apart a mountain (it's the word used in this connection when it happens in front of Elijah in 1 Kings 19). He can supply everyone with food.

For much of its life in Old Testament times, Israel did not see God acting in this way. It lived most of its life under the authority of superpowers such as **Assyria, Babylon, Persia**, and **Greece**, in no position to determine its own destiny and subject to their attack, neglect, oppressive taxation, or persecution. While it sometimes deserved this experience, it did not always do so. It lived in perpetual need of internalizing the truth that God's steadfast love or commitment lasts forever, because it sure didn't look like it. Like Christian worship, Israel's worship involved the people coming into the sanctuary and declaring things to be true that didn't look as if they were true when the people were outside the sanctuary. The worshipers reminded themselves of the facts from their people's story that provided the evidence for the truth of their faith so that they could carry on living in a situation where the truths seemed to be suspended.

PSALM 137

Mindfulness, God's and Ours

¹ By the rivers of Babylon—there we sat;
   yes, we wept as we were mindful of Zion.
² On the poplars in the midst of it we hung our guitars;
³   because our captors there asked for the words of a song,
   our mockers [asked for] celebration:
      "Sing us one of the Zion songs!"
⁴ How can we sing Yahweh's song
   on foreign soil?
⁵ If I put you out of mind, Jerusalem,
   may my right hand put out of mind—
⁶ may my tongue stick to my palate
   if I am not mindful of you,
   if I do not exalt Jerusalem
   above the pinnacle of my joy.
⁷ Yahweh, be mindful for the Edomites
   of Jerusalem's day,
   the people who were saying,
      "Strip it, strip it, to its foundation."
⁸ Ms. Babylon, you who are to be destroyed—
   the blessings of the person who recompenses you
   for the dealings that you had with us!
⁹ The blessings of the person who seizes your babies
   and dashes them on the crag!

The song "By the Rivers of Babylon" was one of the best-selling singles of all time in Britain. In my naiveté, it was some years before I realized its original significance. In origin, it is a Rastafarian song, one of a number based on psalms that provided singers in the Caribbean with raw material for expressing their protest and lament about colonialism and its related oppression, as well as their longing for freedom. The Rastafarians were not campaigning for violent revolution but were issuing a call to their people to stop simply accepting **Babylonian** domination and Babylonian cultural values. They articulated a different voice and a determination not simply to give in to self-pity and hopelessness. The irony of the naiveté of Brits like me, of course, who loved the song, is that we were the Babylon to which it refers.

An awareness of what Psalm 137 has meant for people in the Caribbean who were longing for freedom from their imperial overlords helps us understand the significance of the psalm for the people who originally sang it. Like many other psalms, it can seem offensive to Western readers, and we are right to be disturbed by it because it is about people like us, us people of Babylon. We do have the slight encouragement that as usual the psalm offers no hint that the people who sing it are going to rise up in military rebellion against the overlords. The Israelite people never did so, any more than the Caribbean peoples. They did something more dangerous. They prayed. They told God what they longed to see and then left it up to God to bring it about.

Part of their confidence in doing so would be that they knew they were simply asking God to do what he had promised. Prophetic books such as Isaiah, Jeremiah, Ezekiel, and Obadiah all contain promises that God will punish Edom for its wrongdoing and specifically for its treatment of **Judah** at the time of the fall of Jerusalem. They also contain promises that God will put down Babylon, and the horrific declaration of blessing with which the psalm closes takes up the specifics of what Isaiah 13 says that God will get the Medes to do to Babylon. Admittedly one should perhaps not be too literal in one's understanding of the prophecy or of the psalm. Both are poetry. They compare with the New Testament's talk of people weeping and gnashing their teeth in hell. The presupposition of promises that God will punish Israel's enemies is that God does not permanently abandon people to being under the authority of a superpower that uses them for its own ends, and also that God does judge. The presupposition of a prayer such as that in Psalm 137 is that it is fine to ask God to be mindful of his promises.

Mindfulness is a key motif in the psalm. It is possible for a group of **exiles** to forget where they came from and to abandon any hope or intention of returning. Life did in fact become quite comfortable for many Judahites in Babylon, and many did not return to Jerusalem when they had the chance. While remembering can be a matter of chance, mindfulness is a deliberate act. The people sitting by the irrigation channels that carry the water of the Euphrates around the area and make farming possible are involved in an act of worship as they engage in mindfulness, in deliberate remembering. They are also involved in an act of teaching as they remind their children (who have never seen Jerusalem) of the city's importance. They will resist the chiding of the Babylonians that reminds them of Jerusalem's destruction and mockingly invites them to sing one of the psalms that speaks of the city's impressiveness, the city that does not look so impressive now. The impossibility of singing Yahweh's song on foreign soil does not stem from the conviction that Yahweh cannot be with them on foreign soil, as is indicated by the fact that they go on to pray to Yahweh in the latter part of the psalm. It may stem from the awareness that singing Yahweh's song involves singing about what Yahweh has been doing, and they know that Yahweh has abandoned them and is not acting on their behalf. So they can pray, but they cannot sing in thanksgiving for what God has done for them and is doing for them. Their commitment to remaining mindful of Jerusalem is backed up by their self-curse: may I lose the capacity to play the guitar or sing if I let Jerusalem out of mind. The essential nature of God's involvement with Jerusalem means that such forgetting would be the end of faith.

PSALM 138

How to Be Defiant in Spirit

David's.

1 I will confess you with all my heart,
    before the gods I will make music for you.
2 I will bow low to your holy palace
    and confess your name on account of your commitment
        and your truthfulness.
  Because you have made great above everything
    your name, your word.

³ On the day I called, you answered me;
　　you make me defiant in spirit, with strength.
⁴ All earth's kings will confess you, Yahweh,
　　because they will have heard the words of your mouth.
⁵ They will sing of Yahweh's ways,
　　because Yahweh's honor will be great.
⁶ Because Yahweh is on high, but he sees the lowly;
　　lofty, he acknowledges from afar.
⁷ If I walk in the midst of trouble you will give me life;
　　on account of my foes' anger you will extend your hand.
　Your right hand will deliver me;
⁸　　Yahweh will bring it to an end for me.
　Yahweh, your commitment is forever;
　　do not let go of the works of your hands.

This morning I received a message from a woman who a year ago was attacked and stabbed by a man while she and a friend were hiking in a forest; her friend was killed but she survived because the man mistakenly thought she was dead. She has recently been in court to testify concerning the events; the man was found guilty of the attacks and was sentenced to life imprisonment. People have expressed to her the hope that this judgment would bring her some closure to the experience, but she doubts whether it will. The events were too savage and meaningless, and they are impossible to undo. Her old life has quite gone, and she is not sure who she now is. She is not unhappy that the murderer will not be executed, but she is glad that "God is a righteous judge; he is angry with the wicked every day" (Psalm 7). She does not intend to try to start some new life somewhere other than her home area where the attack happened. There is thus a kind of defiance about her.

Along with Psalm 7, Psalm 138 is a psalm she could echo. On the day she called, God answered her, and he has made her defiant in spirit, with strength. God did not act in the same way for her friend, as God did not act in that way for every Israelite who cried out to him, but the psalm assumes that the occasions when God does so respond are more significant than the occasions when God does not do so. They naturally mean that the people to whom God does respond confess God with all their heart, and they do so before the gods, before earth's kings, and before their enemies (it wouldn't be surprising if the psalm was especially used by kings or leaders such as Nehemiah).

The psalm sees God's entire character expressed in the kind of **deliverance** it looks back on and in the kind of deliverance it now seeks. There is God's **commitment** and God's truthfulness. Perhaps those two are spelled out in the parallel line. God's truthfulness means he keeps his word, his promises. God's **name** or nature is expressed most centrally in the commitment he shows to his people. The acts that express God's commitment and truthfulness are reason for God to be honored by the people who directly experience them and by the people to whom these people tell their story. They are the link between God's being lofty and on high, yet seeing and acknowledging the lowly. God's being lofty and on high means he is in a position to intervene in affairs on earth on behalf of the lowly, to preserve their lives when trouble assails them, to reach out his hand when adversaries attack them. God's being committed and truthful means he has the moral character to make him intervene in that way, to bring trouble to an end, to be persistent in the works that his hands undertake. The fact that his palace is in the heavens means there is a sense in which he is "far away," but it does not mean he stays distant. He does things for us, or for people we know who then tell us about what he did for them.

Therefore it is possible to pray the kind of prayer with which the psalm closes.

PSALM 139

On Openness

The leader's. David's. A composition.

1 Yahweh, you have examined me
    and acknowledged me:
2 you yourself have acknowledged my sitting and my rising,
    you have discerned my intention, from far away.
3 My walking and my reclining you have measured;
    with all my ways you have become familiar.

⁴ Because there is not a word on my tongue—
    there, Yahweh, you have known it all.
⁵ Behind and in front you have bound me,
    and put your hand on me.
⁶ Your knowledge is too extraordinary for me;
    it has towered high, I cannot prevail over it.

⁷ Where could I go from your spirit,
    where could I flee from your face?
⁸ If I were to go up to the heavens, you would be there;
    if I were to make Sheol my bed—there you would be.
⁹ Were I to take dawn's wings,
    dwell on the far side of the sea,
¹⁰ there, too, your hand could lead me away,
    your right hand could take hold of me.
¹¹ Were I to say, "The darkness can certainly seize me,
    light can be night around me,"
¹² darkness, too, would not be too dark for you,
    and night would be light like day;
    darkness and light are the same.

¹³ Because you are the one who created my heart,
    when you wove me in my mother's womb.
¹⁴ I will confess you, because I was set apart in a wondrous way;
    your acts were extraordinary.
    I myself acknowledge you fully;
¹⁵   my frame was not concealed from you,
    when I was made in secret,
    when I was embroidered in earth's depths.
¹⁶ Your eyes saw me as an embryo,
    and on your scroll were written, all of them,
    the days that were shaped,
    when there was not one of them.
¹⁷ So for me, how imposing were your intentions, God,
    how huge is the sum of them!
¹⁸ If I could count them, they would be more than the sand;
    when I have come to an end, I will still be with you

¹⁹ If you would only kill the faithless person, God,
    and murderous people would go away from me,
²⁰ people who speak of you for deception,
    your adversaries who have lifted you up for emptiness.

²¹ Do I not oppose people who oppose you, Yahweh,
  and repudiate people who rise up against you?
²² With complete opposition I oppose them;
  they have become enemies for me.
²³ Examine me, God, and acknowledge my mind;
  test me and acknowledge my concerns.
²⁴ See if there is an idolatrous way in me
  and lead me in the ancient way.

My wife carries in her purse a photograph of her prospective grandchild, an image from her daughter's sonogram. It is extraordinary to have this vivid reminder of the way a baby is steadily developing in the womb. When the prospective mother is sick, as she was a couple of weeks ago, we all worry a little about the effect this may have on the baby's development. In some cultures, mother and grandmother would be knitting clothes for the baby so that the weaving of the limbs of a new person in the womb is paralleled by the creativity that goes on outside the womb. I am not sure whether a sense of wonder at this process is enhanced through our knowing more about the way the baby develops stage by stage or whether it would be enhanced by not being able to trace the fetus's development and instead being confronted by the fully formed baby at birth.

Psalm 139 wonders at this process and marvels at the way God was involved in it. Israelites knew that conception and birth were natural processes at one level, yet they also knew that it was God who worked through the natural process. Likewise, Israelites evidently knew as we do that there is a sense in which everything that we will be and do is shaped before we are born—what kind of person we will be, what will be the nature of our strengths and weaknesses, what achievements will be possible for us, and what infirmities will affect us and limit the length of our lives. It is not that everything is predetermined, but the possibilities and constraints are already set. And the fact that God is involved in the shaping of the person means that God also knows about those data and has the information on file. The sheer quantity of data is staggering, as huge as the number of grains of sand on the seashore. It embraces my whole life and means that I will still be within God's cognizance when I get to the end of it.

The psalm wonders not only at God's involvement but at the process itself. It is very ordinary but also extraordinary, as extraordinary as the process whereby God brought the world into being and brought Israel into being. Talking in terms of being embroidered "in earth's depths" takes up the image of "mother earth" and turns it inside out—it is as if our mother is the earth. The psalm is a piece of poetry and hardly provides a proof text for the conviction that abortion is wrong. Yet its wonder at the process that leads to the birth of a baby and at God's involvement in that process surely makes it hard to see a decision about abortion as merely a decision about a woman's body. It involves a decision to terminate a process in which God is involved and one would need impressive reasons to do so.

Western readings of the psalm have had at least two other angles of interest. One is its implications for God's knowledge of all things and for God's sovereignty over all things. It has often seemed obvious to Western thinking that God is omniscient—that God knows everything. The psalm suggests an interesting take on this assumption: it implies that God can indeed find out anything, though not that God knows everything "automatically," just by virtue of being God. The psalm pictures God finding out about us by examining us, by looking at us, by looking at that process whereby we come into being. Likewise, it pictures God as entirely capable of doing anything with us that he wants to, though it does not imply that everything we do or experience happens because God willed it. God's sovereignty is selective, like God's knowledge. God can know and do anything, but God chooses what to know and what to do in light of initiatives he wants to take or prayers we pray.

The other angle from which Western reading looks at the psalm concerns its significance for our spirituality. It can be extremely encouraging to know that we can never get beyond the realm of God's care for us. Yet there is another side to the significance of God's being able to reach us anywhere. Amos 9 uses the same language and imagery in speaking of people going down to **Sheol** or going up to the heavens and of God's hand being able to reach them there, but it does so in order to remind Israel that it cannot escape God's judgment. Every breath you take, every step you take, God will be watching you. God's capacity to know all about us and reach us wherever we are can be good news or bad news. Indeed, much of the psalm can be read either way. It's almost as if the psalm is systematically ambiguous, careful to state the facts about God's having access to us and leaving it neutral whether this access is good news or bad news. It's almost as if the psalm is daring us to decide. Its technique is an aspect of the way in which the Psalms (and other parts of the Old Testament) are reading us as much as we are reading them, or are driving us to read ourselves. Whether God's access to us is good or bad news for the person who wrote the psalm is neither here nor there. The question is which way the people who use the psalm need to read it.

Through verses 1–18 the ambiguity continues, though the last sections of the psalm may resolve it. The psalm is another that Christians commonly use in a selective way—we read only the first three sections and are rather embarrassed by the last part. Do the last two verses indicate that the psalm recognizes how questionable is the desire for God to kill wrongdoers? How could such a spiritually sensitive person as the one who wrote the first part segue into the harshness of the last part?

Such a dramatic transition comes easily and naturally in light of the ominous side to God's having the kind of access to us that the psalm has described. Not only is it impossible for us to wander beyond some realm where God can look after us. It is impossible for us to flee to some realm where God cannot lay hold of us or cannot get to know all about us. We cannot prevail over God's capacity to know all about us. God can hear even the words we speak in secret. In light of the way the psalm ends, we can see the logic whereby the psalm as a whole works. It is an expression of commitment to **Yahweh**'s ways. The psalmist knows all about **faithless** people who live murderous lives, people who take the **name** of Yahweh on their lips in their oaths and their testimony in court but do so in connection with untruth, "emptiness." There are such people in the community. Maybe he has even been accused of being such a person. He therefore declares that in reality he is totally against them and

201

against everything they stand for. He has nothing to do with them. He treats them as enemies rather than friends (Augustine's comment that we are called to love our enemies but not to love God's enemies is in keeping with the psalm's stance). As a mark of not being such a person, the psalmist urges God to deal with them. It would be too dangerous a prayer if in reality one belonged to such company oneself.

The psalmist's closing invitation to God to examine him is then an opening of himself to God's checking whether this commitment is real. It is the earlier sections of the psalm that add bite to this self-opening. He has made clear that he understands how serious it is. There is no fooling God about the nature of our commitment to God's ways. There is no escaping God if we pretend to be something other than we are.

PSALM 140

The Alternative to a Bulletproof Vest

The leader's. A composition. David's.

¹ Rescue me, Yahweh, from the evildoer,
   save me from the person of violence,
² people who have thought up evil things in their mind,
   who stir up war every day.
³ They have sharpened their tongue like a snake;
   a spider's poison is under their lips.   (*Rise*)
⁴ Keep me from the hand of the faithless person, Yahweh,
   save me from the person of violence,
   people who have thought up how to trip my feet,
⁵   important people who have hidden a trap for me.
   They have spread a net by the side of the track,
      they have set lures for me.   (*Rise*)
⁶ I have said to Yahweh, "You are my God";
   give ear, Yahweh, to the sound of my prayer for grace.
⁷ Yahweh, my Lord, the strength that delivers me,
   you have shielded my head on the day when people took
      up their weaponry.
⁸ Yahweh, do not grant the wishes of the faithless person;
   do not let his plan succeed so that the [faithless] people
      triumph.   (*Rise*)

⁹ The head of those who surround me—
    may the trouble caused by their lips cover them.
¹⁰ May burning coals tumble on them with fire;
    may it make them fall into pits so that they do not get up.
¹¹ May the person of a [poisonous] tongue not stand firm in
       the country;
    the person of violence—may evil hunt him into pens.
¹² I have come to acknowledge that Yahweh makes a
       judgment for the lowly,
    a decision for the needy.
¹³ Yes, the faithful will confess your name;
    the upright will live in your presence.

Not surprisingly (I recently read in a magazine), the best place to buy a bulletproof vest is Bogotá, Colombia, where two students at the University of the Andes noticed that bodyguards didn't wear their bulletproof vests because they were too cumbersome and decided to develop something more wearable. Their company now makes fashion-oriented body armor for politicians, hip-hop artists, and business executives as well as bulletproof vestments for priests, who risk being assassinated if they speak out against drug trafficking or corruption. It also makes a large bulletproof Bible that priests can use as a protective shield.

But you need several thousand dollars to buy one of these garments, and most people who are in danger of violence don't have the money. Psalm 140 exists for such people. You can sometimes get the impression from the Psalms that Jerusalem or some Israelite village must have been nearly as dangerous as Bogotá. The weapons of these Israelite wrongdoers were often not tangible but legal, and the reference to snakes and poisonous spiders shows that they were just as threatening. The story of Naboth and his vineyard in 1 Kings 21 illustrates the vulnerability of an ordinary Israelite to the way "important" people with resources can pervert the legal system in order to get their way at the cost of an ordinary person's life.

When people have designs on your life, then, you are reduced to prayer. All you can do is pray for God to show grace.

Once again the psalm recalls God's own nature as the one who has the strength to protect, and it recalls occasions in the past when **Yahweh** has provided protection. Once again the psalm declares the conviction that God is on the side of the lowly and the needy when they are **faithful** and upright. Once again the psalm urges God to make the would-be killers the victims of their own plans. It would not be surprising if the plotters took part in the same temple services as the person praying such a psalm, and the possibility of God's answering such a prayer might make them reconsider their plans.

PSALM 141

On Keeping One's Mouth Shut

A composition. David's.

¹ Yahweh, when I call you, hurry to me,
  give ear to my voice when I call to you.
² May my plea stand as incense before you,
  the lifting of my hands as the evening offering.
³ Set a watch at my mouth, Yahweh,
  keep guard at the door of my lips.
⁴ Do not let my mind turn to something evil
    to have dealings in faithlessness with people who act
      wickedly.
  So I shall not feed on their delights;
⁵   the faithful person may hit me in commitment and may
      reprove me.
  May choice oil not adorn my head,
    because my prayer is still against their evil deeds.
⁶ When their leaders have fallen on the sides of the crag,
    they will listen to my words, because they will be delightful.
⁷ Like someone cleaving and splitting the earth,
    our bones have been scattered at the mouth of Sheol.
⁸ Because my eyes are toward you, Yahweh my Lord;
    on you I have relied, do not expose my life.
⁹ Keep me from the sides of the trap that they have laid for me
    and from the snares of people who act wickedly.
¹⁰ May the faithless fall into their own nets all at once,
    while I myself pass through.

Sometimes my wife will put her hand over my mouth to stop me saying something or shut me up. It works. A friend once told me, with only a hint of a smile, "You need to learn self-censorship." I am not very good at thinking through the possible effects of what I may say before I say it. Sometimes I find out what I think only by speaking and listening to what I say, but by then it can be too late. I can hurt someone or cause trouble I did not mean to cause. Admittedly there are other occasions when I speak in order to cause trouble and am quite happy when I have done so. It means that some issue that needs consideration is out there and has to be discussed.

The psalm asks God for a form of self-censorship and implies a sense of urgency about this appeal. Its double use of the verb "call" makes the point, especially the peremptory first occurrence of the verb when it bids not merely, "I call to you" but "I call you," more like a master calling a servant than a servant speaking to a master. Its imagery also makes the point. When you offer a sacrifice with its associated incense offering, you can see the sacrifice burn and the incense rise. The uttering of a plea or the raising of one's hands in prayer, especially in some location in everyday life that might be a long way from the temple, might seem less compelling when unaccompanied by those symbols of praise and prayer. So the psalm asks God to treat them just as seriously as if they were complemented by the natural accompaniments of prayer in worship.

Metaphorically, it asks for God to put his hand over my mouth. Of course it may well be that behind what we say is what we think, and so the psalm goes on to ask that God may exercise some control over my mind, too. How on earth would God do so? I assume not by taking command of my thinking by directly determining how my mind works, like a political agency that limits access to certain Internet sites. It would make our lives easier if God would do so, but it doesn't seem in keeping with God's aim that we should learn to live in an adult way. I assume that God works by influencing us in the way parents seek to influence their teenage or adult children, by pointing things out, arguing, setting an example, and persuading, rather than by the compulsion that parents will sometimes exercise on younger children.

The psalmist knows that we need such influence because there are pressures that push us in other directions toward **faithlessness** and its (apparent) delights; the psalm leaves us to fill in the blanks in order to identify the form of faithlessness that would attract us. Far from letting ourselves be drawn to such faithlessness, it invites us to be attracted to the idea of being disciplined by the people we can truly trust and to discipline ourselves. If we are serious about our pleas for God to protect us from giving in to the pressure of other people's delights, we may need to engage in some serious self-denial.

As usual, Western people may be offended at the plea for the faithless to fall into their own traps. One significance of it is that it is a risky prayer, one that people can afford to pray only if they really have turned aside from faithless ways and only if they stay that way.

PSALM 142

How to Get Prayer to Work

An instruction. David's. When he was in the cave. A plea.

1 With my voice I will cry out to Yahweh,
     with my voice I will pray for grace to Yahweh.
2 I will pour out my murmuring before him,
     my trouble before him I will declare.
3 When my spirit faints away within me,
     you are the one who acknowledges my path.
   On the way that I walk
     they have hidden a snare for me.
4 Look at my right hand and see—
     there is no one who pays attention to me.
   Refuge has failed for me;
     there is no one who inquires about my life.
5 I have cried out to you, Yahweh; I have said, "You are
       my refuge,
     my allocation in the land of the living."
6 Attend to my resounding,
     because I have been brought very low.
   Rescue me from my pursuers,
     because they are too strong for me.

⁷ Get me out of my prison,
    to confess your name.
  Around me the faithful will gather
    because you deal with me.

In connection with Psalms 120–121, I mentioned the visit a group of my friends were making to one of the poorest and most dangerous countries in Africa, in connection with their commitment to letting the voice of refugees there be heard in the West. They got home safely this week. There is no formal education in the refugee camps, and one of the supporters of this venture has a vision for getting a handful of the teenagers from the camps to a boarding school in another African country so that they can eventually go back as teachers to their own people. But the obstacles to the fulfillment of this vision are monumentally formidable. Money is the least of them. How can refugees from country *A* living in country *B* get the papers to move to country *C*? How do you get God to make it possible for impossibilities to become realities?

Psalm 142 suggests four insights on how to get prayers answered. First, let God overhear what you are saying and thinking. Often we have good reason to be afraid that God will overhear what we say, but we also know that when we overhear someone saying something that is not addressed to us but does refer to us, it can have a galvanizing effect on our attentiveness. So the psalm begins by talking about God. Second, talk directly to God about your needs or the needs of the people for whom you are concerned. The psalm talks about my murmuring, my trouble, my spirit fainting. The psalm makes explicit our recognition that we are not telling God anything God doesn't know ("You acknowledge my path," the experience I am having to walk through). God knows about all these facts, yet the prayers of the Bible never hold back from telling God things that God knows, any more than a child holds back from telling its mother things she knows. While one point about this telling is to make me feel better, another point about it is to motivate God to act, to make it impossible for God not to answer my prayers.

Third, talk to God about having no one else to turn to. No one else pays attention to me, so you must give me your attention. No one in power cares about those teenagers in the refugee camps. They have the best refuge UNHCR can give them, but in another sense refuge has failed for them. No one asks about them. Nothing will happen unless you make it happen, Lord. Fourth, urge God to take the action you need, and point out how this will bring honor to God.

First Samuel 22 describes the kind of occasion when David was shut up in a cave and we can imagine him praying in this way. The introductions to a number of psalms refer to incidents in David's life, which is told in 1 and 2 Samuel. A look at the account of these incidents commonly produces two results. One can see points at which it is possible to imagine David praying at this point in the way the psalm does. But one can also see other elements in the psalm that don't fit. Psalm 51 provides a good example. The possible implication is that the references in the introductions do not imply that David actually prayed the psalm at this point but rather that it is illuminating to consider the psalm and the story alongside each other because there is this overlap.

PSALM 143

God's Faithfulness, Not Mine

A composition. David's.

1. Yahweh, listen to my plea,
       give ear to my prayer for grace in your truthfulness,
       answer me in your faithfulness.
2. Don't enter into judgment with your servant,
       because no living person counts as faithful before you.
3. Because my enemy has pursued me,
       crushed me to the earth,
   made me live in darkness,
       like people who are long dead.
4. My spirit has fainted away within me;
       my mind is desolated inside me.
5. I have been mindful of the days of old,
       I have talked about all you had done,
       I would murmur about the action of your hands.

⁶ I have spread out my hands to you,
  my heart has been like dry earth in relation to you.   (*Rise*)

⁷ Be quick, answer me, Yahweh;
  my spirit is spent.
Do not hide your face from me,
  so that I shall be like the people who go down to the pit.
⁸ Let me hear of your commitment in the morning,
  because it is on you that I have relied.
⁹ Let me know the way that I should walk,
  because it is to you that I have lifted up my heart.
¹⁰ Teach me to do what you favor,
  because you are my God.
May your good spirit lead me
  on level ground.
¹¹ For the sake of your name, Yahweh, give me life;
  in your faithfulness will you bring me out of my trouble.
¹² In your commitment will you put an end to my enemies,
  destroy all the people who are attacking me,
  because I am your servant.

Contrary to the resolve she had announced a few days ago, first thing this morning my wife sat at her computer checking the news. Eventually I asked her what had happened to her resolve to begin the day with her time of devotion, and in horror she admitted she had forgotten her resolve. She then went off to make breakfast. (She has carried on with her devotions since I wrote this commentary, and you can work out from the acknowledgments section that I would not be including this information without her cooperation, and that she thus did not perceive me as being passive-aggressive.) It is just as well that the relationship between God and us does not depend on our **faithfulness** as much as it depends on God's, and my wife knows that fact and trusts in it, in a good way. It would be possible for us to take God's faithfulness for granted and not feel compelled to be faithful. In contemporary Western Christianity as I experience it, our more prevalent danger is the assumption that our faithfulness determines whether God is faithful, that God relates to us in response to our relating to him.

The opening lines of Psalm 143 open up the question of how God's faithfulness and our faithfulness relate, and they point to the fact that God's faithfulness is the decisive one. Their argument is one that Paul takes up in Romans 3. To show how the Scriptures make clear that we are all wrongdoers, Jews and Gentiles, he explicitly quotes a sequence of passages that come mostly from the Psalms, and he then takes up words from the beginning of Psalm 143 to summarize the point: "No human being will be counted as righteous before you." Paul's point is the same as the psalm's: to establish that the relationship between God and us depends more fundamentally on God's faithfulness than on ours. In effect, when Paul talks about "righteousness," he is using the word in its Old Testament sense that God is doing the right thing and is being faithful. The supreme expression of God's faithfulness is his sending Jesus to redeem us; the only contribution we make to our salvation is our sin and our willingness to trust in Jesus.

The gospel is thus in keeping with the psalm. When the psalm acknowledges that none of us count as being faithful or as doing the right thing when God looks at us (some of us might be satisfied with ourselves when we compare ourselves with some other people), the psalm can face that fact because it has already made its appeal to God's truthfulness and faithfulness. That theme recurs at the end in the psalm's appeal to God's **commitment** and faithfulness.

In between, the psalm also makes clear that recognizing that no one can claim to be ultimately faithful and therefore in the right, and thus to have a claim on God, does not imply that everyone is equally sinful. Both Testaments recognize that there are good people and bad people; most of us come in between. The psalm assumes that my not being ultimately faithful does not give me any excuse for failing to be as committed as I can be, and without any contradiction such commitment is part of the basis for my appeal to God to take my side against people who persecute me. By implication, if I can't make a claim to a reasonable degree of commitment, I had better sort out that question with God before I try to appeal for God's help.

Perhaps more surprisingly, claiming to have shown such commitment in the past is not incompatible with asking for

God to guide me in the right way in the future. When Christians speak of God's guidance or God's leading, they are characteristically referring to whether they should date a particular person or apply for a certain job. God is inclined to leave such questions to us, like a good parent. When the Bible talks about God's guidance or God's leading, it is characteristically referring to our recognizing the morally right path. The psalm implies that having lived the right way in the past does not exclude the possibility that we might deviate in the future.

PSALM 144

A Mere Breath

David's.

¹ Yahweh, my crag, be worshiped,
  the one who trains my hands for encounter,
   my fingers for war,
² the one committed to me, my fastness, my haven,
  the one who enables me to escape,
 my shield, the one on whom I rely,
  who subdues my people under me.
³ Yahweh, what is a human being that you should acknowledge him,
  a mortal that you should think about him?
⁴ A human being is like a breath,
  his days like a passing shadow.
⁵ Yahweh, spread your heavens and come down,
  touch the mountains so that they smoke.
⁶ Make lightning flash and scatter them,
  send your arrows and rout them.
⁷ Send your hands from on high, snatch me away, rescue me,
  from the great waters, from the hand of foreigners,
⁸ whose mouth has spoken emptiness,
  and whose right hand is a deceitful right hand.

⁹ God, I will sing a new song for you,
  on a ten-stringed harp I will make music for you,
¹⁰ as the one who gives deliverance to kings,
  who snatches away David his servant.

¹¹ From the deadly sword snatch me away,
   rescue me from the hand of foreigners,
whose mouth has spoken emptiness,
   and whose right hand is a deceitful right hand.

¹² In that our sons are like saplings,
   nourished in their youth,
our daughters are like a corner pillar,
   carved in the pattern of a palace,
¹³ our storehouses are full of provisions of all kinds,
   our flocks number thousands, myriads in our fields,
¹⁴ our cattle are laden, there is no breach
   and no going out and no cry in our squares:
¹⁵ the blessings of the people that has it like this,
   the blessings of the people whose God is Yahweh!

Some years ago I did a little bit of research into tracing my ancestors. These were pre-Internet days, and the research involved poring over ancient volumes in the repository of such records in London. Sometimes I would discover another "John Goldingay" from more than a century ago. Sometimes I would be reading the marriage certificate of an ancestor who could not write but could only put an *X*, and it made me reflect on how privileged I have been to have grown up when and where I did, when someone from an ordinary background could have as much opportunity of education as someone from a well-to-do background. Sometimes I would be surprised to find an ancestor in the nineteenth century who lived on into his or her nineties, for most people did not live as long in those days as we may expect to nowadays.

There is much difference when we compare ourselves with people from a century or two ago, but there is also much similarity, not least the fact that eventually we all die. A human being, Psalm 144 comments, is a breath; his days are like a passing shadow. The question to which this definition is an answer, "What is a human being?" comes from Psalm 8, but this psalm takes it in a different direction. Psalm 8 marvels that God puts mere human beings in control of the world; Psalm 144 marvels that God puts a particular human being, the king or governor, in charge of Israel. Ironically, another aspect of the answer to the question of why God put a mere human being in charge of

Israel is "Well, I did it because Israel asked me to." First Samuel 8 relates how God appoints a king over Israel because Israel wants it, not because God does. It is a scary thought that what is bound on earth can be bound in heaven (Matthew 16 and 18).

That willingness on God's part becomes both a curse and a blessing for Israel and for its kings. Psalm 144 invites the leader to rejoice in God's extraordinary support and protection. The **commitment** God made to David is for the encouragement of each subsequent David. That support is the basis for the sense of wonder that God pays attention to him as a mere human being. The latter part of the psalm may also add bite to the comment about his days resembling a passing shadow. While a leader will have a better health plan than other Israelites, when battle comes he will also be the prime target of people who may have pretended to be allies but whose words are empty and whose alliance cannot be trusted. He indeed needs to plead with God to rescue him from the right hand that purports to offer treaty relationships but conceals a sword. He is indeed a person whose days are like a passing shadow, possibly a shadow that passes very quickly. He needs God to be prepared to pull apart the apparently continuous firm expanse of the sky and intervene in the world and live up to the description in the psalm's opening lines.

The last section of the psalm looks beyond any crisis that may confront the leader to the blessing that God will bring, and it embodies the reminder that God's involvement with him is not for his own sake but for his people's. Ultimately, it was the people as a whole that God chose, and it is the people God cares about, not David or his successors.

PSALM 145

Thine Is the Kingdom, the Power, and the Glory

An act of praise. David's.

1. I will exalt you, my God, King;
   I will worship your name forever and ever.
2. Every day I will worship you;
   I will praise your name forever and ever.

213

3 Yahweh is great and much to be praised;
   of his greatness there is no fathoming.
4 One generation will laud your works to another generation,
   and tell of your mighty acts.
5 Of your majestic, glorious splendor,
   and your wondrous acts, I will murmur.
6 People will speak of the might of your awe-inspiring acts;
   your greatness—I will declare it.
7 They will pour forth the commemoration of your great
       goodness,
   and resound at your faithfulness.
8 Yahweh is gracious and compassionate,
   long-tempered and big in commitment.
9 Yahweh is good to all;
   his compassion is over all his works.
10 All your works will confess you, Yahweh;
   the people committed to you will worship you.
11 They will talk of the glory of your reign,
   they will speak of your might,
12 to make known his mighty acts to human beings,
   the glorious splendor of his reign.
13 Your reign is one over all ages,
   your rule over all generations.

14 Yahweh supports all who are falling
   and raises all who are put down.
15 The eyes of all look to you
   and you give them their food at its time.
16 You open your hand
   and fill every living thing with your favor.
17 Yahweh is faithful in all his ways,
   committed in all his works.
18 Yahweh is near to all who call him,
   to all who call him in truth.
19 He acts with favor to the people who are in awe of him;
   he listens to their cry for help and delivers them.
20 Yahweh watches all who give themselves to him,
   but he destroys all the faithless.
21 My mouth will speak Yahweh's praise;
   all flesh will bless the name of the holy one, forever
       and ever.

A student once asked me why the Lord's Prayer is so different from the prayers in the Psalms, which characteristically **cry** out to God and issue protests to God because of people's urgent needs. I wasn't sure, but in due course I worked out what I thought was quite an impressive answer relating to the context of the Lord's Prayer in Jesus' ministry. But I won't bother you with it because I have now realized it was mostly mistaken. The Lord's Prayer is indeed different from the protest psalms, but it is quite like other psalms that focus more on praise.

Psalm 145 illustrates the point in a variety of ways. It does so by its focus on God's kingdom or God's reign. The difference in the Lord's Prayer is its expression of the wish "May your reign come." The psalm speaks of God's reign as a present reality. There is some appropriateness in both attitudes. God is sovereign; the world is not out of God's control; and God shows that kingly power in providing for the world and for his people. Yet God's reign is by no means a complete reality in the world or in the church.

In the Lord's Prayer, that bidding "May your reign come" appears in the context of other biddings, "Hallowed be your **name**" and "Your will be done." Such biddings mean more than a commitment on our part to each of these priorities in our own lives. If they were simply disguised acts of self-commitment, they would lose their significance as prayers. But they would also lose their validity as prayers if they did not imply acts of commitment on our part. Psalm 145 focuses on the commitment aspect of our recognition of God.

A third comparison and contrast comes in the talk about food and associated topics. The psalm notes that God gives human beings and animals their food at their needed time. The Lord's Prayer can thus ask for us to be given our daily bread. We might make a further link between the psalm's declarations about **Yahweh's** nearness to people who call on him, especially when they are under pressure, and the plea in the Lord's Prayer for God to deliver us from evil and not lead us into temptation. Yet another link lies in the same context in the plea for forgiveness that appears in the Lord's Prayer, which has its theological background in the fact noted in the psalm that

215

Yahweh is gracious and compassionate, long-tempered and big in **commitment**.

There is a further significance in that last piece of background. The psalm has all those connections to the future, in that Jesus takes up its themes in the Lord's Prayer. It also has an important connection backward, placing it in the setting of God's earlier revelation. When it declares that Yahweh is gracious and compassionate, long-tempered and big in commitment, it takes up aspects of Yahweh's self-description at Sinai, recounted in Exodus 34. When God wants us to know the basic things about him, this is what they are. The description is one taken up a number of times in the Psalms and elsewhere.

Further, it fits with the psalm's forward and backward links that it is another alphabetic psalm, like Psalms 111 and 119. In other words, it has one line beginning with each letter of the twenty-two-letter Hebrew alphabet (except *N* for some reason—hence the fact that it actually has only twenty-one lines). If you want to know what praise from *A* to *Z* looks like, Psalm 145 gives you an answer. I wonder what a prayer or an act of praise would like look like that was based on our twenty-six-letter alphabet?

PSALM 146

Don't Trust in Leaders

1 Praise Yah!
   Praise Yahweh, my soul;
2   I will praise Yahweh through my life,
       I will make music for my God while I exist.
3 Do not trust in leaders,
       in a human being with whom there is no deliverance.
4 His breath leaves, he returns to his ground;
       on that day, his deliberations have perished.
5 The blessings of the one who has Jacob's God as his help,
       whose expectation is of Yahweh his God,
6 maker of the heavens and the earth,
       the sea and all that is in them.
   the one who keeps faith forever,
7   exercising authority for the oppressed,

216

giving food to the hungry—
    Yahweh frees captives.
8 Yahweh opens [the eyes of] the blind;
    Yahweh raises the people who are put down.
  Yahweh gives himself to the faithful;
9   Yahweh keeps the strangers.
  He relieves orphan and widow,
    but subverts the way of the faithless.
10 Yahweh will reign forever—
    your God, Zion, for all generations.
  Praise Yah!

I remember the winter's day when I announced to the students at the theological college in England where I used to be the principal that I would be leaving the coming summer. To my surprise, it aroused a feeling of anxiety among a number of students. Maybe I was deceiving myself in thinking that it wouldn't make much difference to them; the governing body would surely appoint someone else whose views, attitudes, and aims were not so different from mine. Maybe I was deceiving myself about the difference that any individual makes to the leadership of an institution such as a seminary or a church. Still, there is no doubt that many people trust in an institution's leaders if they like the way the institution is being run. Leadership is an idol.

So it's fortuitous and important for the Western church that Psalm 146 warns the congregation not to trust in leaders. The psalm points to three of the host of reasons why it is an important exhortation. First, leaders can't **deliver** or help their people. That may seem an astonishing claim, but those two verbs carry a lot of freight in the Psalms. *Deliverance* is by definition something that only God can do. *To help* is not far from having the same implication; it doesn't denote assisting people with something that they can't quite do on their own but instead rescuing someone who is otherwise sunk.

The second basis for saying you should not trust in leaders points to the particular reason that they can't deliver or help. They die. Or at least, they leave. The plans they have in mind become irrelevant. Their time comes. The faculty of my present seminary know that our president cannot be in his post forever;

sooner rather than later he will retire. And when we think about it, that fact raises some anxiety among us. Who will be the next president? Will we be able to trust and love him or her as we do the present president? When pastors of churches leave or die, congregations are often shocked. Why is it so?

Turn your eye away from those questions, the psalm says, and remember who is really in charge. There is One to whom the expressions "forever" and "for all generations" can be attached. There is One of whom you can have expectations that will not fail to be realized because of his death, retirement, or departure.

The psalm implies a further, third reason for not trusting in leaders. We are always appalled and astonished at the way leaders use their positions to benefit themselves and/or go wrong morally, but we ought not to be surprised, because wanting to be in a position of power often suggests that there is something questionable about a person's character. I write on the day of the death of the writer Christopher Hitchens, who has been criticized for holding the view that politicians do bad things because they are bad men. Even if there is not something questionable about the character of a would-be leader, the position of power will put huge pressures on that character. Leaders will very likely not be the kind of people who keep faith or exercise **authority** for the oppressed, give food to the hungry, look after strangers, or relieve orphans and widows. So we are better off trusting in God, because God is that kind of person.

To leaders themselves, then, the psalm says, "Remember that you can't deliver; remember that you will die; and remember to be like God in the way you act toward people."

PSALM 147

Creation as a Reason for Hope

¹ Praise Yah!
   Because making music for our God is good,
      because glorifying [the one who is our] praise is beautiful.
² Yahweh is the builder of Jerusalem,
      he gathers Israel's exiles.
³ He is the one who heals the broken in spirit
      and bandages their wounds.

[4] He calculates the reckoning of the stars
    and pronounces the names of them all.
[5] Our Lord is great and mighty in power;
    of his insight there is no reckoning.
[6] Yahweh restores the lowly,
    brings down the faithless to the earth.

[7] Sing for Yahweh with confession,
    make music to Yahweh with the guitar.
[8] He is the one who covers the heavens with clouds,
    provides rain for the earth, makes the mountains
        grow grass.
[9] He gives their food to cattle,
    to the offspring of the raven when they call.
[10] He does not delight in the strength of a horse;
    he does not take pleasure in the thighs of a person.
[11] Yahweh takes pleasure in people who are in awe of him,
    people who put their hope in his commitment.

[12] Jerusalem, glorify Yahweh,
    praise your God, Zion,
[13] because he has made strong the bars of your gates,
    blessed your children within you.
[14] He makes your territory peaceful,
    fills you with the finest of wheat.
[15] He sends his word to the earth;
    his command runs quickly.
[16] He gives snow like wool;
    he scatters frost like ash.
[17] He throws his hail like crumbs;
    who can stand before his ice?
[18] He sends his word and melts them;
    when he blows his breath, waters flow.
[19] He declares his words to Jacob,
    his commands and decisions to Israel.
[20] He has not done so for any nation;
    his decisions—they do not know them.
    Praise Yah!

Six centuries before Christ, the city of Jerusalem was destroyed, and many of its people were taken off into **exile** in **Babylon**.

Not surprisingly, over time they became demoralized and found it hard to believe that God was ever going to be involved with them again. The prophecies in Isaiah 40–55 address them in this demoralized state, and one way the prophecies seek to rebuild people's faith is by reminding them that their God is the great creator. The one who created the world at the beginning is capable of acting with creative power in their lives now.

Psalm 147 also mixes talk of God as creator and as the builder of Jerusalem, and maybe it does so for the same reason. The three sections work in the classic fashion of a hymn of praise in the book of Psalms. Three times the psalm urges the people and the city to praise God, and three times it goes on to give the reasons that they should do so, indicating the suggested content of praise. Each time the content of this praise mixes up affirmations about God's relationship with the people and affirmations about creation.

The first section implies the context of the exile. The city has been devastated and denuded of its people, and against all the evidence the psalm declares that **Yahweh** is the builder of Jerusalem and the gatherer of exiles, the healer of broken spirits and the nurse who bandages people's wounds, the one who lifts up the lowly and puts down mighty superpowers. How can you believe such declarations? You can believe them on the basis of the fact that the God of whom the psalm speaks is the one who controls the stars and who cannot himself be put under control. The Babylonians believed that the stars controlled what happened on earth; the psalm does not dispute that belief but points out that there is someone who controls the stars themselves. In theory the Israelites believed it was so; they need to see its implications for their own destiny. In the Western world, we are more likely to assume that we are in control of our own destiny.

The middle section brings the work of the creator nearer home. In theory, the Israelites believe that Yahweh is the one who makes nature work and thus ensures that all earth's creatures have food to eat. In theory they believe that Yahweh doesn't care how strong a nation's army is; this consideration isn't what decides a people's fate. The question is, What attitude does a lowly people take to God? Do they think their destiny depends on themselves?

The third question makes it look as if the restoration of the city has happened, though it might be referring back to God's having looked after the city in its heyday before the exile. Either way, once again the psalm interweaves the work of God as lord of nature and as lord of the city's destiny. Then at the close it ricochets into talk about God's distinctive revelation of his will to Israel. Other peoples didn't know about worshiping Yahweh alone or not using images or keeping the Sabbath. How privileged the Israelites are to know about those expectations. How ironic that they often fail to fulfill them. That failure was the reason their city was destroyed and they were taken into exile.

PSALMS 148–149

Dance and Slaughter

148:1 Praise Yah!
　　Praise Yahweh from the heavens,
　　　　praise him on high.
　2 Praise him, all his aides,
　　　　praise him all his armies.
　3 Praise him, sun and moon,
　　　　praise him all bright stars.
　4 Praise him, highest heavens,
　　　　and you waters that are above the heavens.
　5 They should praise Yahweh's name,
　　　　because it was he who commanded so that they were
　　　　　　created.
　6 He established them forever and ever,
　　　　he made a law and it will not pass.
　7 Praise Yahweh from the earth,
　　　　sea monsters and all depths,
　8 fire and hail, snow and fog,
　　　　storm wind doing his word,
　9 mountains and all hills,
　　　　fruit trees and all cedars,
　10 animals and all cattle,
　　　　things that move and winged birds,
　11 kings of the earth and all peoples,
　　　　leaders and all authorities in the earth,

221

¹² young men and young women too,
    old and young too.
¹³ They should praise Yahweh's name,
    because his name alone is on high.
His majesty is over the earth and the heavens,
¹⁴   but he has lifted a horn for his people,
  [a reason for] praise on the part of all who are committed
      to him,
      on the part of the Israelites, the people who come near
      to him.
Praise Yah!

^{149:1} Praise Yah!
    Sing for Yahweh a new song,
      his praise in the congregation of the committed people.
² Israel is to celebrate its maker,
    the children of Zion are to rejoice in their King.
³ They are to praise his name in dancing;
    tambourine and guitar are to make music for him.
⁴ Because Yahweh favors his people;
    he adorns the lowly with deliverance.
⁵ The committed people are to exult in their honor,
    they are to resound on their beds,
⁶ acclamations of God in their throat
    and a two-edged sword in their hand,
⁷ to execute redress on the nations,
    rebukes on the peoples,
⁸ to bind their kings with shackles,
    their nobles with iron chains,
⁹ to execute on them the decision that is written—
    it will be glory for all the people committed to him.
Praise Yah!

As a teenager, I did not learn to dance or to shoot a gun for different reasons. I didn't learn to dance because my church regarded dancing as "worldly"; it wasn't appropriate to people who were really committed to God. I didn't learn to shoot because I elected not to join the "cadet force" at school (the British equivalent to ROTC), which trained people in the kind of discipline and skills that would be useful (among other things) if in due course you joined the military. I don't think I had profound reasons for not joining; I just have a noncooperative streak. I still don't know how to shoot, and I don't really know how to dance, but this doesn't stop me from throwing myself around the dance floor with abandon.

Psalm 149 implies that one would expect Israelites to be able to dance and to shoot. It assumes that dancing is a natural part of worship, as is the use of instruments such as the tambourine and the guitar (translations usually have "lyre," but the guitar is the modern equivalent of the lyre). Its assumption is that worship involves the whole person; how could you express enthusiasm for your Maker and King if you stood still? That assumption makes Western Christians uncomfortable; at least, not many churches behave as if worship involves the whole person in that way. The smooth transition from dancing to wielding the sword also makes us feel uncomfortable. It is indeed the case that the New Testament makes no reference to dancing or the use of musical instruments in worship; hence some Christian traditions have avoided the latter. The New Testament does refer to the use of the sword (e.g., Romans 13), but some Christian traditions are also diffident about this matter.

The psalm's freedom about worship is thus refreshing, as is its commitment to seeing that wrongdoing is put down. It does not expect the people of God to sit by when wrong is done or to intervene only when our oil supply is threatened. Here, the people of God accept responsibility for putting down wrongdoing. When Israel itself is under attack, the Psalms assume its job is to trust God and not seek to defend itself. But it is a different matter when there is wrongdoing to be punished and defenseless people to be rescued. The assumption that a little people like Israel can put down kings and empires is a crazy one, though not if you believe in God and know there is a decision God has made that needs to be implemented.

The further idea that actually dominates Psalm 148 is also alien to Western Christian thinking. For the same reason that we do not easily think of dancing as an expression of worship, we do not easily think of worship being offered by sun and moon, sea monsters, fruit trees, or cattle. We think of worship as something that essentially involves minds and hearts. The Psalms certainly assume that mind and heart come into it, but they allow for other truths about worship. The expression

"Praise **Yah**" comes at either end of each psalm from 146 to 150; it is commonly transliterated as "Hallelujah." This particular Hebrew word for praise, *halal*, suggests ululating, going "Lala-lala." If words are less essential to praise than we think, and the involvement of the body is more important, it ceases to be odd to think of trees as worshiping when their branches sway and of animals worshiping as they roar, low, or shriek. If there is a "music of the spheres," then it sounds to the praise of God.

If one focuses on the praise offered by sentient beings, once more the psalm expands our horizon by reminding us that the body summoned to praise includes all God's **aides** and armies. Along with the reference to sea monsters (and for that matter to kings, leaders, and **authorities**), the psalm reminds us that there are many entities in the heavens and on the earth that are more interested in resisting God than in praising him, but it has a vision of them all being drawn into praise. Consider the very majesty of God; be realistic, guys. But the psalm closes with a complementary reason for Israel's own praise. How extraordinary that the God of such majesty should have elevated little Israel. How the wordless praise of the heavens and the earth should inspire the wordless and verbal and rational and heart-felt praise of Israel!

PSALM 150

The Praise of God, the Eternal Creator, Is Finished and Completed

1 Praise Yah!
  Praise God in his sanctuary,
      praise him in his strong firmament.
2 Praise him in his mighty acts,
      praise him in accordance with his immense greatness.
3 Praise him with the blast of the horn,
      praise him with harp and guitar.
4 Praise him with tambourine and dancing;
      praise him with strings and pipe.
5 Praise him with loud cymbals,
      praise him with noisy cymbals:
6   every breath must praise Yah.
  Praise Yah!

The heading I have given for this final psalm is the rabbis' footnote to the Hebrew text of the Psalms. We have come a long way from Psalm 1, where we began with an exhortation to pay heed to Yahweh's Teaching, and then with a promise to the king in Psalm 2. You could say that the second psalm from the end (Psalm 149) corresponds to the second psalm from the beginning in its assertions about nations being rebuked and kings being put down, but the very last psalm contrasts with the very first psalm. It also contrasts with the development of the book of Psalms after that opening: the first half of the book was dominated by prayer and protest, but praise is more prominent in the second half of the book, and its ending in Psalms 146–150 simply comprises praise. The Hebrew title of the book of Psalms, *Praises*, is not very appropriate to the book as a whole, but it corresponds to where the book ends, where pain, abandonment, and disappointment have been forgotten—and it corresponds to where everything must end.

We have noted that the praise of the Psalms commonly involves two features: an exhortation or self-commitment to praise and the reasons for or content of this praise. Sometimes a psalm of praise will omit the first feature and jump straight into the second, the content of the praise. Psalm 150 alone comprises only the first feature (though verse 2 alludes briefly to the content of the praise it urges), the feature that elsewhere comprises something more like an introduction. Psalm 150 is not an introduction to anything; it is more like a conclusion. In effect it says, "We have said a lot about God in all these psalms; in light of what we have said, you know all the reasons to praise God. Just do it."

There are people who need to be reminded that the Bible is interested in their showing compassion to the needy and not just in their offering enthusiastic worship. There are other people who need to be reminded that the Bible is interested in their offering enthusiastic worship and not just compassion to the needy.

GLOSSARY

aide

An aide is supernatural agent through whom God may appear and work in the world. English translations refer to them as "angels," but this suggests ethereal winged figures wearing diaphanous white dresses. Aides are humanlike figures; hence it possible to give them hospitality without realizing who they are (Hebrews 13). They have no wings, hence their need of a stairway or ramp between heaven and earth (Genesis 28). They appear in order to act or speak on God's behalf and so fully represent God that they can speak as if they *are* God (Genesis 22). They are involved in dynamic, forceful action in the world (Psalms 34 and 35). They bring the reality of God's presence, action, and voice, without bringing such a real presence that it would electrocute mere mortals or shatter their hearing.

altar

An altar is a structure for offering a sacrifice (the word comes from the word for sacrifice), made of earth or stone. It might be relatively small, like a table, and the person making the offering would stand in front of it. Or it might be higher and larger, like a platform, and the person making the offering would climb onto it.

Asaph

Asaph was one of the leaders of music in temple worship who were appointed by David, according to 1 Chronicles 6. Chronicles often refers to the descendants of Asaph in this connection, and the reference to Asaph in the introductions to psalms may allude to this Asaphite choir, as "David" can refer to the Davidic kings in general.

Assyria, Assyrians

Assyria was the first great Middle Eastern superpower, which spread its empire westward into Syria-Palestine in the eighth century. The

Assyrians first made **Ephraim** part of their empire; then when Ephraim kept trying to assert independence, they invaded Ephraim, destroyed its capital at Samaria, transported its people, and settled people from other parts of their empire in their place. Assyria also invaded **Judah** and devastated much of the country but did not take Jerusalem. Prophets such as Amos and Isaiah describe how **Yahweh** was thus using Assyria as a means of disciplining Israel.

authority, authoritative

English translations commonly translate the Hebrew *mishpat* with words such as *judgment* or *justice*, but the word's underlying connotation is the exercise of authority and the taking of decisions. It is a word for *government*. In principle, then, the word has positive implications, though it is quite possible for people in authority to make decisions in an unjust way. It is a king's job to exercise authority in accordance with **faithfulness** to God and people and in a way that brings **deliverance**. Exercising authority means making decisions and acting **decisively** on behalf of people in need and of people wronged by others. Thus speaking of God as judge implies good news (unless you are a major wrongdoer). God's "decisions" can also denote God's authoritative declarations concerning human behavior and about what he intends to do.

Babylon, Babylonians

A minor power in the context of Israel's early history, in the time of Jeremiah Babylon took over the position of superpower from **Assyria** and kept it for nearly a century until conquered by Persia. Prophets such as Jeremiah describe how **Yahweh** was using Babylon as a means of disciplining **Judah**. Its creation stories, law codes, and more philosophical writings help us understand aspects of the Old Testament's equivalent writings, while its astrological religion also forms background to aspects of polemic in the Prophets.

Canaan, Canaanites

As the biblical terms for the land of Israel as a whole and for its indigenous peoples, "Canaanites" is not so much the name for a particular ethnic group as a shorthand term for all the peoples native to the land.

cherubs

Cherubs were awe-inspiring winged creatures that transported **Yahweh**. There were statues of them in the temple standing guard over the **declaration chest**; they thus pointed to the presence of Yahweh there, enthroned invisibly above them.

commitment, committed

The word *commitment* corresponds to the Hebrew word *hesed*, which translations render by means of expressions such as "steadfast love" or "loving-kindness" or "goodness." It is the Old Testament equivalent to the special word for love in the New Testament, the word *agapē*. The Old Testament uses this word to refer to an extraordinary act whereby a person pledges himself or herself to someone else in some act of generosity, allegiance, or grace when there is no prior relationship between them and therefore no obligation to do so. Thus in Joshua 2, Rahab speaks of her protection of the Israelite spies as an act of commitment. It can also refer to a similar extraordinary act that takes place when there is a relationship between people but one party has let the other party down and therefore has no right to expect any continuing faithfulness. If the party that has been let down continues being faithful, they are showing this kind of commitment. In their response to Rahab, the Israelite spies declare that they will relate to her in this way.

composition

The Hebrew word for composition is commonly translated "psalm." It comes from the Hebrew word for music, so it seems to refer to a musical composition, not necessarily a composition related to praise or prayer. (The Greek word *psalmos* from which we get the word *psalm* denotes a song sung to the accompaniment of a stringed instrument.)

covenant

The Hebrew word *berit* covers covenants, treaties, and contracts, which are all ways in which people make a formal commitment about something. Where there is a legal system that can be appealed to, contracts assume a system for resolving disputes and administering justice that can be used if people do not keep a commitment. In contrast, a covenantal relationship does not presuppose an enforceable legal framework of that kind, but a covenant does imply a formal procedure confirming the seriousness of the solemn commitment one party makes to another. Thus the Old Testament often speaks of *sealing* a covenant, literally of *cutting* it (the background lies in the kind of formal procedure described in Genesis 15 and Jeremiah 34:18–20, though such an actual procedure would hardly be required every time someone made a covenantal commitment). People make covenants sometimes *to* other people and sometimes *with* other people; the one implies something more one-sided; the other, something more mutual. Likewise covenants involving God can be more one-sided (denoting the commitment God makes or the commitment God expects) or two-sided (denoting the mutual commitment between God and Israel).

cry, cry out

In describing people's response when oppressed by others, the Old Testament often employs a word used to describe Abel's blood crying out to God, the outcry of the people of Sodom under their oppression, the Israelites' crying out in **Egypt**, and the outcry of people who are unfairly treated within Israel in later centuries. It denotes an urgent cry that presses God for **deliverance**, a cry that God can be relied on to hear even when people deserve the experience that is assailing them.

decision, decisive, see authority

declaration chest

The King James Bible refers to this chest as an "ark," but the word means a box, though it is only occasionally used to refer to chests used for other purposes. In the King James Bible it is "the ark of the covenant," but the phrase does not use the ordinary word for "covenant" but a word that means a solemn declaration. So the "ark of the covenant" is the "declaration chest." It was a bit more than a yard long, a bit more than half a yard wide and high. The link with covenant is that the "declaration" concerns the kind of expectations God has "declared" to Israel in connection with the covenant, specifically the Ten Commandments with their key significance for Israel's covenant relationship with God.

deliver, deliverer, deliverance

In the Old Testament, translations often use the words *save*, *savior*, and *salvation*, but this gives a misleading impression. In Christian usage, these words commonly refer to our personal relationship with God and to the enjoyment of heaven. The Old Testament does speak of our personal relationship with God, but it does not use this group of words in that connection. They refer rather to God's practical intervention to get Israel or the individual out of a mess of some kind, such as false accusations by individuals within the community or invasion by enemies.

Egypt, Egyptians

Egypt was the major regional power to the south of **Canaan** and the country where Jacob's family had found refuge, where they ended up as serfs, and from which the Israelites then needed to escape. In Moses' time Egypt controlled Canaan; in subsequent centuries it was sometimes a threat to Israel, sometimes a potential ally.

Ephraim

After the reign of David and Solomon, the nation of **Israel** split into two. Most of the twelve Israelite clans set up an independent state in the north, separate from **Judah** and Jerusalem and from the line of David. Because it was the bigger of the two states, politically it kept the name Israel, which is confusing because Israel is still the name of the people as a whole as the people of God. In the Prophets, it is sometimes difficult to tell whether "Israel" refers to the people of God as a whole or just to the northern state. Sometimes the state is referred to by the name of Ephraim, the name of one of its dominant clans, so I use this term to refer to that northern state to try to reduce the confusion.

exile

At the end of the seventh century **Babylon** became the major power in **Judah**'s world, but Judah was inclined to rebel against its authority. As part of a successful campaign to get Judah to submit properly to its authority, in 597 and in 587 BC the Babylonians transported many people from Jerusalem to Babylon. They made a special point of transporting people in leadership positions, such as members of the royal family and the court, priests, and prophets (Ezekiel was one of them). These people were thus compelled to live in Babylonia for the next fifty years or so. Through the same period, people back in Judah were also under Babylonian authority. They were not physically in exile, but they were living in the exile as a period of time.

faithful, faithfulness

In English Bibles these Hebrew words (*saddiq*, *sedaqah*) are usually translated "righteous/righteousness," but they point to a particular slant on what we might mean by righteousness. They suggest doing the right thing by the people with whom one is in a relationship, the members of one's community. Thus they are nearer "faithful/faithfulness" than "righteous/righteousness."

faithless, faithlessness

Words for sin that suggests the opposite of **faithful/faithfulness**, they suggest an attitude to God and to other people that expresses a contempt for what right relationships deserve.

Greece

In 336 BC Greek forces under Alexander the Great took control of the **Persian** Empire, but after Alexander's death in 333 his empire split up. The largest part, to the north and east of Palestine, was ruled by one of his generals, Seleucus, and his successors. **Judah** was under its control for much of the next two centuries, though it was at the extreme southwestern border of this empire. and it sometimes came under the control of the Ptolemaic Empire in **Egypt** (ruled by successors of another of Alexander's officers).

instruction

This introductory term is perhaps an indication that the psalm is particularly designated as a model for prayer or praise.

Israel

Originally, Israel was the new name that God gave Abraham's grandson, Jacob. His twelve sons were then forefathers of the twelve clans that comprise the people Israel. In the time of Saul and David these twelve clans became more of a political entity. So Israel was both the people of God and a nation or state like other nations or states. After Solomon's day, this state split into two separate ones, **Ephraim** and **Judah**. Because Ephraim was far the bigger, it often continued to be referred to as Israel. So if one is thinking of the people of God, Judah is part of Israel. If one is thinking politically, Judah is not part of Israel. Once Ephraim has gone out of existence, then for practical purposes Judah *is* Israel, as the people of God.

Judah

Judah was the **name** of one of the twelve sons of Jacob, then the name of the clan that traced its ancestry to him, then the dominant clan in the southern of the two states after the time of Solomon. Later, as a **Persian** province or colony, it was known as Yehud.

leader

This term in the introductions to Psalms likely denotes a worship leader (see the comment on **Asaph**; and compare Heman in Psalm 88).

Master, Masters

The word *baal* is an ordinary Hebrew word for a master, lord, or owner, but the word is also used to describe a **Canaanite** god. It is thus parallel to the word *Lord*, used to describe **Yahweh**. Further, in effect "Master" can be a proper name, like "Lord." To make the difference clear, the Old Testament generally uses *Master* for a foreign god and *Lord* for the real God, Yahweh. Like other ancient peoples, the Canaanites acknowledged a number of gods, and strictly the Master was simply one of them, though he was one of the most prominent. In addition, a title such as "The Master of Peor" suggests that the Master was believed to be manifest and known in different ways and different places. The Old Testament also uses the plural *Masters* to refer to Canaanite gods in general.

name

The name of someone stands for the person. The Old Testament talks of the temple as a place where God's name dwells. It is one of the ways it handles the paradox involved in speaking of the temple as a place where God lives. It knows this idea is a nonsense: how could a building contain the God who could not be contained by the entire heavens, no matter how far you could travel across them? Yet Israel also knows that God does in some sense dwell in the temple and that people can talk with God when they go there. They are aware that they can talk with God anywhere, but there is a special guarantee of this possibility in the temple. They know they can make offerings there and that

God will receive them (supposing they are made in good faith). One way they try to square the circle in speaking of the presence of God in the temple is therefore to speak of God's name being present there, because the name sums up the person. Uttering the name of someone you know brings home his or her reality to you; it's almost as if the person is there. When you say someone's name, there is a sense in which you conjure up the person. When people murmur "Jesus, Jesus" in their prayer, it brings home the reality of Jesus' presence. Likewise, when Israel proclaimed the name Yahweh in worship, it brought home the reality of Yahweh's presence.

peace

The word *shalom* can suggest peace after there has been conflict, but it often points to a richer notion, of fullness of life. The KJV sometimes translates it "welfare," and modern translations use words such as "**well-being**" or "prosperity." It suggests that everything is going well for you.

Persia, Persians

Persia was the third Middle Eastern superpower. Under the leadership of Cyrus the Great, the Persians took control of the **Babylonian** empire in 539 BC. Isaiah 40–55 sees **Yahweh's** hand in raising up Cyrus as the means of restoring **Judah** after the **exile**. Judah and surrounding peoples such as Samaria, Ammon, and Ashdod were Persian provinces or colonies. The Persians stayed in power for two centuries until defeated by **Greece**.

Philistia, Philistines

The Philistines were people who came from across the Mediterranean to settle in **Canaan** at the same time as the Israelites were establishing themselves in Canaan, so that the two peoples formed an accidental pincer movement on the existent inhabitants of the country and became each other's rivals for control of the area.

Qorahites

One of the temple choirs, according to 2 Chronicles 20:19. The Qorahite psalms (e.g., Psalms 84, 85, 87, 88) presumably formed part of their repertoire.

Reed Sea

Reed Sea is literally "sea of rushes"; the word is the one that came in Exodus 2 where Miriam left Moses in the reeds by the Nile. It might be one of the northern arms of what we call the Red Sea, either side of Sinai, or it might be an area of marshy lakes within Sinai.

restorer, restore

A restorer is a person who is in a position to take action on behalf of someone within his extended family who is in need, in order to restore the situation to what it should be. The word overlaps with expressions such as next-of-kin, guardian, and redeemer. "Next-of-kin" indicates the family context that "restorer" presupposes. "Guardian" indicates that the restorer is in a position to be concerned for the person's protection and defense. "Redeemer" indicates having resources that the restorer is prepared to expend on the person's behalf. The Old Testament uses the term to refer to God's relationship with Israel as well as to the action of a human person in relation to another, so it implies that Israel belongs to God's family and that God acts on its behalf in the way a restorer does.

rise

The Hebrew *selah* often comes at the end of lines in psalms, and sometimes in the middle. It means something like "rise," but we do not know what sense attaches to the word there. Were people to stand, or did the tune rise, or what? My favorite theory is that it was what David said when he broke a string—which fits the fact that we cannot see a pattern in the word's occurrence.

Sheol

The most frequent of the Hebrew names for the place where we go when we die. In the New Testament it is called Hades. It is not a place of punishment or suffering but simply a resting place for everyone, a kind of nonphysical analogue to the tomb as the resting place for our bodies.

Songs of the Ascents

These are Psalms 120–134. They do not have much in common apart from this title, so they do not look as if they were originally designed to be used together. More likely they came to form a collection of originally separate psalms that were used by pilgrims "ascending" to Jerusalem for a festival.

Sukkot

The word *sukkot* means "shelters" and is the name of the festival in September/October that marks the end of the harvest and also commemorates the way the Israelites had to live in makeshift shelters on the way from **Egypt** to **Canaan.**

Torah

The word *torah* means "teaching," and in the Psalms and elsewhere it can have that general meaning, but it is also the Hebrew word for the first five books of the Bible. It is then commonly translated as if it means "law," but this title gives a misleading impression. Genesis is nothing like law, and even Exodus to Deuteronomy are not legalistic books. The word *teaching* gives a clearer impression of the nature of the Torah.

Well-being, see peace

Yah

Yah was either an earlier version of the name of God, of which **Yahweh** is then an elaboration (cf. the story in Exodus 3), or an abbreviation of the longer name.

Yahweh

In most English Bibles, the word LORD often comes in all capitals thus, as does sometimes the word GOD in similar format. These represent the name of God, Yahweh. In later Old Testament times, Israelites stopped using the name Yahweh and started to refer to Yahweh as "the Lord." There may be two reasons. They wanted other people to recognize that Yahweh was the one true God, but this strange foreign-sounding name could give the impression that Yahweh was just Israel's tribal god, whereas anyone could recognize a term such as "the Lord" or "God." In addition, they did not want to fall foul of the warning in the Ten Commandments about misusing Yahweh's name. Translations into other languages then followed suit in substituting an expression such as "the Lord" for the name Yahweh. Unfortunately this practice obscures the fact that God wanted to be known by name and the fact that often the text refers to Yahweh and not some other (so-called) god or lord. It also gives the impression that God is much more "lordly" and patriarchal than actually God is. (The form "Jehovah" is not a real word but a mixture of the consonants of Yahweh and the vowels of that word for "Lord," to remind people in reading Scripture that they should say "the Lord," not the actual name.)

Yahweh Armies

This title for God usually appears in English Bibles as "the Lord of Hosts," but it is an even more puzzling expression than that translation implies. The word for Lord is the name of God, **Yahweh**, and the word for hosts is the regular Hebrew word for armies; it is the word that appears on the back of an Israeli military truck. So more literally the expression means "Yahweh [of] Armies," which is just as odd in Hebrew as "Goldingay of Armies" would be. Yet in general terms its likely implication is clear; it suggests that Yahweh is the embodiment of or controller of all war-making power, in heaven or on earth.

Zion

Zion is an alternative name for Jerusalem. Whereas Jerusalem is a more political or geographical term, Zion is a more religious or theological one (ironically, given the modern meaning of Zionist). Zion stands for the place where Yahweh dwells among his people and the place they meet with Yahweh.